ANIMAL MAGIC

ALSO BY ANDREW BARROW

Gossip
International Gossip
The Gossip Family Handbook
The Flesh is Weak
The Great Book of Small Talk
The Tap Dancer
The Man in the Moon
Quentin & Philip

For Anne

ANIMAL MAGIC

A Brother's Story

Love from
Andrew B.

ANDREW BARROW

JONATHAN CAPE
LONDON

Published by Jonathan Cape 2011

2 4 6 8 10 9 7 5 3 1

Illustrations by Jonathan Barrow

First published in Great Britain in 2011 by
Jonathan Cape
Random House, 20 Vauxhall Bridge Road,
London SW1V 2SA

www.rbooks.co.uk

Addresses for companies within The Random House Group Limited can be found
at: www.randomhouse.co.uk/offices.htm

The Random House Group Limited Reg. No. 954009

A CIP catalogue record for this book
is available from the British Library

ISBN 9780224090599

The Random House Group Limited supports The Forest Stewardship
Council (FSC), the leading international forest certification organisation.
All our titles that are printed on Greenpeace approved FSC certified paper
carry the FSC logo. Our paper procurement policy can be found at
www.rbooks.co.uk/environment

Typeset in Bembo by Palimpsest Book Production Ltd
Falkirk, Stirlingshire

Printed and bound in the UK by
CPI Mackays, Chatham ME5 8TD

For Simon, Julian and Martin

CONTENTS

Prologue   1
1. Lancaster   9
2. Cumberland   21
3. Turleigh Combe   27
4. Hens   34
5. Clifton   44
6. Gilda   59
7. Harrow: Part One   71
8. Frere and Christie   79
9. Harrow: Part Two   89
10. Show Business   106
11. The Dorchester   124
12. Yellowstone   140
13. Hotel School   147
14. Claridge's: Part One   160
15. Claridge's: Part Two   180
16. Office Life   204
17. Return to Tite Street   225
18. James Graham and Mr Grant   247
19. Living Alone   265
20. Anita   277
21. Engagement   292

Epilogue   303
Bibliography   323

PROLOGUE

In Market Street, Poulford, our coach is delayed
by a large crowd outside St John's Church. I shout
to a passer-by and he tells me there has been an
incident in the church. Apparently Roger Cooke
is marrying Cynthia Rachel Charte. Guests were
asked to be in their pews by two-thirty and everything went according to plan until the procession.
The organist played Bach's 'Unititi Un Die' and
the proud relatives turned their heads to the aisle.
But the bride is not there. Instead three men in
black are carrying a coffin, followed by weeping
parents. There has been a mistake. Vicar, what has
happened? The whole congregation are in uproar
and the Best Man runs to the pulpit. He addresses
the people: I'm sorry there has been a mistake. The
Vicar has made an error. He is not a machine.

The Queue, Chapter Six

I AM ONE of five brothers, four of whom survive and are
now shuffling or strutting towards retirement. We are not
particularly alike but get on well together, touch wood, in
spite of our differences. Between us, we have fifteen children, some of whom are themselves married with children
of their own. Our youngest brother, Jonathan, escaped these

blessings and booby prizes. On 5 April 1970, at the age of twenty-two, in the full flush of youth and promise, and only a few days before his wedding at the Brompton Oratory, he was killed in a car crash. His twenty-three-year-old fiancée, a Roman Catholic, died with him in broad daylight on a Sunday afternoon. A wooden bench bearing their names and put up by my father still marks the scene of the accident.

Tragic early deaths, even double deaths, are alas not rare, but Jonathan's case is stranger than most. Days, even hours, before he and Anita Fielding crashed into another car at Olney in Buckinghamshire, my brother had finished, at least in structural terms, a short novel in which road accidents, especially head-on collisions, feature often, and in which he had predicted and described his own violent death in excruciating semi-comic detail.

I was closer to Jonathan than my other siblings and it fell to me to clear out his desk at the advertising agency where he had recently started working. In a drawer I found the closely typed, much scribbled-upon manuscript, littered with word-counts and entitled *The Queue*. He may have finished the story, but he was still writing material that could be added to make it a more publishable length. On the page still in the typewriter he had with him on that fatal weekend he had even addressed the idea of a wedding being replaced by a funeral. Which indeed is what happened. Instead of getting married at the Brompton Oratory on 23 April, Jonathan and Anita had their double requiem there, with many if not almost all the potential wedding guests – the embossed copperplate invitations had already gone out – now in the role of mourners. In the passage quoted at the start of this chapter Jonathan expands upon this irony with comic relish, and goes on to describe how the bride runs from the church, fails to see an oncoming bread van, and dies under its wheels.

There are dozens of other defiantly nettle-grasping scenes in *The Queue* and, though a similar morbidity pervades much of Jonathan's other writings and the drawings he had done from an early age, a vein of tenderness, humour and affection, not least a love of nature, also runs through his work. In *The Queue* there are many gestures of absolution and it seems generally agreed that Jonathan himself was outwardly pleasant, good-looking, stable, reliable, honest and hard-working. A few months after his death I showed *The Queue* to the soon-to-be-famous Quentin Crisp, whom Jonathan and I had met in a Soho café called the As You Like It. The author of *The Naked Civil Servant* had immediately pronounced on the discrepancy between Jonathan's inner and outer selves. 'Your brother looked healthy, happy, natural,' Quentin told me after reading the typescript. 'He could have played head prefect at Eton. They all adored him in the As You Like It. But everything *else* about him is extremely odd. Not faintly odd. *Extremely* odd. Except in appearance.' Then came the complicated bit. 'He's the *opposite* of you.'

One of the oddest things that Jonathan had done in the last year of his life was to befriend a homeless, friendless, alcoholic old schoolmaster and pursue this relationship even when, a few months later, he found The Love of His Life. He had met Mr Grant in a wine bar in the Strand. Soon he would welcome this courtly, vintage figure into the flat he shared with Anita on Chelsea Green. Later the old man would sleep in his car. In a tribute to Jonathan, published in *The Times* after his death, the writer Jonathan Gathorne-Hardy, who would have been best man at his wedding, did not touch on these oddnesses and ended his eulogy: 'He was

3

quite delightful to be with, warm, gentle, generous, very swift with a quick highly idiosyncratic wit.'

For several months after my brother's death, Jonny Gathorne-Hardy tried to get *The Queue* published, and I also touted the typescript in other directions, including that of Quentin Crisp. Though the book was unedited, repetitious and often excessively scatological, it appealed to me immediately and seemed to encapsulate and advance many of the ideas, subjects and private jokes Jonathan had first broached in tens of dozens of letters to me, in scraps of autobiographical writing he had dashed off for fun and in the two stories which, six months before his death, he had published in the *London Magazine*. The typescript reduced me to tears of laughter. I found it screamingly funny and so did some of the people I showed it to who had no direct knowledge of Jonathan.

The Queue is written in a complex style of its own – part journalese, part satire, part Beatrix Potter, part Marquis de Sade – but its plot is only too simple. The narrator leaves boarding school in a hurry and arrives at Euston Station

where he is approached on the concourse by an elderly dachshund called Mary, who has problems of her own. Immediately they form a bond, walk together to the station cafeteria and queue for twenty-five minutes to get tea and pies. Mary turns out to have no interest in the pie but is 'greedy' for the hot tea which the boy cools for her in a saucer. Soon a manageress appears and tries to take the dog away — but then gives in and passes the narrator some wrapped-up scraps and a collar and lead a customer had once left. For the next eighty pages the narrator and his dog have a series of stupendous adventures in and out of London, including court appearances and sexual encounters, until eventually, on the last page, Mary is sent off by train to a maternity home in the provinces. She has turned out to be not only an alcoholic and a drug addict but also 'four-months pregnant'.

Within moments of starting to read the book, I was aware of the eerie links between Mary and Anita Fielding — who was in her own way extremely wild — with Mr Grant and with a dachshund called Gilda whom we had known and loved as children. On the other hand, I still do not know, or care, what the story really signifies. My cousin Tim Behrens, author of a book about his own younger brother, *The Monument*, admired *The Queue* for its 'energy' and 'authority' but also wondered if it were not 'a veiled oblique extended suicide note'. A more recent reader, the poet Charles Boyle, sees the book as 'a kind of love letter, written by a man in the high of love'. I only know that in scholastic terms Jonathan had been a dunce — he had left Harrow without a single O level — and during our shared schooldays I had sometimes thought of him as a slight embarrassment. Then, almost overnight, he had blossomed, become self-sufficient and overtaken me in many ways. Jonathan had worldly ambitions and was on the crest of a wave at the time of his death. He had a well-paid job in a fashionable firm, he had already sold several large pen-and-ink drawings at the Redfern Gallery and had expectations of becoming a successful writer in his early twenties. The sequence in *The Queue* describing a highly eventful train journey ends with a self-mocking self-portrait of the person he might have become:

> A man in a corduroy suit, red socks and dishevelled hair is leaning out of a window. He looks wretched. His eyes are red with weeping. There has been a tragic incident. Last Tuesday he had finished his 90,000-word novel which had taken nine years to write. He was now on his way to London to present the manuscript to Gilda & Godwin, Gilston St publishers. But as he was passing an open window, a strong gust blew every sheet out of his hands. He was left clutching an empty file. I held his hand and comforted him. But, overcome with sorrow, he lowered the sill and threw himself out. I got a turn-up but, because the material was cheap, I was left with just a handful of corduroy. Far below on Exton High Street, I saw a crowd of shoppers gather round his body. That night the editor at Gilda & Godwin was told the news. A man of action, he cabled Exton Technical College and asked them to send out volunteers to search tracks, sidings and cuttings to gather the lost work. With great diligence, the task was successfully completed and four days later all 14,000 sheets were dispatched to London . . .

At the end of this book I will describe what happens to this 'sodden and almost illegible' manuscript, the young author's posthumous acclamation as a genius and subsequent memorial service in Westminster Abbey. Full of foreboding though this extract is – the bizarre flash-forward and the illogical number of scattered pages are typical of *The Queue* – it also bursts with good humour and, like all Jonathan's writings, seems motivated by a love of life rather than some morbid desire to mourn its shortness.

CHAPTER ONE

Lancaster

A priest comes running from a nearby farm. He
does the last rites. Then a storm begins. The skies
open. Lightning and thunder. You can just see the
ambulance making its way down the rutted farm
track. But the rain is so dense that they have difficulty. Rigor mortis has set in and the Magistrate
is hard to move. The stretcher-men use crowbars,
winches and pulleys. It takes over an hour. I tip
them 10/- each.

The Queue, Chapter Six

THE QUEUE WAS written in a hurry during the winter of
1969–70 and is ostensibly set in that period, but there is an
old-fashioned desolation about the landscapes (and town-
scapes) through which the dog and her young master travel
which might have belonged to a much earlier time. Adjectives
like 'gothic', 'primeval', 'diabolical' or even 'hellish' could be
applied to some of the characters, places and events described,
and the portrait of England that emerges is as bleak, distorted,
over-simplified and gaudy as a medieval map.

Geographically illogical, vaguely intersected by the Great
North Road and a wonky railway line, criss-crossed by random
highways and deserted country lanes and dotted with faintly
satirical, upliftingly meaningless landmarks like Carter Bridge

9

and Frampton Corner on the B34, this is a landscape both cosy and inhospitable. Jonathan was acutely aware of the sinister aspects of farms and smallholdings and what Sherlock Holmes described as the 'record of sin' that lies behind the 'smiling and beautiful' English countryside.

The weather is bad. There are strong winds. The going is soft. Many events take place beside main roads, in transport cafés or on the verge itself. Passing vehicles fling up 'dense black mud' as the 'sodden and filthy' narrator and his plucky old dog pass on their way. The scenario quoted at the start of this chapter gives the meteorological flavour of the whole book, but barely hints at the perversions, oddnesses and dangers which lurk on every corner.

I make these opening remarks merely to set the scene for my brother's birth – or perhaps to compare the world into which he was born with that of his imagination. Jonathan Head Barrow – his slightly eerie middle name came from a remote ancestor of my father – was born at Sawbridgeworth in Hertfordshire on 10 April 1947 after one of the coldest winters on record, a winter during which birds froze to telegraph wires and American millionairesses arrived in Britain carrying hot water bottles.

I have no memories of Sawbridgeworth, which – in *Queue* terms – is somewhere on the A1184 between Harlow and Bishop's Stortford. The Barrow family comes from the north of England and we were only living in the south so that my father could take the train each day to London where he worked in the prosecution department of the Board of Trade. For the previous eighteen months we had been living in a wing of a nearby mansion called Briggens, rented from a man called Lord Aldenham, a member of the Gibbs family, whose fortune derived from the guano trade. Though we soon left Briggens – the house is now a hotel and conference centre – its name and titled owner would occur often in subsequent family conversations. Towards the end of his life my father remarked about our time at Briggens: 'We did jolly well to get in there.'

My father's snobbery is worth mentioning early on. From his engagement diaries I see that three days after Jonathan's birth, he spent the afternoon at Easneye, a nearby country house helping its owner, H. F. Buxton, sometime High Sheriff of Herts and a distant cousin of my mother, cut his beech hedge. Note my father's use of initials, which was a habit of his generation – and a constantly used device in *The Queue*.

Jonathan was the fifth and youngest of us Barrow boys. I am the second youngest and was one-and-a-half when he was born. Our athletic oldest brother Simon, aged nine, was already at a prep school in Yorkshire called Aysgarth, run and owned by a terrible-sounding figure called Tommy Thompson. Julian, a podgy seven-year-old, would join him there soon. Our brother Martin, now three, and not yet bespectacled, would for many years act as leader of what my father later called the Little Boys, still in the care of our long-suffering but very capable mother.

We remained at Briggens for only a few weeks after Jonathan's birth. At the end of May 1947 .the family moved back to Lancaster, the north country county town and former port where the Barrows had lived and worked for five or six generations. My father remained in the south, living in comfortable bedsitting rooms in Kensington and visiting us at weekends. His work for the Board of Trade took him all over England: during the first few weeks of Jonathan's life he visited Bristol, Chesterfield, Daventry, Wolverhampton, Guildford, Luton, Horsham and other places faintly sugges-tive of the urban desolation in *The Queue*. I never asked him what he did in these towns and cities but years later I came across a cutting from a provincial newspaper which had him standing up in court haranguing some poor shopkeeper who had infringed Board of Trade regulations: 'I put it to you that your evidence is a pack of lies from beginning to end!'

Throughout these perambulations, my father gave a great deal of thought to his growing family in Lancaster, where his mother and aunt also lived. I had been born in my grandmother's house on an Edwardian development outside the city and must have already been taken to see my aged great-aunt, who lived in the family mansion closer to the city centre, built with money which may or may not have partly derived from the slave trade.

Are these prehistoric details relevant to my story? Does it matter that my father's family had been Quaker from the early eighteenth century and had later forged two marriages with the Cadbury dynasty and even, according to my father, put money into their first chocolate business? And what about my mother's ancestors, also partly Quaker in origin and tastes? Do I need to claim Elizabeth Fry as a remote aunt? Or mention my mother's cousin, Edward Johnston, who revived the lost art of calligraphy and designed the typeface the London Underground still uses today?

Bearing in mind the strangeness of *The Queue*, it may be more relevant to dwell upon the darker aspects of our family background, in particular the early deaths of both my grandfathers. In the summer of 1910 my father's father had been knocked down by a bus in Threadneedle Street and died before reaching St Bart's. As children we were dimly aware of this tragedy without considering its effect on my father, his only son, brought up alone by our grandmother, whom I later looked upon as a source of bohemian sophistication — she scattered sugar on salad — but whom others later pronounced to be 'a little on the queer side'. And the same might well have been said of my mother's father who had died in 1914, after suffering from a mental illness so severe that the psychiatrist treating him had begun his letter of sympathy to my grandmother with the words, 'What am I to say? It would be such hollow mockery to pretend we were not genuinely glad to think of that poor troubled spirit at rest and knowing how unfounded all his darkest fears have been all these years.'

And what of Lancaster itself? And how far removed was it from the landscape of *The Queue*? Perhaps prejudiced by his mother's experiences in a mental hospital there, Alan Bennett expresses a hearty dislike of the city, describing its inhabitants as 'less amiable and appealing than elsewhere in Lancashire'. I can only say that, revisiting the town in the late 1990s, I realised for the first time how beautiful it is. From the roof of the centrally located Music Room, an ornate edifice of which I was quite unaware as a child, Lancaster's skyline seemed almost Italian with its spires and domes. Small children have a limited aesthetic sense. One may have appreciated Lancaster Castle — also used as a prison — but must have missed out on so much else. As a child, one notices not cornices and finger-plates but noises and smells. Indeed there was a road on the outskirts of the town which we — or our mother — had renamed 'Smelly Street'.

Jonathan's first home in Lancaster was a small three-storey Victorian villa set at a junction of a main road, part of the A6 itself, down which huge lorries thundered day and night. The cabins in which the drivers of these 1940s juggernauts were housed were often primitive and exposed, lacking the creature comforts such trucks have today. I remember our mother pointing out a poor, suffering figure, perched high above his vast vehicle in a fluttering tarpaulin tent. And then being jolted awake in the night when one of these ghastly lorries took the corner badly and crashed into the houses opposite.

The house where we lived between 1947 and 1950, originally called 1 Meadowside and renamed Ash Tree House by our father, was set on an asphalt triangle called the Pointer, close to the family mansion, Baldrand, now a veterinary practice. Our great-aunt had by now had both of her legs amputated – one of the operations being performed by the father of Nicholas Monsarrat, author of *The Cruel Sea* – and was confined to a wheelchair, possibly engendering Jonathan's costermongerish interest in wheeled vehicles and handcarts. A love of such contraptions and the pretence of 'digging up the road' played a central role in the games that Martin, Jonathan and I soon began playing in the small front garden at Ash Tree House.

This 'senior clerical worker's house' – my father's description – is still standing today. Across the Pointer is the site of a shop which never closed, even on Christmas Day, and where we went to get sweets or more basic provisions. Years after we left the town we were shocked to hear that the popular proprietor had been charged with molesting small boys. Further up the Scotforth Road, as this bit of the A6 is called, was a shop called Howarth's which sold meat pies. I mention this because there is a passing reference in *The Queue* to Howarth's Debt Collection Agency. Even as a small boy, Jonathan had an acute ear for a potentially comic name, especially multi-consonanted ones, and an ability to store away this sort of material for future use.

Another neighbour who played a crucial role in our upbringing was Margaret Richardson, known as Richie, who lived with her mother at 19 Meadowside and for the next seven years would act as our mother's part-time help. The formal nannies and nurses who had looked after our older brothers Simon and Julian were a thing of the past. Richie was a fanatical Anglican and vegetarian with a pioneering interest in fresh air and food. She slept with her bedroom window wide open even in winter and cooked delicious things in ancient skillets in her back kitchen at 19 Meadowside. We sometimes spent the night in her house and shared the breakfast cereal called Fru-Grains served with black treacle, grated apple and an early version of yoghurt. Richie did not offer us her own home-made yoghurt, created by what appeared to be live maggots, strained through muslin, but these early experiences, along with trips to Lancaster market where Richie bought fresh shrimps and other luxuries we did not get at home, may have helped promote Jonathan's lifelong interest in cooking.

Richie's churchgoing activities focused on St Thomas's in Penny Street and we often went there with her as we grew older. Was this rather exotic pinnacled place of worship a forerunner of the church featured in *The Queue* being converted out of a dirty bookshop? Describing this particular enterprise, Jonathan mentions the stained-glass windows, rare surplices and eight-ton E-flat bells being cast, and then goes over the top by talking about *kennels*: 'Five hundred must be ready by August 1st.' Why on earth would five hundred dogs be needed

in the church? What demon was in him when he wrote those words? And what would Richie have made of this description and the book it comes from? Would she have been disappointed in her former charge?

Though we were constrained and exposed to the roar of traffic, there were plenty of excursions outside the narrow perimeters of Ash Tree House. We visited Baldrand often, played in the large garden there and attended upon our aged, legless great-aunt. We also went, via Smelly Street, to High Bank, our grandmother's house on the outlying Haverbreaks estate where Martin and I had been born. Here there was a grass tennis court and a small field in which our mother kept a pony or two. One of these animals was used to pull a simple wooden trap which we sometimes took into the town, even to meet visitors at Lancaster Station. At what point in history did we acquire our Austin A40? And how did we get out to places like the Ingleborough Caves, Heysham, Glasson Dock, Cockerham and Hest Bank? Or attend the Blackpool Tower circus, where one summer we saw a highly trained horse climbing into bed, pulling up its blanket, and switching off the light? Or visit my parents' friends in the Lune Valley? Or so often get over Shap Fell to see our other grandmother in Cumberland?

Anyway, we were not at Ash Tree House long. In the summer of 1950, when Jonathan was still only three, we moved to Bowerham House beyond Baldrand, a handsome square house built by a ship-owning ancestor in the 1820s, secluded within its walled garden and approached by a short private drive called The Grove. I don't know if my father had inherited this house or repurchased it. Here we had a bad-tempered mongrel dog called Jake who had to be put down, and a cat with a cauliflower ear called Pebble. Here too,

Jonathan's and my education began. Every morning, a Miss Randall came to the house and taught a handful of local children. Somewhere there is a photograph of us standing in a line. I am tall, pale and thin, Jonathan is as tubby as a pastry chef. And I remember Bowerham House in other ways. Thanks to the proximity of a cobbled working-class alleyway behind the house, odd things were sometimes thrown into the garden: pieces of fetid white bread and on one occasion an entire sheep's head.

At Bowerham I also became more aware of Jonathan's emerging personality. I remember cosy times with him and our mother, and how she even took us to a café in Lancaster called the Cosy Café. I also remember a timid, frightened side to him. Having a bath in Bowerham House, he was afraid he might go down the plughole. Exploring the attics with me, Martin and my mother, he was terrified that he might fall through a tiny hole in the floorboards, a hole so small that even a matchbox covered it. But such fears are surely not uncommon in small children? And there is a photograph of him from this time, blond-headed, curly-haired, grinning jubilantly and far from insecure, astride a broken tank up on Ingleborough Fell. I cannot tell you when his peculiar love of animals first manifested itself. Did Jake and Pebble mean much to him, I wonder? And though *The Queue* shines throughout with what Tim Behrens called a 'transcendent innocence', there is nothing in it which throws light on Jonathan's character as a child.

In July 1953, a month after the Coronation, when Jonathan was six, we moved again, this time to High Bank, the home of the mainly bedridden grandmother we knew as 'Grandmama'. From this temporary home – my father was already planning his big move south – I attended the Mount Independent School in Morecambe and was followed to this establishment by Jonathan. Here I became exaggeratedly aware of my brother's mild backwardness in academic terms when a teacher asked me to help him with his sums and spelling. And back at High Bank there were also signs of what would now be called 'behavioural problems'. One day on the drive, Jonathan spat at our grandmother's cleaning lady, Annie. And I have a sharp memory of the family ganging up on him one lunchtime, causing him to leave the dining room, his face contorted with rage.

Madness, anyway, was in the air. Though *mad* was then a word usually applied to *me* rather than Jonathan. On holiday from Harrow, our oldest brother, Simon, tended to tease his youngest siblings. At High Bank, he went through a phase of pressing his face into mine and saying, 'Here's the mad boy!' This was a little undermining but I never at this time thought I *was* mad, only that I *looked* mad – which is perhaps just as bad. And this problem was dramatised by the fact that close to High Bank was a lunatic asylum called the Royal Albert. The somewhat sinister silhouette of this institution, not the one in which Alan Bennett's mother was held, was visible from the house and is also within view of those travelling into Lancaster on the train. According to the architectural historian Nikolaus Pevsner, the Royal Albert was built in 1867–73 and has 'a steep French roof rising between pinnacles and accompanied to most of its height by a chimney'. There were many family jokes about this place. Some of them cruel. Whenever my behaviour seemed to merit it, my older brothers went through the motions of telephoning the Royal Albert and arranging for me to be collected. Right away.

I imagine Jonathan took all this in. Later on, during our teenage years, my father rammed home the message with arch comments about mental deficiency – he was keen on the expression 'MD' – and occasionally reproved us with remarks like: 'People will think you're from the institution.' When eventually, at the age of twenty-two, Jonathan came to write his book, he featured innumerable institutions, and let his hair down when describing the asylum to which the narrator and his dog are bundled so unceremoniously. 'The inmates gather round us,' he wrote. 'Ghastly figures

without proper form or construction.' He then switches into a monologue by the superintendent Miss Uinne: 'You cannot expect them to behave like humans. They were brought here in cages. This is not really living. The trouble is that they have long, long lives. Many here are well into their 100th year. On the ninth floor, we have a human sheep who remembers Disraeli. Look through that window. There's our burial ground.' This episode culminates some paragraphs later with the asylum's demolition in the middle of the night, one of the many holocaust-like scenes with which *The Queue* is filled.

By the end of August 1954, my father was ready to

leave Lancashire for ever and re-establish us all – including Grandmama and the cat called Pebble – in south-west England. Earlier that summer I had followed my older brother Martin to a boarding school in Bristol and my father had already started looking at country properties in Somerset and Wiltshire. His engagement diaries mention houses he looked at – and rejected. A place called Ashley Grove was said to face the wrong way – and so on. On 10 June 1954, my father offered £6,000 for a south-facing house called Turleigh Combe, on the edge of a village called Winsley, one-and-a-half miles west of an ancient and semi-picturesque Wiltshire town called Bradford-on-Avon, famous for its Saxon chapel. The offer was instantly accepted.

CHAPTER TWO

Cumberland

The journey to the police station was not without incident. At the junction of Pell Street we ran over a toad that was trying to get from Cumberland to the South Coast. His legs were badly crushed and his neck was severed. I looked back as we sped away and saw him trying to get to his feet again. Just as he was up a City Council gutter-cleaning machine came past and swept him into the machinery. After he had gone I found a tiny suitcase where Toad had been struck down. I opened it and found 2 pairs of toad's socks, a change of underwear, a cheap toad's plastic mac and a pair of slippers.

The Queue, Chapter Six

BEFORE EMBARKING UPON our life at Turleigh Combe, which would remain my parents' home until after Jonathan's death, I must explain and describe the role that our other grandmother's house in Cumberland had already played in our lives. And in Jonathan's life in particular. Perhaps I should have mentioned our holidays in the Lake District earlier, and the powerful but peaceful counterbalance they offered to our grimy, semi-urban existence in Lancaster, where a factory horn rang every morning to wake the mill-workers.

My grandmother's house in the village of Dacre near Ullswater had a Beatrix Potterish charm. I remember its scrubbed red sandstone floors and the elaborately chiming clock. I remember the cat known as Lord Grey and the rough-haired dachshund, Rudy, named after the infamous Rudolf Hess. And the Chinese print in the upstairs lavatory whose caption 'The Earthly Paradise. By an unknown Painter of the Latter Part of the Ming Period 1368–1644' was later seized upon by Jonathan and became one of the sacred texts of our shared private world.

My grandmother had moved to Dacre before the war along with my mother's unmarried older sister, Aunt Jean. For most of the time I knew it the house was run by a man called Ferguson who lived across the village green, kept ferrets, and came over each day to light fires, clean shoes and help my aunt in the garden. In the orchard, Aunt Jean kept pigs which we sometimes could hear being slaughtered, and in the small field was a hen-run. Jonathan's intense attachment to hens may have begun at this point – the smell of the mash Aunt Jean cooked up for them was a dominant presence – but they were only one element in a richly rural environment. Farm milk was collected each day in a lidded canister. The villagers included old-fashioned characters like Miss Bonus, who dressed in black and kept a cow down by the beck. There were village boys who scared and teased us and there was my grandmother's cleaning lady, Miss Titterington, widely known, even by my grandmother, as Miss Titty.

Dacre was, and is, a lovely village. It has an old red sandstone church and a fourteenth-century castle, a former border fort or peel tower, used as a farmhouse at this time but later to play a rather weird and wonderful role in this story. The castle – Pevsner states that it contains 'a pretty *lavatorium* . . . with a twelve-petalled drain like that of a piscina' – and all the land around it had belonged since the 1680s to the Hasell family, whose shimmering pale-pink stately home Dalemain is fully visible from the Penrith road and is now open to the public. Major Edward Hasell was Lord of the Manor throughout our childhood and was the first and perhaps only squire Jonathan and I were conscious of as children. Clad in astonishingly heavy tweeds and with the face of an old lion, he delivered the lesson each Sunday in Dacre Church in the tones of a dalesman, not a toff. This rare countryman, who never went to London, would inevitably feature later in Jonathan's writings.

So too would our Uncle Gurney, who lived in a large, attractive villa on Ullswater where he and Aunt Betty – she celebrates her ninety-first birthday as I write these words – taught English to foreign students and later prepared boys for Common Entrance. Though our mother's older brother was an unusual man, he bears no resemblance to the uncle mentioned in *The Queue*, a pistol-wielding ex-commando later seen through a window indulging in sadomasochistic activities with a Mr L. B. Yonne. Nor was Uncle Gurney the sort of man who would make you promise, as the uncle in *The Queue* does, to get in touch if you were ever in trouble.

In other ways, Uncle Gurney did fuel Jonathan's imagination, and so did the Lake District as a whole. In *The Queue,* there are several lapses into rural idyll. From inside a hessian sack on his way to the Home for Imbeciles, the narrator suddenly notes everything is peaceful. 'It is very quiet. I hear larks, thrushes, and, in the distance, a tractor ploughing.' And lovely though Dacre was, its inhabitants were not entirely immune to the darker side of country life. A woman had drowned herself in a deep pool in the beck where we played. Miss Titty would go mad and throw her purse into the same

23

river. And one holiday we learnt that a local farmer had found his prize bull threatening a farmhand — and shot it dead. *The Queue* is full of farm stories and even in the Home for Imbeciles there is a bull that has gone off the rails, got drunk, raped the farmer's wife and ever since has been slowly growing the features of a human being.

Though half-human animals and other oddities like a one-legged cat crop up often in *The Queue*, most of the animals mentioned, including Mary, have some human character-istics. With a storyteller's disregard for logic, Jonathan gives his animals, birds and fish attributes, instincts and origins which render them utterly unworldly. Inspector Snaith has looked after the highly trained official Police Cod, used for complex underwater retrievals, since it was *a small child*. One of the sewer rats plans to keep Sir Roland Humphrey's missing brooch for *his little girl* when she's grown up. A trout *drowns*. Hens who refuse to help the police with their inquiries are *punched in the face*. Rats on a refuse truck 'all know each other and chatter incessantly'. During a scene at a dogs' home, a bulldog borrows sixpence for a cup of tea and Sir Ivan Cutt's shepherd's dog has a favourite TV programme it wants to watch. Many of Jonathan's creatures also have very flex-ible identities. The friendly sparrow who appears at the end of the story first rests on the narrator's shoulder, then, minutes later, carries both narrator and dog on its back and even offers them the loan of his *pyjamas*.

Jonathan's humanisation of birds and animals reminds one again of the works of Beatrix Potter, whose animals all speak and dress like humans and who in some cases — what could be more chilling than *The Tale of Jemima Puddle-Duck*? — act in an extremely violent manner. The animals in Jonathan's imaginary world, like the accident-prone toad mentioned at the start of this chapter, are more complex, urban and eccentric, but Beatrix Potter's stories were certainly familiar to him. Among his possessions when he died was *The Tale of Little Pig Robinson* and towards the end of *The Queue* there is a moment when the sparrow begs the narrator and his dog to exert themselves, which is exactly what the sparrows did when Peter Rabbit got caught in a gooseberry net.

I must not forget my mother's role in all this. Born and brought up on farmland twenty miles north of the Lake District, she was also a passionate animal lover who often amused us as children with tales about the horses and dogs she had known before the war, without glossing over any grizzly details. I still remember how spiritedly my mother and Aunt Jean had talked of the dog they had known as children. 'Binkie once caught a rat by its tail. The tail came off with *several inches of pink innards.*' Like Beatrix Potter, my mother had also been a painter. During a spell at the Edinburgh School of Art she had painted an oil of the school's donkey which now hangs above my younger son's bed in London. She had also received private lessons from an illustrator called Vernon Stokes – learning how to paint and draw dogs and birds – but had completely given up this pastime on marriage and now only showed off her artistic skills in paper and pencil games.

I will later write of how my mother raised her animals and even her hens to almost human status. Here I am concerned with the early influence of Cumberland on Jonathan. As so often, he took matters to extremes, extracting amusement even from the names of Cumbrian fells and other landmarks. Writing to me in the mid-1960s from Wyoming and then the South of France, Jonathan revived the names of places we had known as children. Some of these names, like Moor Divock, Motherby and a hillock known as Chinaman's Head, are celebrated for their inherent, intrinsic humour. Others like Skiddaw, High

Street (the range of fells south of Ullswater), Great Dodd and the hill closest to Dacre known as Little Mell are given human identities – and even cast as defendants in police court dramas. Great Dodd, he tells me, 'has done three years in Newcastle for being found on enclosed premises'. High Street 'had been assaulting people in a Motherby toilet.' And Skiddaw, he says, had 'lost its PO book and suspects Little Mell of its theft'. However nonsensical this stuff is, mountains and hills *do* have disquieting qualities. And I still remember those family walks across the fells with Jonathan, perhaps by then ten or eleven years old, lagging a long way behind us and calling out, more than once, *'What would you do if the whole mountain came rushing towards you?'*

CHAPTER THREE

Turleigh Combe

At 4.38 a.m., just as the sun is coming up over
Gorley Woods, I hear a strange rustling in the grass
beside me. I peer closely but can see nothing. But
there it is again. Suddenly I leap to my feet and
go pale. For there, just a few feet away, is a 19-foot
Viper. It is curling itself into a ball, ready to strike.
He is as thick as a man's neck . . .

The Queue, Chapter Seven

TURLEIGH COMBE, INTO which we moved in the middle of
September 1954, had its own kind of eeriness but was as
different from my grandmother's house in the Lake District
and the whole Cumberland ethos as my father was from
my mother. However much my mother may have objected
to the original purchase of this Victorian villa on to which
a fake Georgian wing had been attached, she would do her
best to eradicate some of its pretensions, making a large
kitchen garden and populating the place with dogs, hens,
geese and ponies. Visiting the house a few weeks after
Jonathan's death, his friend Gathorne-Hardy remarked, 'I
now see why Jonathan wrote as he did.' Had he perceived
the tensions or contradictions in the air, the solid north-
country furniture, some made by Gillows of Lancaster,
and the rather bogus even gimcrack twentieth-century

turlish Camh

refinements? Or perhaps the differences between my mother and father?

My mother was shy and country-loving. She was bored by London – where my father continued to work until 1957 – and inclined to be disparaging about 'towny' behaviour and 'hotel' food. Later in life I noticed how she would listen in a sullen manner to my father's observations on city life and accompanying vulgarities. She was at her best dealing with animals and plants and had learnt over the years how to manage children, even if it sometimes meant playing off the majority of her sons against the offending minority. For as long as I can remember my parents had separate bedrooms. My father would sleep at the top of the house and had his own bathroom to which the hot water never came – or came very slowly. My mother slept a flight of stairs away, where she was sometimes joined in bed by Jonathan, only seven when we moved south.

And also – how can I have forgotten? – there was

Grandmama. Now eighty-seven, my father's mother had arrived at Turleigh Combe only eight days after us and was immediately and permanently installed in the bedroom next to my mother's. Grandmama is one of the many dark horses in my story. As children, Jonathan and I took her presence for granted and were utterly unaware of any burden she might have placed on our mother. I have already touched on her difficult 'queer side'. She was also amusing. She took her meals on a tray in bed and wrote notes to my mother in French, stating that she could only eat with silver spoons. She received saffron cake from Cornwall where her own childhood had been spent and packages from her bank containing crisp new ten-shilling notes. Later she gave me a set of George Eliot's works, carefully inscribing each volume to me, though I would not start reading these until long after her death.

Today, I look upon Grandmama and the family she came from – Tim Behrens, her great-nephew, later boasted that all his female relations looked like the comedian Larry Grayson – with a certain admiration, but she does not feature in any shape or form in Jonathan's writings. Grandmama died soon after our arrival in Wiltshire and perhaps made more of an impact on my oldest two brothers, Simon and Julian, both of whom were now at Harrow. Even today, I notice that Julian sometimes uses Grandmama's expression 'Please to . . .' instead of plain 'Please . . .'

Anyway, my father was not directly involved in the care of his mother or his children. Or even of his wife. He had not been present during the move south, leaving all practical arrangements to our mother. During the first three years at Turleigh Combe, my father continued to work in London and kept a permanent bedsitting room in Holland Park. Writing this book obliges me to reappraise both parents.

In the past I noticed that my father got on wonderfully well with barmen, waiters, taxi-drivers and policemen, but also thought of him as friendless. Perhaps this is how he became in the late 1970s when finally self-marooned on the Isle of Man, but according to his surviving engagement diaries he had quite a busy, sociable existence in the post-war years. In 1949 he had joined the Treasury Prosecution team. Whatever that meant, he now worked permanently in London and no longer out in the sticks.

My father's diaries give a vivid impression of his life as he approached early retirement. He attended fittings at Kilgour & French in Savile Row and saw his dentist Mr Maloney. By 1954, he was a member of the Reform Club and dined there often with his stockbroker, Sir Charles Hobhouse, and others noted only by their surnames. He also dined, admittedly often alone, at the Hyde Park Hotel's Buttery Bar. Also alone, he frequented the Metropolitan Music Hall in Edgware Road – and went there twice in May 1955 to see the so-called 'Mighty Mannequin', Joan Rhodes. My father's brief subsequent friendship with this remarkable woman, who bent iron bars and tore up telephone directories on stage, had prolonged repercussions. Driving through Exeter in the late 1950s, on our way to a family holiday in Cornwall, my father was convinced he had spotted Joan in the street and had to be prevented stopping the car.* Such incidents and the names of other variety stars hung over our early life. So did jokes about Wormwood Scrubs, where for several years during the same period my father was a regular prison visitor. He did not boast about this work, which may have owed something to his Quaker blood, but often talked about the criminal types he'd

---

* Joan Rhodes died in 2010. I played Scrabble with her a few weeks before her death.

met and even once described being locked in a cell with a convicted murderer.

None of us can claim to have done anything so obviously charitable but all five of us inherited or acquired a great deal from *both* our parents. In Jonathan's case the mixture of town and country, domestic and metropolitan life and other opposites would eventually create a highly volatile situation, even a violent combustion. At this early stage my father was a semi-absent figure, and the scatological, medical and legal aspects of his character, which arguably had such an effect on Jonathan's writings, were less evident. My mother's character and use of language, on the other hand, must have been already familiar to him. When *The Queue's* unnamed narrator tells the insects circling around them, 'Go away, you brutes,' he was using the very phrase my mother often employed during those wasp-infested picnics of our childhood.

What more can one say about Turleigh Combe that has bearing on this story? The village of Winsley, to which it was attached, had some attractive old buildings, a post office run by Mrs I. R. Evans, a pub called the Seven Stars, a famous chest hospital and a modern housing estate – but no squire. Turleigh Combe itself was set in seven acres and approached by a long curling drive between paddocks, along which my father would later plant enough shrubs to render it as oppressive as the long, steep drive leading to the Home for Imbeciles in *The Queue*, which Jonathan describes as winding through privet, laurels, antirrhinums and rhododendrons. At Turleigh, the drive culminated in a sloping gravelled area my father called the forecourt and to which, in a letter from the South of France many years later, my brother would give a human identity. The view south was one of our new home's most impressive features, extending ten miles and offering a distant view of the Westbury White Horse and in the middle distance the ghostly ruin of a stately pile called Rood Ashton, which might itself have come from the pages of *The Queue*. Down below our garden and the wild, sloping combe itself was the village of Turleigh, a much more significant place than Winsley, with a grand little manor house and a few stately cottages, which meant something to me but nothing, I daresay, to Jonathan. And below this village, at the bottom of the valley, was a tiny hamlet called Avoncliff which had a pub called the Cross Guns and a railway station called Avoncliff Halt. I mention this place only because it would become the inspiration for 'tiny Rollscliffe Halt with two stopping trains a day', where *The Queue's* narrator and his dog are thrown off a train and bombarded with rotten fruit, vegetables, dead cats, bad eggs, sewerage and chemicals.

Significant though Avoncliff was – the Cross Guns later became a private haunt of ours – Jonathan was always, from the very start, more excited by the farm to the north of Winsley run by a man called Godwin. On 3 October 1954, only a week or two after our big move south, my father noted in his diary: 'Walk with Jonathan. He loves Godwin's farm!' I remember Mr Godwin, who looked more like what my father would have called 'a senior clerical officer' than a farmer, on account of his wife, May, who soon became one of the cleaning ladies at Turleigh Combe. Mrs Godwin would later excite us by describing a large snake she had seen crossing the drive – 'as thick as a man's neck' – and with the information that terrible things went on in Winsley that we, in our relative isolation down at 'the combe', were unaware of.

By the autumn of 1954, Jonathan was the only one of us left at home. Earlier that year I had followed my brother

Martin, nicknamed by our older brothers the Brainy Pup on account of his slight resemblance to the Rupert Bear character of that name, to Clifton College Preparatory School in Bristol. I don't know how Jonathan's education continued. Was there a school in the village – or in Bradford-on-Avon, our local market town? For the next year or so, he must have spent a lot of what is now called 'quality time' with our mother. I remember no 'behavioural' issues at this point.* I know that in the kitchen a special stool was introduced so that he might cook things on the Aga and that in the garden he helped my mother in all kinds of ways.

---

* Yes, but in my pocket diary for 12 January 1957 I find I have written, 'Jonny off his head. Mrs G tried to comfort him.'

CHAPTER FOUR

Hens

We walk down a narrow path between laurels and come to a big grass area, at least the size of a tennis court. But there are people already there. Hundreds and hundreds of hens are lined up. Each carries a small bundle. I ask what happened. Apparently 500 chickens from Coddfird Friendly Society were taking a rail excursion to Clacton-on-Sea. There had been an accident. A collision with an oncoming goods train. Terrible slaughter and every chicken lost its life. The dependants have bagged the whole area for a mass burial. The clerk protests. There's a three-week waiting list. Immediately he is set upon by the angry hens. Some go for the neck. Some go for the eyes. He is down on his back in seconds and dead within the minute. Twelve minutes later all that is left are buttons, bones and shoes.

The Queue, Chapter Fifteen

I IMAGINE MY mother began keeping hens fairly soon. Or bantams. I remember a tin on which Jonathan had written and misspelled 'bantams carn'. Hens were part of the domestic culture of the mid-twentieth century, not an aspect of my mother's personality as they were of Aunt Jean. Jonathan already knew all about Aunt Jean's hens at Dacre and was

34

aware of the comic possibilities of feathered creatures. In the Winsley Post Office, he was delighted by Mrs I. R. Evans's bleak response to a customer asking if she sold whitewash: 'Is that for fowls houses?' And in Bradford-on-Avon he soon noted the jolly, red-faced butcher who accosted passers-by with the question: 'How about a nice cockerel?'

There are, alas, no drawings of hens by Jonathan, but they play a central role in his writings. Of course he was not the only author to use hens – or cocks. Shakespeare did so. So did Chaucer. And Flaubert. And isn't there a character called 'Cocky Locky' in the old fable 'The Sky is Falling'? Hens appear along with other poultry in the works of Beatrix Potter and in an unaccountable number of lesser children's stories. They also feature, it hardly needs to be added, in great paintings of all nations. Their appeal is obvious: they are colourful, picturesque, fierce, brave, half-tame and beloved by children. In his book *Memoirs of a Public Baby* Philip O'Connor remembers how as a boy he loved lying in the hen-run. The hens themselves he loved for 'their sharp matronly scrutiny out of eyes like the slits in castles, their eccentric movements expressing an uncompromising thoroughness of purpose.' The hen or chicken has enriched our language, provided dozens of metaphors and played a singular role in the Barrow family. I sometimes thought Aunt Jean looked like a half-plucked hen and, soon after moving to the south-west, we began to attend meets of the Beaufort Hunt, where we were riveted by a smartly dressed, but bleak-looking lady who rode side-saddle. We nicknamed her The Hen-Without-Feathers.

Hens make dozens of appearances in *The Queue* and there are several lengthy set pieces in which they appear as both victims and aggressors. On other occasions the narrator's dog is the chief troublemaker. Following the accident near the start of the book, Mary ducks into the plucking room of an abattoir and gets a live broiler by the leg. In the pandemonium that follows, five hundred 18lb turkeys break out of the next hutch and wreak revenge on the dachshund. Hundreds of beaks begin to peck her and it is only the narrator's 'quick reaction' that saves Mary from what he describes as 'a terrible death'. Later Mary shakes with fear, apologises for her behaviour and promises it will never happen again. But of course it does happen again. And again. One of the worst skirmishes occurs when boy, dog and the friendly sparrow get a lift in a truck carrying 4,000 eggs to a supermarket in Middlesex:

> After travelling for an hour, the driver suddenly brakes and the truck stops. I look out of the ventilation window and realize we have been picketed by angry hens. They have erected barricades across the road and it is impossible to continue. I step into the cab through the dividing-door and find the driver is in hysterics. At least five thousand hens are striding about on the road in front of us and many others are perching on the windscreen and bonnet. A Senior Hen comes forward and asks us to explain our load. What are you doing with those eggs? How dare you take them away. Unless they are returned immediately, you will not be able to continue. The driver loses his temper, grabs the Senior Hen and wrings its neck in front of the five thousand. It was a stupid thing to do. There is pandemonium. The hens are now pressing against the windscreen and thousands of beaks tap angrily. In the back of the truck I hear Sparrow and Mary crying for help. A new band of hens has arrived, and they are trying

to force their way in through the rear doors. I slash at them with a broom-handle, execute several, and frighten the others away. At the front of the truck, things are getting desperate. They have tapped a small hole in the windscreen and already claws and feathered legs are trying to enter.

Fortunately, we are saved from almost certain death by the discovery of a large can of petrol under the front seat. I open it, light a match and climb rapidly out of the skylight onto the roof of the truck. The astonished hens do not realize what is happening as I spray them with petrol. I drop the match and it is all over. A dreadful screaming, and feathers, claws, eggs and sinews explode in all directions. There is a strong smell of burnt feathers. The few that escape instant death are so badly burnt that they die within minutes. Others, unable to face such an overwhelming defeat, take their own lives.

As so often in *The Queue*, Jonathan uses illogic as a comic device. How do hens take their own lives? Another awesome scene involving humans and hens, quoted at the opening of this chapter, ends with the crematorium officials running for guns, hand grenades, pikes and muskets and taking revenge on the intruders. Twelve minutes later all 500 hens sprawl across the grass and the victorious humans move in to examine their kill: 'They choose two dozen of the plumpest birds for their own larder. That afternoon a buyer from a big local firm of poultry packers pays 2d each for the remainders. He leaves 36 behind. Too badly shot-up. Rooks, vultures and carrion-crows from local woods consume these unfit carcasses over the next few weeks.'

Here we touch on the heart of the matter. The hen is not just a picturesque and ferocious creature — if you disagree with ferocious, consider the cannibalism that occured in hen-runs like Aunt Jean's. Its alter ego, the chicken, also plays a central role in cooking and catering. The fact that Jonathan would become a very good cook and work for some time in grand hotels makes his interest in hens all the more pointed, even though he cannot, it seems, resist putting a macabre spin on many aspects of the catering trade. Consider this typical high-street scene from *The Queue:*

> Mary is now in an extremely difficult mood and refuses to walk any further. Instead, she crosses the main road and gazes into the window of a butcher's shop. The business does not appear to be in a very good working state, and sirloins, best-ends and offals are rotting in the hot sun. There does not seem to be any organization. Recently-slaughtered beasts are stacked on the pavement, awaiting dissection. And, inside the shop, the butcher is behaving oddly with some chicken carcasses. He was unable to sell them and they have gone bad over the weekend. At his feet there is a large basket of feathers and he is trying to stick them back onto the carcasses with glue. They smell horribly and he uses liberal amounts of aerosol disinfectant. Tomorrow, he will try and sell these carcasses to other dealers, pretending that they were alive-on-the-farm that morning.

During the train journey in *The Queue,* there is a bizarre red herring about a solo naked hen. First encountered in a restaurant car being tortured by galley hands, the bird's corpse

is then chucked out of the window, skids down the embankment and rolls onto a main road. A motorist pulls up and,
thinking the object to be a human limb, places it in his boot.
After a few miles, clucking is heard and the hen manages to
open the boot from the inside. The driver loses concentra-
tion, swerves into the wrong lane and dies in a collision with
a laundry van. The hen, with amazing agility, jumps out just
before impact and flies to a nearby poultry farm. Here she
is welcomed by the farmer Mr Mille and offered tea and
biscuits. Later that night he shows her to a hutch but the
23,000 Rhode Islands already in residence take an instant
dislike to the newcomer. Mr Mille decides to keep the hen
in his own house, soon finds her 'the ideal hen' and grows
passionately fond of her. Unfortunately a local gossip named
Miss Cudde starts a rumour that the farmer is having an
affair with the hen, which reaches the ears of the CID. Police
cars, Alsatians and a Black Maria roll up at the farmhouse.
Mr Mille, clad only in a jockstrap, is forced to admit them
and Hen is found in the farmer's bed, 'naked and in a high
state of sexual excitement'. This long paragraph ends with
court proceedings: Mr Mille is sentenced to twenty-eight
years' hard labour for his 'bestial and hideous crime' and the
hen, brought into court in a crate, is granted a free pardon,
only to get beaten up by a gang of youths at a bus station,
and finally commit suicide – had Jonathan run out of better
ideas? – by flushing herself down the toilet.

Here we have bits of the criminal court, the language
of sentencing and sexual knowledge that have no bearing
on Jonathan's character as a small boy but faithfully reflect
the world in which he grew up, the paraphernalia of the
hen-run and the feel of the farm. Having police crawling
about farmland reminds us of Sherlock Holmes's wise words
about the English countryside and of Mrs Godwin's sinister

hints about village life. During another of *The Queue's* rural raids, armed police enter a battery cage, wake up 300 Sussex, tear away blankets draped over one hutch – inside a cock is discovered having sexual intercourse with a young Rhode Island – and cross-examine the whole lot of them. Returning to their cars, the disappointed detectives stumble upon the body of the man they were hunting. He has been horribly gored by a bull. In a typical flash-forward the narrator then tells us that the farmer is furious with the bull and orders him to be chastised in front of his herd: 'There were pictures in all the farming press.'

As a child and later as the author of *The Queue*, Jonathan's tender, violent, humorous interest in birds and animals seems to have encompassed all living creatures in an almost Francis of Assisi-like embrace. And the creatures he writes about often show a similar mixture of violence and tenderness themselves. Tearfully explaining his plight to another cross, snorting bull, the boy notices that tears are also rolling down the animal's cheeks: 'Cautiously, fearing a hoax, I approached and put my hand on his neck. Suddenly he went down on his knees, blinked and began to weep . . . Between sobs, he explained to us that the man from the Corned Beef Factory had arrived last night and selected his carcass for the abattoir.'

Not only are animals given joke human characteristics, human beings are also jokily treated on a par with animals. Reunited with his pet cod, Inspector Snaith becomes extremely emotional, weeps copiously, cuddles the fish in his arms and tells onlookers: 'It can't be true. My cod has come back to me. All of you, go away. I want to be alone.' And though often handled with humour if not actual *joie de vivre*, death is everywhere. In another crematorium scene, mourners queuing with their dead bodies include humans, toads, bantams, rooks, pheasants, stoats and sheep – 'One crow has a handmade coffin. About £8 I think. Stoat cannot afford anything and has a paper bag' – but are soon upstaged by the unpleasantness of the priests in charge: 'We do not take cheques. We do not have change for £5 notes. We mean to be as disagreeable as we can. Take your bodies elsewhere if you like. We don't mind.'

In the Animal Hospital, to which the narrator takes his new friend on the day they first meet, there is an even more

extraordinary parade of sick and injured animals and insects: a rat that has damaged its foot in a culvert, moles, hedge-hogs, bats, flies, gnats, cats, stoats, shrews and dormice. Then 'a most terrible howling' from the Casualty entrance announces the arrival of a badger who has been hit by an articulated wagon on the A33. Later, orderlies rush in with a tabby cat, which has taken an overdose, and a barn owl who's been found with her head in a gas oven.

Suicidal animals are a particularly poignant invention, but this sequence hints at the delight in all animals which Jonathan had begun to show during those early days at Turleigh Combe. The first real live pets, or living creatures, that Jonathan knew were Rudy, Pebble, Jake, Lord Grey, Aunt Jean's hens and pigs and my mother's bantams.★ And to this motley crew would be added, on 31 March 1955, a pony. I remember quite well the arrival of this animal at Limpley Stoke Station, down Winsley Hill. In those days, British Railways were happy to transport pet animals and for all I know the same train could have borne gorillas, orang-utans, pet rats or any of the other creatures which pop up in *The Queue*. The liver chestnut pony which we rode home that day was called Flash on account of the white diamond on her forehead. Almost exactly Jonathan's age, she would become his first real special, four-legged friend, and live on until a few weeks before his own death.

Some sixteen months later, in the autumn of 1956, life at Turleigh Combe was further enriched and Flash was to some extent upstaged by the arrival of a brown, smooth-haired, half-miniature dachshund. My father, who was good at this sort of thing, gave her the name Gilda. My mother would later pronounce Gilda to be 'bad, greedy and fat'. I do not know what Jonathan made of this newcomer in those early days, but I do know that Gilda would preside over the rest of our childhood, and become the inspiration for hundreds of Jonathan's drawings, some of them scatological, and for imaginative writings of every sort. Above all, she

★ Jonathan also had a beloved toy dog, Jackie, with heavily patched, tubular legs, that had originally belonged to our father.

would provide the model for Mary the sexually promiscuous, fun-loving, alcoholic dog in *The Queue*. And Gilda retained her allure by being wrenched away from him – or was it the other way round? A year before her arrival, Jonathan had joined Martin and me as a boarder at Clifton College Preparatory School.

CHAPTER FIVE

Clifton

This morning, sugar buns for three hundred were delivered at the school. As the roundsman drove away, I heard Mr Prente come up from his basement room. He opened the confectioner's box, counted numbers, and found three buns missing. Immediately, he rang the little hand-bell that he carries in his trouser pocket. Every boy came into the preparation room. Then Mr Prente searched the lockers. He had difficulty with No. 19 and used a tool. A moment later there was a scream and Mr Prente ran up the stairs: his gown had blood on it and his underpants were at his ankles. On the way up he bumped against the school hairdresser and oils, clippers, combs, knives and clips fell from the little attaché case which he always carries. This means the end for the school hairdresser. Only yesterday he had cut off a boy's ear with a clipper and the Head Master now wants to talk to him.

The Queue, Chapter One

THE CHOICE OF Clifton College Preparatory School was odd, and underlined the oddness of Turleigh Combe. Both places were, in culinary terms, neither fish nor fowl. Our oldest brothers Simon and Julian had been sent to a conventional preparatory school – never mind its scary-sounding Head Master – which had long acted as a feeder school for Harrow where we were all in theory heading. Clifton Prep had no connection with Harrow nor any public school other than Clifton College itself. Here there *was* a link. My father had been a boarder at Clifton College for a few terms in the 1920s and then moved to the Quaker school Leighton Park, near Reading. In some draft instructions to his executors dated 1948, my father had written, 'Clifton would not be my choice as I was permanently unwell there.' In spite of these misgivings, he had nonetheless, long before the move south, decided to send his three youngest sons to its prep school. Martin had started at Clifton in September 1952 at the age of eight and I had joined him there for the summer term of 1954.

Clifton College and its Preparatory School are set in the suburbs of Bristol, nestling against Clifton Downs and within a few minutes' walk of Clifton Suspension Bridge, from which people occasionally threw themselves in despair or accidentally fell off when they were trying to rescue blown-away mackintoshes caught in its cables. The prep-school building had gone up in 1933 and consisted of class-rooms, the Head Master's office and a school hall. The surrounding streets were full of mid-Victorian stucco houses, some of which served as boarding houses for both the upper and lower schools. And within a stone's throw of the complex was the famous and popular Bristol Zoo. Considering Jonathan's intense interest in animals it must be of some significance that he spent four formative years a few yards away from – and in some cases within earshot of – a memorable collection of live wild beasts. There was a famous gorilla at Bristol Zoo called Alfie. There were also caged eagles, snakes as thick as a man's neck and, I daresay, orang-utans.

The proximity of such howling, wailing and hissing creatures was one of the oddnesses of Clifton College Preparatory School. Another oddness was the fact that fifty per cent of the pupils were day boys, the sons of local merchants, garage-owners, solicitors, clergymen and the like. This introduced a roughness – or richness? – into the mix which in the long run benefited us all. Clifton College Preparatory School was not set, like most prep schools, in some isolated, converted country mansion, but on the edge of a huge, proud city, the ingredients of which fed into Jonathan's mind from an early stage.

I dwell on these details partly because *The Queue* begins at a school and carries several subsequent references to its Head Master, and partly because there are elements throughout the book which relate to Jonathan's time at Clifton and which became a source of our private folklore. Since a lot of this material is dark and deeply sinister, I should quickly explain that Clifton College Preparatory School was, and probably still is, an exceptionally well-run establishment and things that went on there were a good deal less odd than what went on at other schools at that time, and that there is really very little to connect it with the school in *The Queue*, which was anyway set in a remote rural area and depicted with the purposeful illogic that Jonathan applied to so much of his writings. According to the book's third paragraph, the narrator is nine years old. A few lines later he states that he has already been at the school for eight years.

The story begins, however, with a very particular real-life incident, the theft of the sugar buns. The inspiration for this occurred early on in Jonathan's time at Clifton and he had already used it in one of those scraps of writing he turned out long before he wrote *The Queue*. I remember the actual event well and how the Head Master's wife, Mrs

Hankey, played down its criminal aspects, comparing it with the theft of apples from an orchard. All she wanted was for the culprit or culprits to own up. Although *The Queue* kicks off with this pretty harmless affair, Jonathan's macabre imagination takes over immediately. The reference to the school hairdresser – there really was one at Clifton – and his little attaché case may provide temporary uplift or absolution but the narrative is soon darkened by the appearance of the Head Master and his astounding nonchalance about the extremely serious injury inflicted by the hairdresser on one of his charges.

The unnamed Head Master in *The Queue*, who pursues the narrator after his escape from the school, is an utterly preposterous figure – alcoholic, murderer, thief, spy, sadist and pederast – and physically fit, active and agile into the bargain. The opening pages of *The Queue* are full of his misdeeds. He keeps gin in a flap of his gown, is sick in front of the class he is teaching, and overreacts murderously when a pupil giggles on hearing that three teachers have died in a train accident. Summoning the offender onto the platform, the Head Master takes out an enormous pair of scissors from a leather sheaf and cuts him in two. Jonathan then minimises this horror by stating: 'This alarmed the entire school, including staff,' and launching into a description of the boy's funeral and how his father, an assistant meteorologist from a weather station in the Hebrides, cannot afford the fare home. 'We decide to have a collection for the poor man and I raised £3-16-7 from my class alone,' he boasts, 'but, as I was putting this money in a safe place, the Head Master entered. He took away the money and cycled off to the Three Crowns. There he drank heavily and was sick under a laurel as he walked home.'

A few paragraphs later the narrator is caught in a noose and winched up into the Head Master's special study at the top of a tall, lighthouse-like building and waking from a coma finds his trousers have been tampered with. Worse is in store. Next day, the Head Master asks Miss Jogge, the school cook, to place a substance called 'Methlyne Oxide' in the narrator's roly-poly pudding. But, before raising the tin spoon to his lips, the boy detects a curious expression in the Head Master's eyes. His suspicions raised, he tries a spoonful on the mongrel who lives in a basket under the top table. 'She took it greedily and died four seconds later with a wail so terrible that Mr Vizze could not be heard to say Grace.'

These atrocities – the Head Master also goes for him with a jack-knife – are followed by a chase through the school kitchens. Here the Head Master gets the tail of his gown caught in a dishwasher and is dragged inside. Now the narrator has a change of heart and switches off the machine: 'I take him in my arms and watched by an enormous crowd carry him gently to his bedroom.' The relentless illogic to all this – how could a fully grown man have been dragged into a washing-up machine and how could the same man be carried by a small boy? – perhaps reminds the reader not to take it too seriously.

It is tempting, nonetheless, to ask whether the Head Master of Jonathan's imagination has any basis in fact. The actual Head Master of Clifton College Preparatory School in those days was L. H. A. Hankey. Immensely dapper, well-born and well-tailored with a terrifyingly sleek bald head, he dominated the school, boys and staff. When years later, he came to Harrow to give a sermon and was sat in a choir stall, he appeared in Jonathan's eyes like a 'huge double-yolker egg', dwarfing everyone around him, even the formidably stylish Harrow master J. P. Lemmon, of whom more in a moment. When Hankey and his wife Vicky came to say goodnight in our dormitory, they came across as an extremely glamorous couple and their allure was underlined by the knowledge that Hankey was a friend of showbusiness characters like Dickie Valentine and Stanley Holloway. And I see from *Burke's Peerage* — Hankey's uncle was made a lord in 1939 — that his father had been secretary of the Athenaeum Club and his great-grandfather Governor of the Bank of England, connections which would not have been lost on my father and may have removed his original prejudice against Clifton.

So far so good, but I also remember that Hankey was a bad-tempered man, famous for what school-boys call 'bates', and that he cut himself often when shaving — blobs of cotton wool sometimes adorned his face when he shook hands with us all in the morning — and he could speak ferociously, shaking with rage like the Head Master in *The Queue*. When

the dormitory immediately above his private quarters in Matthews House had misbehaved, he had shouted, 'I'll thrash the lot of you,' and while reading to us in his study he had suddenly bellowed at a boy, 'Take your filthy hands off my leather chair!' Catching me one morning in the matron's room to see if any letters had arrived for me — a lifelong obsession — he had thrown me out of the room, causing me to fall against a radiator, wetting my pants. Later that morning, during break, he had appeared at my side and asked me to forgive him. I also remember the Hankeys' rather punitive attitude towards soiled underwear. And so did Jonathan, who wrote about the regular pants inspections at Clifton in some uncharacteristically straightforward jottings several years later: 'Mrs Hankey, the Head Master's wife, would come round and check while we were washing in the evening,' he recalled. 'I can't remember if we actually took the pants off or just lowered them. Any boy who had dirty pants *had to wash them in front of the Head Master!!!!!*'

It's conceivable that only serial offenders were punished in this way. I also wonder if this was normal practice in preparatory schools. Does it suggest anything especially sinister about Hankey? Did such experiences contribute to the severely scatological aspects of *The Queue* I am reluctant to quote? Alas, I know little of Hankey's direct dealings with Jonathan, only that in one school report, the Head Master observes in his rolling italic that Jonathan might develop into an interesting boy. When Jonathan wrote *The Queue,* was he thinking of Hankey or of Harrow's Head Master, Dr James, who would prove an even more scary figure? Or neither of them?

In those early, angrier writings by Jonathan, which he would eventually bind together under the title *Squabbling Blackbirds*, I spotted a passing throwaway reference – 'I saw my old Head Master in Mayfair. He was being beaten up by 14 thugs' – and in *The Queue* itself the Head Master makes several reappearances, long after the narrator's departure from the school. Though the Head Master is portrayed as the vengeful one, the narrator always ends up getting the better of him. Marooned on the Great North Road or some other godforsaken highway, the boy and his dog are offered a lift in a red Consul driven by a friendly dress-shop assistant. Opening the rear door, the narrator finds his old Head

Master hunched in a corner seat. While Mary dances about, boy and man immediately attack each other's private parts in the most violent possible manner. Finally the Head Master attempts to bugger his former pupil and the boy grabs a pair of dressmaker's scissors and snips at his oppressor's sexual organs. 'He manages to dodge but, all the same, I take a size-able chunk from the scrotum and he is now out of action.'

Nasty stuff – childish too? – but Hankey was not the only character at Clifton who may or may not have haunted Jonathan. And, anyway, haunted is the wrong word. Jonathan simply derived endless amusement from these early days at boarding school, had a far sharper memory than I had and was far more observant than me in the first place. For the rest of his short life, he seemed to cherish the slang, the abbreviations, the trivia, the paraphernalia and personalities of prep-school life. These memories came up often in conversations, in scraps of writing, in letters to me – and in *The Queue*.

The names of other masters besides Hankey were constantly celebrated. There was Mr Lewin, for example, and Mr Barker, who had famously stood up during tea at Matthews, asked for silence and announced, '*The currant scones do not need butter.*' There was an elderly master called Mr Read whose style of tailoring Jonathan may have recalled when he came to describe a Rolls-Royce-driving homo-sexual in *The Queue*: 'Though in his seventieth year his trousers were extraordinarily tight around the crotch and his testicles protruded in an unpleasant fashion.'

And there was Mr Frampton, whose purple tracksuit much amused us and whose multi-consonanted name was used more than once in *The Queue*. There were also teachers called S. P. T. Wells and P. E. M. Holmes and W. F. M. Jones, whose names along with others already mentioned would crop up years later in letters that Jonathan sent me long after he had left the school. As would the names of the school's porters and under-staff. The man who was meant to ring the bell was called Pritchard. Some years later Jonathan sketched this man on his bicycle and added the caption: 'Pritchard home to Speedwell Av for beans.' Another of Pritchard's duties was to hand out compasses and the powdered ink which, Jonathan remembered, was then put into plate glass or bakelite inkwells. Jonathan also noted and recalled the names, and sometimes addresses, of staff he had never met. There was the viola instructor Miss V. Pryce-Lucas and the Swedish masseur Steen Folke. In the autumn of 1964, he signed off a letter from Edinburgh with 'Mr Leadbetter 12 Henleaze Park Bristol 10'. And of course there were the school matrons, like Betti Vine,★ Freda Heath and Lettice Rose – or were these last two ladies at Harrow?

Jonathan's memories of Clifton College and its environment grew stronger with the passing years. In a letter from Cannes in August 1966 he says nothing about the girl he was travelling with but instead plunges back into the Clifton world. 'Hankey went to referee a Bigside game but his leg fell off after a Woolaston (WH) try.' By this stage I had forgotten about Bigside, the senior school's chief sports ground, and Woolaston's, the name of one of the senior school's boarding houses usually known by initial letters. At an even later date he was referring to the Nissen huts where we went for most of our meals and where a woman with incredibly short hair, appropriately called Mrs Mann, was in charge in the kitchen. At breakfast, Hankey sat at the top of his table here opening

★ When writing about Hankey, Betty Vine and others in his past Jonathan often jokified their names in one way or another.

his letters and at the end of lunch our brother Martin some-times carried a horrible dish of meat scraps back for Mrs Hankey's corgis. Jonathan also remembered things I never noticed in the first place. Like the sign in the Sick Room, bearing George VI's words: 'It is to the young that the future belongs.' And the collection of butterflies in the Prep Room. And the way that house prayers often began with Hankey intoning: 'As another day is over . . .'

He also, of course, recalled the names of fellow pupils. Names like R. K. Stott, T. T. Pratt and G. T. Fripp would become the inspiration for the strange short names that adorn *The Queue*. Surnames and initials crop up on almost every page and the surnames are generally double-consonanted, monosyllabic and carry an additional *e*, like G. L. Husse, C. E. Vonne, O. L. Pivve and K. O. Putte. Even a wasp is given a full human name – S. G. Hoode. This amusing device may suggest a detachment from real people and certainly perpetuates the institutionalised and alien nomenclature of boarding schools in general and Clifton in particular. Among new boys who joined the school at the same time as Jonathan was a pupil called – it sounds too good to be true – J. R. Batte. At least ten years later my brother would sign off letters with the names of Clifton contemporaries who had somehow caught his imagination. On 19 October 1966, he bundled four names together, ending his letter, 'Love from Kahil & Caish & Dobson & Gas.' According to the *Clifton College Register*, Caish went on to work for thirty-one years at the National Westminster Bank. Dobson and Gass (note the correct spelling) never filled in their questionnaires and the more ethnic-sounding Kahil doesn't appear at all.

And how did J. H. Barrow fit in with these contem-poraries? How did he get on at prep school? Was he as satirically aware or humorously mature as this subsequent jokiness suggests? How unhappy was he? Certainly the letters he wrote to our parents during his first few terms at Matthews House sound cheerful enough on the surface. Though sometimes filled out with tedious stuff about sermons – 'E. F. Fisher is preaching today' and 'the preacher today is V. E. D. Haggard Esq.' – they carry no aura of oddness about them. 'I like school,' he wrote in one of his earliest letters. His note on 9 October 1955, 'We often have tined [sic] meat for lunch,' is the only early reference to food and not necessarily a derogatory one. On 27 November 1955, he notes 'Only twenty more days till the end of term' and from time to time there are typical schoolboyish boasts about his sporting prowess. 'We played football on Friday. Our team won,' he writes in his very first letter home and the following summer would brag, 'On Tuesday I stumped someone and scored 12 runs.'

Fourteen years later the author of these pleasant, friendly, normal little letters – far happier, I guess, than the ones I wrote home at the same time – would pen a horrific account of an aeroplane crash-landing onto a school playing field:

> Our aeroplane has been repaired and refuelled, and we are once more moving along the runway. After we have been airborne for about ten minutes, I hear the public address system being switched on. The pilot tells us that we are about to crash-land. He has a choice of a ploughed field, an arable pasture with grazing Friesians, or a school football pitch with game in progress. An impossible decision: ploughed field would mean buckled undercarriage and possible explosion, arable pasture is almost suicidal – too many Friesians about to obstruct.

Only real choice is the playing-field. But young boys in the prime of life could lose limbs and possibly life.

We fasten safety belts and grip seats. Mary's heart beats fast. We are going for the football pitch. I see the pilot switch on a hazard warning horn. Just a hundred feet below, I see the horrified games master blowing his whistle. Run boys, run for your lives. But many do not hear, they are too involved in the game. I see the pilot close his eyes and cover his face. Now the games master is running just a few yards in front of the propeller. Then, unaccountably, he trips and falls. The propeller catches the seam of his flannel jacket. He is thrown up, sliced and taken to bits. The blood splashes on my viewing window. (I must try and stop his wife identifying him.) We've touched down now. Boys are tumbling about by the undercarriage. Games shorts are shredded and many boys lose their lives. Staff run from the schoolhouse, but they've only got one first-aid kit to tend the 23 wounded. I hear ambulances trying to get along narrow lanes. There's a herd of bullocks blocking the entrance to the field and the driver's going frantic. They abandon their vehicles and run across three fields with stretchers under arms. The bullocks, annoyed at the noise and interruption, charge at them. They shield themselves with stretchers. The pilot, unable to face the terrible responsibility, has jumped into a propeller. Poor soul, the extrication takes hours and we call urgently for aeronautical mechanics. Through the schoolhouse window, I see the Head Master on the phone. Judging by his pale face,

I guess he is telling next-of-kin. There is a list of deceased in front of him.

Whatever such imaginings may reveal about Jonathan's subsequent inner life, in academic terms he remained backward – even if his letters sometimes contain boasts like 'I got an A for Gog and french' – and as we will see his spelling and handwriting remained bad for some time ahead. His Easter 1957 maths report, written by a master with illegible initials, states, 'He seems to be unable to grasp the fundamentals, whether tables or methods. His memory also appears bad. He has been rather a disappointing pupil.' Hankey's reports were more generous. While admitting that Jonathan was 'a little old for his form' he goes on to say, 'Out of school he is becoming more mature . . .' He also won the approval of the art master, P. R. Clay, for whom in May 1958 he did a drawing of a clown to which he added a dachshund on a lead★: one of the first of many dachshund pictures which showed his confident hand and humorous line. Jonathan would later express mixed feelings about life in the art room: 'The master-in-charge-of-art used strips of hardboard as a deterrent,' he recalled in one of those early scraps of autobiographical writing and then, more personally and addressed to me, 'Do you remember the satisfactory feeling of using a wet sponge to clean off clay from the work tops?'

By this time, our elder brother Martin, who deserves a larger part in this narrative, had left Clifton and followed Simon and Julian to Harrow, and I had moved into a house for older boys called Hartnells. For a while, I saw Jonathan only during morning break and noticed that his breath sometimes smelt of

★ Featured on the title page of this book.

the bread he had been eating. Or perhaps a stolen sugar bun?

Jonathan's last year or two at Clifton were spent in Hartnells with me. Here I have more vivid but slightly sadder memories of him. I recall that, instead of playing with other boys, he spent a lot of time gazing unblinkingly out of a downstairs window in a daze of homesickness which caused concern to the house matron. I also remember him asking this lady if he could help her sort out the socks and handkerchiefs just back from the laundry. *'Matron, can I do the handkerchiefs, please'*, became a family catchphrase for many years. Clearly there was something about the smell and touch of folded linen and newly laundered socks which soothed him, reflected his deep love of domesticity and perhaps pointed forward to his subsequent interest in all aspects of the hotel trade.

Another element of those final days at Clifton was our shared interest in a master called Moorhouse. G. D. W. G. Moorhouse, or D. M. for short, was for some time house tutor at Hartnells. Moorhouse had served in the navy during the war and was a fierce disciplinarian addicted to some unusual corporal punishment rituals – senior boys were strapped to a table in order to be chastised – not entirely unlike those featured in *The Queue*. 'Do what you like but be prepared to pay for it' was a Moorhouse maxim Jonathan quoted later and he also recalled with glee how Moorhouse had pronounced on the quality of other masters' gowns. 'You will find that most masters do not have ermine trimmings. They have rabbit.'

I left Clifton in March 1959. Jonathan stayed on for only one term, during which it was decided he needed special tutoring to get into Harrow. Shortly after going back to Clifton on his own he wrote a long letter to me at Harrow, in which he comes across as a normal, happy twelve-year-old schoolboy. He boasts that he has jumped 14 feet in the long jump and had other successes on the cricket field. 'I have just bowled someone, caught (twice) someone, stumped someone.' He also mentions, 'I am having proper drum lessons

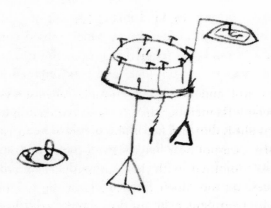

now plus proper stand.' Only when he mentions Moorhouse's sartorial style does he show some hint of oddness and originality. 'D. M. is ill at the moment but latest fashions have been cap (pulled well forward), sports jack., and Marks and Spencer trousers!!!!!!' I will use these multiple exclamation marks to conclude this chapter.

CHAPTER SIX

Gilda

Mary, lost and perplexed, stumbles against every
passer-by. Remember that she is an old dachshund.
Her sight is dim and her limbs, stiffened by terrible
arthritis, cannot bear her weight for long distances.
This, combined with her unfortunate circumstances, are too much for her and at the junction
of Moorsom Street she sits down and weeps. I take
her gently in my arms and walk with her to the
Animal Hospital in Ferry Place.

The Queue, Chapter Four

IN THE MISSPELT and poorly punctuated letters Jonathan had
sent home from Clifton, he had asked constantly about the
animals at Turleigh Combe. When staring out of the window
at Hartnells with such a vacant expression, was it the animals
he missed most? During that first autumn term of 1955, he
had asked, 'Are the babby chicks any bigger' – his letters are
oddly devoid of question-marks* – 'Is Pebble lonely' and
'Can Flash jump over the rope'. During his time at Clifton,
my mother's animal kingdom continued to expand. Soon
Flash was sharing her field with some geese – 'I don't think
the geese like her,' Jonathan observed in a letter – and then

* Hardly a single question-mark appears in *The Queue*.

a horse arrived called Tango, on which my mother would ride. On 14 May 1957, Jonathan had asked, 'How is Flash, Tango and the kittins. Are the kittins any bigger yet. When does the woman come to take some away.' His very first letter from Clifton had begun, 'How are the aniamalis', and this misspelt word had immediately become a family joke or umbrella word for all the pets at Turleigh Combe.

Jonathan's unpunctuated questions about the 'aniamalis' may sound fairly cheery but he undoubtedly found separation from these creatures – I include the hens in this category – very painful. At the end of one holiday, I remember a heartbreaking scene on Bradford-on-Avon station where his brave but stilted words to my mother were, 'Make sure all the animals are well!' At the end of another holiday, Jonathan became so unhappy about leaving home, so ill in the car, that my mother – usually so tough in this area and disinclined to commiserate with sick animals – decided to keep him at home for a few days. I was jealous and disturbed over this decision and remember Jonathan's triumphantly contented expression in the back of the car.

The arrival of Gilda, an indoor domestic pet, must have made departures from Turleigh Combe even more traumatic. This bad, fat, greedy dachshund soon became the presiding force in the house and garden, a potent matriarchal symbol, the focus of a great deal of love and endless source of jokes, fantasies and anecdotes. At the risk of offending lovers of other breeds of dogs, I must argue that dachshunds have particularly strong, semi-human personalities. Other breeds have poker faces. You often don't know what's going on under, say, a bulldog's mask. Dachshunds relate brilliantly to human beings, they have warm eyes and an understanding manner. Is it surprising that Picasso and President Kennedy were both intensely fond of their pet dachshunds? The smooth-haired variety like Gilda also have a comfortable, rounded and silkily tactile physique. And Gilda was a prime specimen of her breed. She would have twenty-one puppies, in three litters, but none of the offspring we kept had their mother's imposingly attractive presence. You wanted to touch her, to cuddle her and, since she was choosy about whom she'd allow to befriend her, for her to love you in return.

As Gilda was to a large extent the inspiration for the *The Queue's* heroine, it's relevant to describe her character, or since she arrived as a small puppy in the autumn of 1956, the character that she soon became, and to see how much the fictional Mary owes to her. Just how bad, greedy and fat was Gilda? There is no reference in *The Queue* to Mary being fat, nor do I remember Gilda as particularly overweight. But both real and fictional dachshunds were exceptionally naughty – Gilda killed more than one of my mother's hens – and bad-tempered. Everything that Mary does, one could imagine being done by Gilda. Like stealing velvet from a haberdashery counter. Or going missing. Or lapping up milk 'from an overturned lorry' and then being truncheoned on the neck by a police constable.

There is also a sexual side to Mary which she shared with Gilda. I can remember various times when Gilda escaped while on heat and purposefully stalked off to the village in search of rough trade. She returned to have her private parts examined for telltale evidence. On one occasion we found curious wood chippings and fragments of dry leaves stuck onto her nether regions. Mary was apparently known for her licentious habits before she meets the narrator. The doorman at a striptease club seems to know her and lets them in at half-price. She then behaves in an obscene, delinquent and foul manner on stage. Encountering three

perverts in a bed in the asylum, she immediately jumps up and asks if she may join in. As my mother would have done with Gilda in such circumstances, the narrator pulls her off and scolds her.

There is also an alertness to both dogs, perhaps to all dogs, that is appealing. Mary has 'a dog's sense of direction'. Realising the narrator is in trouble, she runs 'as fast as her four legs can carry her'. Under real pressure she is capable of great intuition and almost acrobatic efficiency. Spotting a murderous railway official trying to direct an express train onto an old branch line, Mary jumps at him, tears a wound in his neck and averts 'the worst rail accident in history'. And when Mary and the narrator steal a boat, she shows herself fully capable of handling a rudder. I do not, of course, suggest that Gilda was capable of such feats, such circus tricks, only that there was something about her personality that suggested near-human qualities: wisdom, tenacity, experience. Our oldest brother, Simon, who had left home by the time of Gilda's arrival, once remarked, '*Gilda knows a thing or two.*'

Gilda had come to us a puppy but soon grew matronly, as dachshunds do. And tattered. She tore an ear out hunting, grew a lump on her stomach, began to go grey around her chops. Her fictional counterpart is also ageing and showing increasing signs of wear and tear, but like a cartoon character, she bounces back after a setback and is soon as alert and as mischievous as ever and up to any number of new tricks. Is she really ill? Or just naughty? Near the end of the book, a vet drives past, lowers his side window and starts haranguing her keeper: 'Your dog is in a shocking condition, she's in no fit state to be walking to London,' but the narrator tells the reader in an aside: 'I'm not unduly worried. She has coped remarkably well over the past difficult weeks and, apart from exhaustion and grime, there is not much wrong with her.' In a later chapter, I will draw parallels between Mary and Jonathan's friend Mr Grant, the down-and-out schoolmaster, who also showed extraordinary resilience and was in his own words, 'not in the least rheumaticky'. For the present, we must just accept that Mary – like Gilda, like many dogs – is a complex and contradictory character. Drawn to the fleshpots, she is also extremely prim and sensitive. We are told at the outset that Mary 'cannot bear unpleasantness' and that she hates death. Though often the author of her own misfortunes, she is horrified by what she sees, hides her eyes or has her eyes hidden for her by the narrator. She also inspires mixed feelings in people she meets. Drivers at first refuse to give her a lift, then change their minds and finally offer her a cushion for the back seat. In the middle of some of the worst calamities, Mary lays her head down and falls asleep. On arrival at the asylum, stiff and perplexed, she even refuses to leave the sack in which she's been carried. Like many vagabonds and men-of-the-road, she has had enough. 'She longs for a warm fire and a basket and a regular hot dinner,' the narrator tells us. 'She is tiring of the scraps that I give

63

her. Things like crisps, cheap cakes, chocolate and currant buns. She longs for proper meat.'

It is worth noting that throughout *The Queue*, the narrator and his dog are homeless hitch-hikers. In real life, Jonathan and Gilda had an utterly secure if slightly peculiar home in Turleigh Combe. We no longer led a peripatetic life. We had our holidays in Cumberland or Cornwall. Even my father was soon permanently at home, retiring from the Board of Trade on his fiftieth birthday in June 1957. At this time, his personality was still fairly shrouded: he may have tap-danced on the kitchen floor but he didn't yet imitate judges pronouncing sentence or display his taste for esoteric, forensic detail or lavatory jokes. By the end of the 1950s, Julian as well as Simon had more or less flown the nest. Simon had already done his military service and was now in his last year reading Geography at Oxford. He had turned twenty-one in November 1958. Julian was already intent on becoming a painter but had left the art school in Bristol after one term and was now working in the restoration department at the National Gallery in London. Holidays at Turig – Jonathan's wild misspelling of Turleigh in a letter from prep school had now become our nickname for the place – revolved chiefly around the animals or whatever local activities Martin, Jonathan and I evolved or had imposed upon us.

During the late 1950s and early 1960s, we went to the pantomime at the Bath theatre, attended meets of the Avon Vale and Beaufort Hunts – once or twice Jonathan may have ridden Flash at the more local ones – and walked with our mother on the Kennet and Avon Canal which, like the railway, ran through Avoncliff at the bottom of our valley. When we were a little older, the three of us went off by bus to

Trowbridge Fair where we saw the world's largest and smallest women – or so they were billed – and slipped into a sideshow called 'Naughty but Nice' where a buxom girl performed the 'Dance of the Seven Veils'. On excursions like these Jonathan may have picked up some of the local place names like Norton St Philip and even the Hook of Newbury, along with catering terminology like 'choice teas', 'creamed carrots' and 'Welsh saddle of lamb' which feature in some of his later writings. In Bradford-on-Avon he learnt the names of shop-keepers like Mr Uncles and from Winsley itself took on board the names of village characters like Mrs Moorsom, her cousin Miss Clayton and an old man my mother had renamed 'Old Sweetie Dagger'.

At home, we soon smoked cigarettes in the wood, made fires using what Jonathan later described in *The Queue* as 'twigs and twigling', and built and rebuilt an elaborate semi-under-ground house, which we called the U. H. We also waited for the postman to come down the drive. For several years we were addicted to the catalogue of jokes and novelties – they included sneezing powder and false protruding teeth – that came from a shop in High Holborn called Ellisdon's. And for many months Jonathan also collected Kiddicraft Miniatures, tiny replicas of products like Gordon's Gin and Cadbury's Dairy Milk, with which he set up an imaginary shop. In the same vein, he was soon collecting point-of-sale placards for household goods – and asking for these things in every shop we called at.

In spite of these towny diversions, the holidays at Turig still revolved firmly and irresistibly round Gilda, Flash, the new horse Tango and the hens and geese, all of whom my mother elevated to nearly human status by inventing stories about them, told in what she imagined their voices to be like. My mother was far more confident when dealing with animals than humans and she was also a gifted story-teller. Once she had given a man lift somewhere in the West Midlands – *Queue* territory again – and he had come out with a riveting bad-luck story that she had later related to us. Around the Turig fireside, she often read aloud. I remember her reading John Buchan's *The Thirty-Nine Steps* and *Huntingtower*, chapter by chapter, with Gilda no doubt on one of our laps, her front paws curling inwards rather than spread out. In the dining room my mother lifted Gilda's feet up to the table, and folded her floppy damaged ears into different shapes as if they were fashionable or silly hats. And made her speak to us in a grumpy woman's voice.

I imagine Jonathan took all this in. When he came to write *The Queue* he filled it with talking animals, some of them imaginary and faintly obscene or freakish, like soot-rats and jumping sewer-mice.* The relationships between Mary and the other creatures in Jonathan's bestiary are drawn with great vigour and tenderness. There is a particularly touching moment when the plucky little sparrow tries to sooth the suicidal dachshund: 'Don't worry my dear. You're in kind hands now,' he tells her, but Mary, bitterly ashamed, jumps off her bench and disappears. In the subsequent chase, Sparrow – key animals are soon favoured with capital letters and stripped of their definite or indefinite articles – offers to search from the sky, calling in pigeons, chaffinches and robins to help: 'Find the little brown dachshund. She may try to take her life. She answers to Mary.'

---

* During his prep-school days Jonathan had written to a children's comic claiming that, on a recent visit to a trout-hatchery, he had been amazed to spot *a fish with two heads*. The editors had published this letter under the title *Freak Fish*.

A few paragraphs later, Sparrow is carrying the boy and dog to his own nest. A mid-air collision with a crow shows how the creatures in *The Queue* sometimes relate to each other. 'Apparently Sparrow owes Crow seven pence and Crow wants it back,' the narrator explains. 'I shoo the crow away, telling him to grow up and not be so fussy over such a small sum. (Crow is a well-known local miser and is reputed to own over 37 nests).' And soon after arrival at Sparrow's home there is further battle between animals when Mary falls down the chimney to the intense annoyance of the resident soot-rats, some the length of a cat. Head Soot-Rat immediately wants to know Mary's business in his flue: 'You can't just come wandering in like this. Didn't you know this was private property. Who do you think you are?' Sparrow then tells Head Soot-Rat to shut up. He explains that it was an accident and Mary had no wish to interfere. Head Soot-Rat realises he has made a fool of himself, apologises and grudgingly asks if any help is needed to get Mary down. He then calls an assistant who brings rope ladders and axes.

Though this change of heart on Head Soot-Rat's part is pleasing to witness, many of Jonathan's creatures have unpleasant characters and unpleasant human characteristics. The pike that rescues the suicidal drowning dachshund has 'a disagreeable expression on his face' – do pikes ever look agreeable? – and other creatures are far more sinister. The non-stop Perth-London Express that hurtles through the station carries gorillas, giant bats and orang-utans, many of them dead. The train on which the narrator is travelling is not being driven by a human being at all. 'Crouching at the controls is a giant rat at least twice the size of a man. Sweat pours from his face and he is obviously in difficulties.' Ditto the driver of a black Cadillac which pulls up in the middle of the night beside the narrator and his dog. Peering in, the boy finds his wrist grasped by a feathered claw. Soon he is face-to-face with a giant wood pigeon, at least the size of a fully grown man, and with vicious sexual intentions. Within seconds, it has the narrator's penis firmly in its claw, but once again Mary comes to the rescue, taking a deep bite into the bird, who drives off alone with the car hopelessly out of control. A collision with a Morris Estate follows, Wood Pigeon is flung through the windscreen and spins three hundred yards, ending in a tall elm, and the narrator is forced to conclude: 'I should imagine he would have lost his life.'

Some of the animals in *The Queue* are good souls, however, with powerful characters of their own, who help the narrator and his dog on their way. None more so than the rook who comes to the rescue when the tiny aeroplane carrying our heroes runs out of fuel and begins to lose its propeller. Suddenly Mary tugs at her friend's cuff and draws attention to the rook, which has settled on the wing. 'He seems friendly,' the narrator tells us, 'and, in seconds, his quick brain has grasped our plight. With great haste, he departs in the direction of a nearby rookery and returns in three minutes with 800 rooks. They settle themselves on wings, fuselage and nose. They flap like hell and keep us up until we are in sight of the airport.' The episode ends with the boy spluttering to his feathered friends: 'I can't thank you enough. You've saved our lives. Is there anything I can do in return?'

I will describe what the narrator tries to do for the rooks in a later chapter. Here I am concerned with those early days at Turleigh Combe, with Gilda herself and the connection between my mother's imaginative regard for animals and Jonathan's subsequent delight in humanising fish, fowl, mammals and reptiles – even insects. I have already mentioned that wasps featured often at Turig, and have no doubt that my mother warned us that if you kill a wasp many more will come to its funeral. Perhaps this ancient adage was the inspiration for the passage in *The Queue* which begins with the boy discovering a wasp nest under his taxi seat. Suddenly surrounded by furious, flapping wings, he learns that one of their number had been killed that morning

by flying in front of a bus in Park Lane. The driver had tried to swerve but there was no hope. 'The wasps, angry and upset, will attend a memorial service tomorrow. The famous wasp named S. G. Hoode had written an obituary for insertion in *The Times* − but the Editor has just rung to say it is unacceptable. Illegible and badly constructed. You must do better than this.' The introduction of a wasp with such a sophisticated name gives a depth and comic complexity to this episode, and the phrase 'You must do better than this' was one of those warnings Jonathan must have heard only too often at prep school.

During his last year or two at Clifton, doubts were indeed expressed about Jonathan's ability to get into Harrow. For some time my father looked around for residential tutorial establishments where his youngest son might be crammed for the entrance exam. One such place in the south of England he turned down on hearing from a neighbour 'I have enquired in the village and rumour has it that the —s are queer people.' I don't know how many other places were considered. I do know that in September 1959 Jonathan, still only twelve, was sent to Cumberland to receive the appropriate coaching from Uncle Gurney. My mother's older brother had stopped teaching English to foreign students but was still living at Beauthorn, one of those 'houses-with-property' on Ullswater, of which Jonathan would write later, where he was tutoring boys for the Common Entrance exam.

CHAPTER SEVEN

Harrow: Part One

The train passes the bloody school where I went.
I see the ghastly building on the hill. The sun is
setting beyond Pinner. Is it my imagination or do
I hear *a school song*?!! No . . . I am wrong. There is
a huge picture across the sky. Or rear-projection.
It is my old headmaster.

Squabbling Blackbirds, 1968

JONATHAN'S FIFTEEN MONTHS' tuition in Cumberland paid
off. Not only did he gain a place at Harrow, he also strengthened his rural awareness, increased his independence and
began to display his powers of observation. To start with, he
had lived in our grandmother's house at Dacre and bicycled
each day to the lake. At Dacre, he eyed the household with
amusement and had much to report on a lady called Theo
Fox, who now lived there as my grandmother's companion,
secretary and driver – in addition to Aunt Jean. He noted
the exact moment Theo always changed gear when collecting
him from Penrith Station and how, when listening to a concert
on the 'Third Programme', she shut her eyes and *cocked* her
head on one side.

After a few months, he had become a resident at
Beauthorn where there were six or seven other pupils. One
of them was his first cousin Miles – Uncle Gurney's son was

heading for Rugby where he would briefly overlap with the *Queue*-like named writer A. N. Wilson – and within a month or two, the two cousins started a newspaper, the *Beauthorn Echo*. A surviving copy of this amateurishly roneoed news-sheet contains indications both of Jonathan's subsequent interests and the bleakness of *The Queue*. A headline proclaims 16 dead this Whitsun on the roads' and in the General News section it is reported, 'On Saturday and Sunday night the wind reached gale force causing accidents all over the country and causing a tree to fall down on a car travelling on the main Carlisle–Penrith road, killing a woman.'

I know little else about Jonathan's time in Cumberland and draw no significance from the fact that he returned home one holidays wearing his pyjama jacket instead of a shirt.★ On 4 November 1960, he had written to me at Harrow wishing me a happy fifteenth birthday and telling me that the pipes had burst at Beauthorn. 'There is no water so we *trundle* water up from the lake for lavatories etc.' As with his earlier emphasis on the word *cocked*, the underlining of *trundled* indicates that he was fully aware of its comic properties and also reminds us of Jonathan's early interest in handcarts and the like.

★ I certainly do not trust Jonathan's account of a school outing to Carr's biscuit factory in Carlisle and his claim that our uncle had suddenly started shouting, '*Watch out! There's a boy in the dough!*'

In the same letter, he offers a further taste of things to come by adding: 'Good character forms and papers to sign have come from Harrow.' Things like good character forms belong to the world of law courts and other institutions he would later satirise in *The Queue*.

With or without these commendations, Jonathan entered Harrow on 17 January 1961, aged thirteen and three-quarters. Martin and I escorted him there that evening after spending the day in London, visiting Floris Chocolates, the Hong Kong Restaurant in Shaftesbury Avenue, Fleet Street, St Paul's and the Stock Exchange. What impression did the three of us make as we eventually made our way to Baker Street and took the Metropolitan Line to Harrow-on-the-Hill? Martin and I, now sixteen and fifteen respectively, were tall, thin and bespectacled. Jonathan or Johnny – his name had various versions – was by comparison small and sturdy, with still something of the pastry chef about his features. And what impression, if any, did Harrow make on the brother who had spent most of the previous fifteen months on a beautiful English lake?

Those who have never been there may be glad to know that Harrow is indeed set upon a hill, surrounded by places with names like Kenton, Roxeth, Northwick Park and Pinner. According to Pevsner, the school buildings exude a 'hearty and confident gloom'. Some of the boarding houses are of 'towering height' and built of 'purple brick with bands and diapers in vitrified blue or yellow brick'. These 'overwhelmingly assertive' buildings find parallels in the institutions described in *The Queue* but I suspect caused Jonathan, and me, little trouble at the time.

Our first point of call on arrival at this ancient establishment was the school shop, where Martin and I helped Jonathan choose an umbrella and get it stamped in gold, there and then, with his initials. I remember the pleasure

Jonathan took selecting the letters J, H and B from a box on the counter. Soon afterwards we deposited him at a house for new boys known as The Foss. From here he wrote several letters to our parents which my mother fortunately preserved. His handwriting and spelling are now much improved. On his first day at school he describes the trip to London and states, 'I have been put in form S.2.B. (not the bottom form).' He carries on, 'We have seen the Head Master today' and concludes 'It is still rather muddling where to go but I am finding out.' Jonathan started at Harrow sharing a room with another new boy called W. R. Bennett who I see from the *Harrow School Register* qualified as a solicitor a year after Jonathan's death. Later in January he writes that he is finding his feet, has had percussion lessons and taken part in the school steeplechase. 'Running to Wembley and back, about 8 miles, very exhausting. Especially as most of the ground was under-water and our clothes stank when we got back.' He also states, 'I have been moved down into the IV form after a fortnight because my Latin was not good enough!' Squeezed in between two lines, almost as an afterthought, he adds, 'I hope all the animals are well.'

There is nothing in these letters that suggests home-sickness or unhappiness. I suppose it helped a little that, as at Clifton, he had two older brothers still at the school. I see from my own 1961 diary that I walked in the park fields with Jonathan and went down into Harrow town with him and bought buns. I also see that on 2 March he 'hurt and split' his elbow in the gym. His end-of-term reports confirm both that he was settling down well and that he still had serious academic difficulties. His famous English teacher, J. P. Lemmon – he was widely known as Jeremy, but I use his initials to remind us of *The Queue* – writes in a fine italic hand, 'He has had some difficulty finding his feet; his work shows imagination and his vocabulary is good but he writes carelessly and his grammar is poor.' His Maths teacher J. M. Rae, later headmaster of Westminster, describes him as 'far too disorganised and scatterbrained'. These judgements were summarised by Harrow's Head Master, Dr R. L. James – 'There are signs in these reports that he is beginning to get on top of his difficulties' – and expanded upon by our housemaster Mark Tindall.

Tindall and Dr James would remain dominant influences for the rest of our shared schooldays and, along with Hankey, may or may not have contributed to the Head Master figure in *The Queue*. Writing about Harrow forty years on in *The World of Interiors*, I described Dr James as 'a chiselled monolith of unfaltering gravity' and claimed that he had ruled the school with a mixture of 'clockwork dignity and subtle showmanship'. His arrival in the Speech Room on Monday mornings was dramatically announced by the slamming of the building's doors, and in one-to-one encounters he made his presence felt by standing as still as a bird of prey in his floor-length gown. Tindall was a more restless and athletic figure, conceivably capable of some of the physical contortions practised by the fictional Head Master in *The Queue*. Tindall's letters and postcards to my father also show that he was conscientious and responsible and had a powerful turn of phrase, but as a teacher and housemaster he was often menacing and manipulative. Long after leaving Harrow, Jonathan still quoted Tindall's gravel-voiced comments and, when he was actually writing *The Queue*, during the last month of his life, said of Dr James: '*Even now I could send him a solicitor's letter which would give him the shakes.*'

Such cockiness came later. For the first year or two at Harrow, Jonathan remained as submissive as he had been at

Clifton, patiently learning the ropes and absorbing the school's rituals and slang. He would later relish the expression for the severest non-corporal punishment available, a Georgic, which I think meant the writing out of five hundred lines. In May 1961, Jonathan moved from The Foss and joined Martin and me at Bradbys where Mr and Mrs Tindall lived on the Private Side. One of the highlights of this early period was Hankey's visit in June 1961, and the extraordinary impact he made in the chapel stalls, upstaging even the normally flamboyant J. P. Lemmon. In my diary I describe Hankey's sermon as 'moderate' and my new friend Mike d'Abo dismissed it as 'absolutely hopeless'. I also remember an amusing incident that term during an art-school lecture. A glass plate had broken inside the projector and the efforts of the nice art teacher R. W. Treffgarne to deal with the problem – he cut his hand in the process – could be seen on the screen: blood, handkerchief and all. An obscene version of this episode appears in *The Queue* when homosexual activity in a cinema's projection room is somehow thrown onto the screen causing gasps and then excitement in the audience.

Otherwise this was a quiet period in Jonathan's life. He was, it seems, holding his fire and even the impressions he took in at this time had virtually no outlet. End-of-term reports, accompanied by austere two-line summaries by the Head Master in which the word 'difficulties' invariably appears, suggest that during his first two years at Harrow he plodded away at his work. He is also accused of laziness. 'I am gaining the impression,' wrote Tindall at the end of the spring term of 1962, 'that there is a touch of, shall we say, not going "flat out" about him which really must be eliminated.' 'I believe he could make a more strenuous effort,' echoed his Latin teacher, M. G. Balme. His geography, writes C. D. Laborde, is 'very weak I'm afraid', an impression, some might feel, borne out by the unmapped quality of *The Queue*. At the end of the following term, J. P. Lemmon has more complex thoughts to impart. 'He has remained rather inattentive and idle; this is all the more a pity because he expresses himself well and can write stylishly.' Only the art master strikes an entirely good note. R. W. Treffgarne praises Jonathan's 'well-shaped hand, fluent and with a sense of style' and the promise he shows with his pottery. There are also compliments from his music teacher. During the summer term of 1962, Jonathan began to play the tympanii in the school orchestra. All these judgements were to some extent irrelevant. On Jonathan's fifteenth birthday, 10 April 1962, Tindall had written to my father saying that he believed that any idea of Jonathan going to university had been 'discarded in your mind, I think'. The same letter makes a passing reference to me: 'Andrew is merely going through a stage of rather prolonged "intellectual arrogance". I don't imagine it will last indefinitely.'

Readers will have their own ideas on this last point. And, anyhow, there were now only the two of us left at Harrow for my parents to worry about. Martin had left the school in December 1961, failed to get into university but made his first step towards his subsequently successful career as an international businessman by going round the world. Our parents had other matters on their minds. Letters from our mother remained what our older brothers called 'doggy'. Gilda had long ago had her first litter and one of the seven puppies, Candy, had been kept. In a letter to us at Harrow, my mother wrote, 'The naughty dogs have chewed two large holes in my green cardigan!' In another undated letter, she writes: 'Both dogs are now on heat. Gilda may see her former husband Bertie next week. Dog Plenty and Keckery are in constant attendance.' In another, 'Gilda has just eaten quite a big bit of that lovely Cadbury's Dessert Chocolate which

I had unwisely left out on the floor.' My father's letters were fewer and his occasional use of words like 'septicaemia' and a passing reference to seniority in the police force give a foretaste of things to come and the medical-legal standpoint from which he had now begun to look upon life.

Jonathan was far better at processing our mother's 'dogginess' and our father's taste for forensic detail than I was. Instead of being irritated or disgusted, he simply took it all in and bore it in mind until the time came for him to use it in writings or drawings. Commenting on my younger brother at this time, Mike d'Abo, who had now become head of house at Bradbys, commented that Jonathan in his quiet, cool way had us all 'taped'.

Underneath his dogged, academically handicapped façade, Jonathan underwent a transformation halfway through his Harrow years which makes it tempting to divide this Harrow chapter in two. Most, if not all teenagers undergo such a change. In Jonathan's case it meant changing from an utterly innocent child into an immensely knowing adult. I imagine there were many factors involved but I must mention two powerful and unconnected outside influences on him. Both of these are very strange indeed and both met a need in the pair of us and reflected the sort of people, quite different in many respects, we were becoming. In these two twin preoccupations, we aided and abetted each other. Was it a 'close collaborative relationship' as Jonathan Gathorne-Hardy later wrote in *The Times*, or was it what is sometimes called an unholy alliance?

CHAPTER EIGHT

Frere and Christie

The castle of Dacre is now converted into a
commodious farm-house. The moat is filled up;
the out-works destroyed and the chief parts now
standing are four towers of excellent workmanship,
and built of a durable stone calculated merely for
defence, with narrow grated windows and other
dark remains of the feudal ages.

William Hutchinson,
The History of the County of Cumberland

You will not find Rillington Place in any street
map of London as a result of the fearful things that
happened there, it has changed its name to Ruston
Close. It is a mean shabby cul-de-sac of ten houses
on either side. Although the houses have three floors,
they are small, almost miniature houses, and their
most striking characteristic is peeling paint and
rotting stucco.

Ludovic Kennedy, *Ten Rillington Place*

BOTH OF OUR two new preoccupations had sexual, literary
and criminal ramifications. One of my stories is bleakly and
horrifically urban. The other, which I will start with, is both
quaintly rural and outrageously upper class. I have already

mentioned the castle in my grandmother's village and promised that this impressive and romantic border fort or peel tower would feature again in this narrative. Dacre Castle, which still stands proudly but moat-less a couple of hundred yards from my grandmother's old home, had been used as a farmhouse for a century or two. Indeed, I imagine it had been the home of the farmer, Mr Guy, who had reluctantly shot his prize bull when he found it threatening an employee. We had known the building well as children and accompanied by Aunt Jean, who was loaned a key, had often climbed the stone spiral staircase which led to the large empty room which occupied the top half of the building or climbed even higher and out onto the roof. From here we could look down on our grandmother's house, then painted yellow with brown cornerstones in the Cumbrian style.

In the spring of 1962, we were very interested to hear that Dacre's landlord, Major Hasell, had let the castle to a man named Frere, a former officer at the College of Arms. According to our grandmother's *Who's Who*, James Arnold Frere was an Old Etonian who had served as Bluemantle Pursuivant of Arms and then as Chester Herald. He was unmarried and we later learnt that he was sharing the castle with a man called E. W. Sharpe. That this exotic, grandiose creature had suddenly surfaced in my grandmother's beautiful, quiet, humble village was extremely exciting for both of us. Jonathan and I were beginning to become acutely class-conscious – partly the effect of being at the fundamentally middle-class Clifton and then at posh semi-upper-class Harrow and partly the effect of our father's multiple snobberies – but were also class ignorant. We both had an oversimplified view of toffs and grand country life, as witnessed at a distance in Wiltshire, Savile Row tailoring and the typical Harrovian's respect for and fear of Etonians. The fact that Frere – even the name carries a hint of depravity — was a bachelor living openly with another man also appealed to the sexually confused side of our adolescent natures.

Our interest in James Arnold Frere, then only forty-two, greatly increased when we spent part of the 1962 summer holidays at Dacre. We saw his flag fluttering over the castle and saw him from a distance, walking past our grandmother's house dressed in somewhat preposterous belted tweeds. And

a tweed cap. We fed off the gossip about him and the dis-approval he provoked in our father and some of the villagers. And his power over us was cemented when one day during those holidays we went to the castle, climbed its steps and knocked on its front door.

After a long delay and various sound effects, Frere himself stood before us. We were both immediately aware of the dark circles under his eyes. Without introducing ourselves or explaining that our grandmother was his nearest neighbour, I asked if he could show us round the castle. His reply – 'No, certainly not!' – and the slamming of the door in our faces was crushingly decisive but did nothing to dispel the myth.

It wasn't just the circles under his eyes. We soon learnt that Frere was an unsavoury character, a seedy but picturesque representative of the upper classes and 'a most unhappy man'. He lived in debt. He owed money to the Dacre pub, the Horse and Farrier. He couldn't drive a car – a distinction I shared with him until I was thirty-five – and had been sacked from the College of Arms. And, better still, we soon learnt that he was a friend of Vassall, the Soviet spy arrested later that summer. But he carried all this off with commendable, semi-comic arrogance. Jonathan and I needed heroes or comic characters – Jonathan had a genius for spotting them – but almost overnight Frere had supplanted all those figures from the past, like the Hen-Without-Feathers and the schoolmasters we still grappled with. Though personally unavailable, his existence offered us a yardstick by which to judge other toffs and an insight into court circles and worlds we hardly knew. In particular, he alerted Jonathan and me to the glorious, comic richness of the College of Arms and we quickly memorised the names and titles of Frere's former colleagues at this extraordinary institution. Among them were Trappes-Lomax, the Somerset Herald, Robin de la Lanne Mirrlees, the Rouge Dragon Pursuivant, and the Norfolk Herald Extraordinary, who went under the decidedly *Queue*-like name, G. D. Squibb.

Frere's visit to Cumberland lasted only a few months. Writing to us the following spring, my grandmother added an uncharacteristically gossipy postscript to her letter: 'Mr Frere who was at Dacre Castle has gone off and left it without paying his bills!' Major Hasell would later describe his tenant as 'a man of straw', but Frere retained a hold over Jonathan for the rest of his life and interested me for long afterwards. During our remaining Harrow days, we gathered a great deal of information about him. I soon found a photograph of him in his tabard beside Winston Churchill at Windsor Castle. And another in a book about the Coronation.

Though Jonathan tagged along with me in these pursuits, as always seeing the funny side to everything, I was the prime motivator. Frere stirred my emotions. For Jonathan, he was simply a source of weird and wonderful ideas, an odd angle on the upper classes or landed gentry but not in any way a forerunner of Mr Grant, the down-and-out schoolmaster he befriended at the end of his life, or even of the predatory homosexualists who populate *The Queue*. Yet even today I cannot quite make out this business with Frere. And the odd coincidences involved. On 11 April 1963, I was changing trains at Plymouth, on my way to Cornwall, when I thought I spotted Frere on the platform. When the Truro train pulled in, I followed this faintly familiar stranger into a first-class carriage, sat down opposite and started a conversation with him. It *was* Frere – but the conversation didn't come easily. What Jonathan would have called the 'best' moment was when the ticket inspector entered our carriage. Frere produced a ticket but declared, without a trace of embarrassment, 'This doesn't go far enough. I haven't got any money so I'll have to give you my name and address.' Two months later Frere's book *The British Monarchy At Home* was published but contained very little of interest to us, aside from the author's encounter with a heavily tweeded King George VI, whom he described as 'looking for all the world' like Farmer George

– a syntax or idiom that Jonathan would later employ in letters to me.

Much more rewarding was the visit that Jonathan and I paid in August 1963 to the now empty Dacre Castle. Finding that the key to our grandmother's bedroom also fitted the door to the castle, we let ourselves in, crept around and filled our pockets with odds and ends that Frere and his friend, secretary and companion Mr Sharpe had left behind them. We found unpaid bills for milk and laundry and an empty box of Roger & Gallet Carnation Soap. These and other more mundane items found their way into the first of two scrapbooks about Frere which Jonathan and I created together and which I still have beside me as I write these words.

The second of these volumes contains material from a secret visit we later paid to Frere's new home in Herefordshire. Frere had moved directly from Dacre Castle to a twenty-room mansion called The Mynde near Much Dewchurch. Jonathan and I would wander the lanes around The Mynde – the name has its own *Queue*-like resonance – never straying near the house but catching glimpses of it through the mist. At 10 o'clock that night we spotted a light on. Anyway, Frere was not at The Mynde for long. Rumours would soon reach our ears that he was in prison for debt.

Whether or not this was true, it fed our imaginations and, for years ahead, Frere, The Mynde, Dacre Castle and the College of Arms featured in our letters and conversations. Writing to me on 22 July 1965 from the Lake Hotel, Yellowstone Park, Jonathan plunged straight into an item headed 'Frere's Trial':

As Frere was led out of the courtroom in hand-cuffs, he asked the Judge if he might be spared being sent to the same prison as Colonel Squibbs. In the end they didn't send him to Pentonville. He did go, however, to where he had some old friends. The prison was Strangeways and Major Hasell, serving 12 years for larceny, was working in the laundry.

The casually delivered insult to Frere's former colleague at the College of Arms – Squibb didn't have an 's' to his name and he wasn't a colonel – and the fictional comeuppance for the immensely worthy Major Hasell has an anti-establishment ring. The whole paragraph also reads like an extract from the ghost-written memoirs by criminals that were more popular at that time than they are today.

Jonathan was not a great reader during his schooldays – or afterwards – but, as we know, possessed the ability to pick up the style and content of books and reproduce them at random. One of few books we both enjoyed at this time was *The Truth About Dartmoor*, written by an ex-convict called George Dendrickson and full of the kind of anecdotal material parodied in 'Frere's Trial'. Around the same time, we both became hugely interested and entertained by Ludovic Kennedy's book about the Christie and Evans miscarriage of justice. *Ten Rillington Place* was published in January 1961 and its subject matter would become Jonathan's second great preoccupation during his mid-teens. Strange though it is to relate, *Ten Rillington Place* meant more to him than any other book – and he effortlessly reprocessed its contents and style in all manner of ways, turning its minutiae, language and intrinsic black humour to good use.

My older brothers had given the Ludovic Kennedy book

to my father as a Christmas present. My father had read it
quickly beside the fire and laughed out loud over the fact
that the murderer Christie had given his dog Judy a meal
of fish and chips. Months later, the book had fallen into the
hands of Martin, Jonathan and me. All three of us had
been fascinated by it, and made it our cult book for a while.
We were not alone in our interest in the case. Eight years
earlier Terence Rattigan, Cecil Beaton, Edith Sitwell and
other members of the intelligentsia had attended Christie's

trial at the Old Bailey. Edith Sitwell had even paid several
visits to the house in Notting Hill where the murders had
been committed. But Jonathan went further than anyone,
almost to the point of glorifying the agonisingly genteel,
moralising murderer, certainly making him into a comic
character.

Ten Rillington Place is written with passion and indignation – it led to a pardon for the utterly innocent Timothy Evans – but its text is full of murky forensic detail and the picture that emerges of working-class London in the early post-war years is chilling. It evokes the metropolitan underworld and twisted sexuality with detachment and disdain, and concerns itself not only with the lifestyle of Christie himself but also with transport cafés, cemeteries, doctors' surgeries, nosy neighbours, CID officers, prisons, court cases and judges' pronouncements. There are many links here with my father's medico-legal viewpoint and many foretastes of the grim and grotesque landscapes of *The Queue*. There was even a photograph of the large, untidy, *Queue*-like graveyard visible from the bedroom Christie occupied as a child. *Ten Rillington Place*, you could say, portrays another England, the flipside to the weird and wonderful court circles occupied during those very same years by the tabarded James Arnold Frere.

Ludovic Kennedy's authoritative, almost patrician style and liberal use of quotations – he often refers to another book on the case written by a man called Jesse – may have provoked my brother into parodying it. Writing to me from Harrow during the spring term of 1964, he begins, 'Dear Christie' and asks: 'Did you know that every other word in the Christie Book is in inverted commas? e.g. An example of "care and neatness" & Dr Odess observed that the pain was so bad that Christie was "hardly able to get off the chair". Which chair?' Jonathan was not only delighted by phrases like *in flagrante delicto*, he also reworked Ludovic Kennedy's material, applied it to unlikely subjects and incorporated it in letters to me and anything else he could lay his hands on. The photographs in the album he had started keeping in 1960 had originally carried banal and conventional captions.

By 1963, many of these had been amended and in several instances carried material from *Ten Rillington Place*. Thus, a photo of Uncle Gurney's dog Henry was now accompanied by the words: 'The sort of dog one came across in the army, fool enough to forge his leave pass (see Jesse II)' and a picture of Mrs Godwin at her sewing machine in the Turig kitchen was given the face of Mrs Christie which Jonathan had cut out of the book. Around this time, Jonathan had also stuck Christie's face on the handle of a tennis racquet, replacing that of the tennis star Fred Perry. Using this racquet later to play tennis with Wiltshire neighbours, our oldest brother Simon had carefully unpicked the murderer's portrait.★ From Harrow, Jonathan had also sent me a pen-and-ink cartoon he had done of Christie standing beside the Thames where he was eventually arrested, but again improves upon the idea by making Christie's penis stick through the embankment wall.

And so it continued. The worlds of Frere and Christie had several elements in common but were chiefly linked by our interest in them. Lexicographers use the word 'corpus' to describe a source of written material from which words, phrases and ideas can be extracted. In the case of the Frere and Christie sagas, both offered an exhaustive fund of dark and light material and modes of expression which would educate Jonathan far better in the ways of the world than any schoolmaster could.

★ To be fair to Simon, he now admits he destroyed a masterpiece.

CHAPTER NINE

Harrow: Part Two

I cannot go on like this. Since arriving here as a
new boy some 8 years ago, I have learnt practically nothing and seem to spend my life between
dramas, police raids and court-room evidence. Some
O-levels, which once seemed certain, are now
rapidly diminishing and I am writing a letter to
my father with instructions for my removal from
the school.

The Queue, Chapter One

DURING HIS LAST few terms at Harrow, Jonathan ceased to
be the submissive, docile, plodding, untidy figure of the past.
In a matter of months my younger brother would be trans-
formed from a potato into a peach. He turned sixteen on
10 April 1963 and by then his interests had expanded in
many directions, as well as those discussed in the last chapter.
One of these was in the field of personal grooming.

In the middle of this transitional stage, between 19 May
and 8 June 1963, Jonathan kept a revealing private diary of
his life at Harrow. In it, he notes his bowel movements – or
lack of them – and homosexual assignments. On Sunday, 25
May, there is a meeting with someone in the Vaughan Library,
followed by a visit to a place called the Farmers Room. In
the same breath, he records his visits to the Art School. 'I was

pleased to see the glaze was adhering to my bottle,' he notes on one occasion, and on 1 June reveals, 'I moulded faeces.' He has favourable things to say about the art master, R. W. Treffgarne, describes him as 'entertaining' and savours his utterances. One afternoon, 'Treffy' or 'Truffles' calls Jonathan a 'villain' and on another occasion, begins, 'I say, artists extraordinary . . .' To his contemporaries, Jonathan shows a certain aloofness. On 30 May he notes, 'Borrowed 2/6 from B.S. who is a failure and a bore,' and on 6 June declares, 'Stevenson behaved like a child.' Several entries conclude with the statement, 'Watched street,' which means he sat at the window of his room observing the passers-by. This shows a touching interest in the outside world, also explicit in his misspelled references to 'Profumo Scandle' and 'Stephen Ward Scandle'.

These diary jottings strike the same confident note as the narrator's pronouncement in *The Queue* – 'I had a homosexual affair with Lord Fuck at School' – and compare favourably with the forlorn description of boarding-school life quoted at the start of this chapter. In fact, Jonathan's last

two terms at Harrow were full of ups and downs – even dramas – unmonitored and unwitnessed by me. I had left the school at the end of 1963 intent on becoming a stand-up comedian – and intent on dragging Jonathan with me in this venture – but had begun the new year at an art school in Florence, where I would study for a few weeks under the eye of our brother Julian, now a pupil of Annigoni.

Separated from Jonathan for the first time in three years, we had immediately begun to dash off letters to each other. Those I received from Jonathan at this time contained his first surrealist offerings, were often composed entirely of nonsense, shaggy-dog sentences and non sequiturs, enriched with filthy drawings and innumerable references to Christie and a few to Frere, whose signature I had been startled to find in the visitor's book at the British Consulate in Florence. Had our hero now served his prison sentence? Or was he still on the run from the law?

The first in this new series of letters came from Turig, was dated 11 January 1964 and ran to six pages. The second paragraph begins with a reference to our parents whom we now knew by their initials: 'GEB & MAB discuss among themselves how Andrew will behave at night and they wonder whether you are keeping clear of Firenze Benvenu, Florence's "Red Light" district.' He added nudgingly, 'By the way how are the red lighters?' and continues somewhat pretentiously, 'I am writing in the drawing-room. Gilda is lying at the fire, looking for all the world like a mushroom in heavy traffic,' and then, shaggy-doggily, 'Mrs May "Don't pull my hair" Godwin is . . . guess what . . . scrumming around in the cupboard.' Later there is a reference to Mark Tindall and my future, still very unresolved from everyone's point of view except my own: 'MT has written a bitter little card about University. It makes Catto's letters to Theophilus look like the paper that Christie used to wrap fish and chips in for Judy.' Another paragraph, wholly fanciful, about my parents' part-time gardener and a feeble offspring of Gilda called Tiger, offers a foretaste of the court-case scenes which litter his subsequent writings and come to full fruition in *The Queue*. Our gardener, he explains, is 'up before Bradford Courts for the attempted theft of Tiger, who was found in his car.' And he adds the soon-to-be-familiar words, '46 previous convictions were taken into account.'

This letter, written on flimsy airmail paper, also contains several drawings. A man in a car with the darkened silhouette of a dachshund on the back seat has run over someone. Our mother is out riding a horse which has a dog dangling from its mouth by its penis. And there's a cocktail party scene with one of our Wiltshire neighbours, a Mrs Leavey, 'taken bad' and lying on the floor. All the figures, including the stricken lady, have TV aerials sticking out of their heads.

In a subsequent airmail letter from Harrow, dated 27 January, he pleaded, 'Do tell me "more" of Florence's "seamy" district,' – alas, I had nothing to report in that vein – and concluded with a reference to my Old Harrovian friend Mike d'Abo, who was now taking his first steps as a pop singer. Jonathan tells me there has been a photo of d'Abo in the *Sunday Telegraph* and adds, 'Inevitable – Treffgarne has put it on the Art School board.' A postcard dated 3 February informs me that 'M. d'A' has been practising in the Music Schools with the Band of Angels and that an article about Harrow in the latest *Tatler* includes a photograph of myself. Added in pencil are the words: 'getting fish for Judy'.

Later that spring I was back in Wiltshire, at Turig, attending a tutor's with a view to obtaining more A levels while dreaming only of my career as a stand-up comic. Here Jonathan wrote to me on thick yellow writing paper which came with matching envelopes from Truslove and Hanson, explaining, 'Bought by me because Father has been generous enough to give me an adequate allowance here.' I fell upon these letters, or the enclosures addressed to me included in letters for my parents, with great excitement. Jonathan was, at this stage, practically my only friend and certainly my only correspondent.

The letters he continued to write to me during the spring term of 1964 contained the same mixture of sense and nonsense. They also contained serious information and real emotion. Poor old Mark Tindall is described as '"foul"' – note the triple inverted commas – and Jonathan's fellow three-yearers at Bradbys dismissed as 'revolting' and 'loathsome'. A loaded question from Tindall – 'How is your extraordinary brother?' – is passed on without comment but the revelation that Jonathan may have an operation on his bunions is embellished with the semi-surrealist information that the operation will take three weeks. Some items begin straightforwardly but rapidly go off the rails. In a letter mysteriously signed 'Love Peter' he urges me to see a film called *The Living Desert*, which apparently features 'brilliant triangle-shaped "girda" snakes chasing scorpions'. In another, he starts by mocking our friendship – 'The things I really miss you for here are the sort of observations that no other creature in Europe "would" understand.' – but restores normality with a reference to Mark Tindall 'trying to make his Whitworth & Co suit look badly fitting,' a reference to how our house-master's natural angularity and often expressed disapproval of slickness or smoothness was reflected in his clothing.

Many of Jonathan's letters were enriched with material from *Ten Rillington Place*. I have already relayed his observation about the number of words and phrases in the Christie book put in inverted commas. His own use of this practice, or parody of it, gives his letters a sinister aura. With or without the inverted commas, the Christie story was still very much on his mind. One letter begins 'A fantastic thing has happened here' and then lifts a whole section of *Ten Rillington Place* and sets it in the school context. 'Old Mrs Eady,' he begins about some imaginary Harrow resident, 'died last month and was buried in her own garden. Now this afternoon I was gardening and there leaning against the fence was – guess what? Mrs Eady's right thigh bone had worked itself loose from the soil and Tindall is now using it to prop up the garden fence! This shows his astonishing effrontery!!'

The same letter continues by parodying Ludovic Kennedy's revelation that Terence Rattigan, watching the Christie trial from the public gallery, had been caught staring at the defendant and turned his head away: 'This afternoon Tindall was walking in the street and he started staring at my window. I returned his glance, but then Tindall felt ashamed at being "caught" staring and turned his head away.' A few days later, he wrote again, reviving an occasion when Mrs Christie or Christie himself had refused to open the door to a caller: 'As I was returning home from the Dining Club last night, I found MT's door locked. Then I saw Mrs Tindall peeping behind her curtain so I continued to knock until she had opened the door.'

Many of Jonathan's letters also mentioned show business, the world I had set my heart on, partly inspired by the ease with which my friend d'Abo had cruised into the pop world and the whole burgeoning youth culture. Jonathan

94

was still to some extent under my power and more than happy to be dragged along by me in this straw-grasping venture. As long ago as 22 October 1963, he had even written to Aunt Jean: 'I have decided that I want to go to a London stage school when I leave next summer. Father is dubious, of course!' Quite so, but our plans were still vague and peripheral. In several letters that spring, Jonathan encouraged me with ideas and information, none of it directly relevant. 'I have spoken to Monty Berman, the costume hire man', he soon tells me 'and he can let us have stage glitter suits for 3 gns to 5 gns per week.' Another long letter that spring strikes a more businesslike note:

Dear Andrew,
A few more ideas for revue & cabaret. The tiresome Show-biz woman at the Teashop says the Astor Club are always wanting comics for cabaret. Her son writes scripts for Charlie Chester, and he sent up some material to the Stork Room, and they 'pinched it'.

She says the idea is to get a show at either the Stork Room or the Astor and then phone up the Jack Hylton agency who will send a talent 'scout' along.

You may have read the weekly magazine 'Stage'. They have a page devoted to auditions, etc.

If you can come up on April 1st, I suggest we go to Fielding's Music Hall at the Prince Charles Theatre. It sounds brilliant. Satirical bar bending acts, fat women, 71-year-old Billy Russell sings 'When the midnight Choo-Choo goes through Alabama.'

Another idea. For your revue have you thought

of the Tower Bridge 'man-in-a-sack-with-two-swords-through-him' act.

> How about it?
> See you Wednesday week.
> Yours 'Faithfully'
> TONKS

However feeble these schemes – Tonks was a nickname Jonathan enjoyed for a while at both home and school – neither of us had other plans for the future. Nor do I remember any serious opposition to these aspirations from our parents. Our father, perhaps, had so far been kept out of the picture. 'Don't worry,' Jonathan had added in response to my concern that he might be becoming less rebellious, 'the Barrow legend grows larger every week, e.g. my appearance in a black velvet faced overcoat.' One of these letters from which I have already quoted is headed 'The Victorian Suite, Bradbys', and it might be argued that he had now completed – and overshot – the 'tidying up' process.

Near the end of that spring term – and almost in the same post as a letter from our oldest brother Simon, announcing his engagement to a girl called Caroline – a letter arrived for my father in Tindall's angular and symmetric handwriting. I do not know where this letter is today but I remember well its decidedly oblique opening lines. 'Jonathan seems to have landed himself in a spot of bother. Of the smutty nature, if you take my meaning.' Tindall had gone on in mild, vague terms, telling my father that it was not something 'to get wildly het up about' but that the two men should meet some time to discuss the matter. As on other occasions, my father's initial reaction was mild and even jubilant, singing out, *'Johnny's in the dog house!'* as if the whole thing was a big joke. My mother's response was anxious and grim. Within hours, however, my father was similarly worked up and not at all mollified by an end-of-term report from the Head Master, Dr James, which concluded: 'He certainly creates a very odd impression of himself on the Hill. He must do, or I would not have such a clear impression of him in various postures, as indeed I do.'

Jonathan never discussed this episode with me in any detail – he had apparently had unspecific liaisons with two younger boys from another house – and it had no effect on our joint plans to enter show business. On 1 April, at the beginning of the Easter holidays, we obtained an interview with the Bernard Delfont Agency in Jermyn Street, then one of the top variety agencies in the country, representing acts like the Beverley Sisters, Mike and Bernie Winters and the Three Monarchs. This was our first glimpse of the real thing. And our hopes were raised when Delfont-director Keith Devon, who wore orange-framed spectacles, offered us a cold audition ten days later at the Talk of the Town. Alas, this was not a success. Our satirical stuff was not at all what they wanted – we were politely advised to go to RADA, an option we considered beneath us – but I still dine out today on the fact that I have performed on the stage of this famous nightspot, now known by its original name, the Hippodrome.

My father was meanwhile still brooding about Jonathan's incident at Harrow, and was later even accused by Mark Tindall of overreacting. My father had his own theories about adolescent homosexuality: Jonathan might have been badly circumcised, thus placing too much attention on his own and other people's penises. On 15 April, Jonathan was sent to see a psychiatrist or specialist my father knew called Mr or Dr Harland Rees with a WELbeck

97

telephone number. After conducting a thorough physical examination – Jonathan reported that a small towel had been briefly draped over his private parts – Harland Rees had written a calm and sensible letter to my father, saying that he believed Jonathan to be going through a temporary phase and there was nothing whatsoever wrong with his circumcision. He had discovered, however, 'a fairly marked degree of constipation', the remedies for which he had gone into in some depth. The letter concluded that in the doctor's view – some may think it comical in the circumstances – Jonathan was completely serious about wishing to go into the theatre.

My father was not content to leave the matter there, however, and soon organised for a clergyman he knew, a cousin of our mother called David MacInnes, to visit Harrow on a weekly basis during the following term and give Jonathan one-to-one confirmation classes. Jonathan would soon put a mischievously ironic twist on these arrangements, claiming that he and the clergyman had been spotted lying in a meadow reading the Bible together and immediately reported to the Head Master.

In other respects, Jonathan's life seems to have expanded and stabilised – on 10 April he had turned seventeen and obtained his provisional driving licence – and he had returned to Harrow for his final term there in good spirits. His first letter to me – his handwriting had also become enviably confident – starts on a wholly fictional note and shows that the Rillington Place story still amused him: 'It is incredible. There are two new boys this term. One is call Vincent (notable sex murderer) and the other is, oh no, but yes, Christie, P. J. P. . . .' In other correspondence, there were oblique references to the two boys he had supposedly been involved with the previous term, and the touching information that one of them was now getting confirmed. There were also copious further references to Christie – 'Meanwhile Ethel and Christie snuggled up together in their double bed' – and to the murderer's dog Judy, who had somehow caught up with and almost supplanted Gilda in Jonathan's imagination. There was also a reference to Frere whom we liked to believe was back in prison. 'Frere will probably be in Brixton,' he wrote at the end of May, 'Visiting hours are 8–6, and the Governor, Somerset, will give you a list of inmates.'

There was also a mention of the famous escaped prisoner Foxy Fowler, who, Jonathan suggested, might be in our part of Wiltshire and a threat to Gilda. Several letters parodied, in part, the sort of letters our grandmother still wrote from Cumberland. 'I hear you have floods' and 'I fear it means Garlands' – a reference to the mental hospital where Miss Titterington would end up. There were also assorted allusions to Clifton, which had by no means lost its grip on him, and endless cartoons – even one of a boy washing out his pants in front of the Head Master – and a letter signed Jarrett-Kerr, a Cliftonian name which had somehow caught his attention. There was also a full-page drawing headed in capital letters, 'DO YOU REMEMBER LUSH-O AT CLIFTON?' showing the way Cliftonians responded to good news during morning assembly by spouting the invented word 'Lush-o' and flicking their wrists in unison. In the corner he had drawn the singing teacher, Miss V. B. Sutton, hammering out 'Oh Praise Ye the Lord', a hymn he particularly liked on account of the joyful musical build-up to its second line. In retrospect, this faithfulness to his early school-days is touching, even generous and, as we know, it did not cease at this point.

During this summer term, there was the amusing diversion of our oldest brother Simon's wedding, which took
place on Friday 5 June at Holy Trinity Brompton, followed
by a large reception at Claridge's. This was attended by, among
others, our cleaning lady Mrs Godwin, who was placed on
a special staff table. That night – Jonathan had been allowed
out for the day by Mark Tindall – there was a family dinner
in the Buttery Bar of the Hyde Park Hotel. I mention these
arrangements partly because both Claridge's and the Buttery
Bar would feature later in Jonathan's life.

And the following day Jonathan wrote blaming the
'bustle of the buttery' for the fact that he had forgotten to
hand over the latest comedy script he had written. We had
been writing these things – none of which survive – for
some months now and Jonathan now hoped these would
soon be 'girating' the London agencies and give 'all at Delfonts
a good giggle'. We also exchanged more general comments
about showbiz personalities. That summer I discovered Tommy
Cooper, and Jonathan still harped on about Jimmy Mac,
perennial star of the Bath pantomime. 'Jimmy Mac is in a
summer show at Cliftonville with Tommy Trinder,' he told
me. There was also quite a lot about Mike d'Abo, whose
career as a pop star was already going through ups and downs
and who for some reason or another paid frequent visits to
his old school. In May Jonathan asks, 'Did you watch M. d'A
on ITV on Saturday. Very excellent.' A few weeks later he
offers a more mixed account of my old friend: 'Michael d'A
came up yesterday looking extremely smooth. The disc has
flopped completely, and I am told he came up by tube.
However he starts filming at Shepperton on June 21st. <u>ALSO</u>
he is appearing on ITV's "Discs Ago-go" which is either
tonight (Monday) or sometime on Thursday.'

Other letters mentioned teaching staff. There is a passing

reference to my old history beak D. J. Parry coming into chapel wearing sunglasses and 'looking exactly like Dr Strangelove' and accounts of dialogues he has had with a teacher called Palethorpe and R. W. Treffgarne. With Palethorpe, the conversation is distinctly dull – 'Sir, do you ever have goose pimples?' 'Only when I'm in a draught' – but things are much livelier in the art school, especially when Treffgarne's sidekick Harvey is present:

> J. H. B.: Sir, what d'you know of Black Magic?
> R.W.T.: Oh, Barrow, that's old, and very stale, cake.
> (Mr Harvey is hiding behind the screen & interrupts)
> Harvey: Excuse me, but there's some truth in it.
> R.W. T.: Look, shut up, would you, Harvey!
> Harvey: We don't normally shut till 6pm on Tuesday!
> Barrow: Sir, look out (pointing to Shakespeare bust) that statue's moving:
> R.W. T. (keeping up the joke): Oh, he gets a bit restless in the summer!
> Barrow: Does he?
> R. W. T.: No!

Characteristically, Jonathan has nothing to say about the pictures he was doing in the Art School, some of which are propped against the walls around me as I write these words. One is an oil painting of an imaginary market scene, with stout men and women selling fruit and vegetables. The jaunty angle of their hats, the sharp look on their faces, the careful depiction of the trestle tables laden with produce and the prominence of a cash register reflect Jonathan's down-to-earthness.

The presence of two men pushing, one might almost write *trundling*, a cart or wheelbarrow in the background is almost his signature. Unlike the illustrations included in his letters, these pictures were not intended specifically for my eyes but appealed to me none the less.

Jonathan also had a lot to say about Tindall, distorting him and demonising him to some extent. A few weeks into the new term, Tindall had written a postcard to my father beginning 'All goes well here, as far as one can possibly tell . . .' and made some attempt in person to keep Jonathan on the straight and narrow during those last few weeks. Finding the dressing table in Jonathan's room laden with cosmetics, scent and the like, Tindall had growled, 'Those little bottles have got to go.' We gathered Tindall had also told a house monitor that during a visit to the school from our father, he had caught them both 'going at each other hammer and tongs'.

In letters to our parents, Jonathan adopted a subversive attitude towards his long-suffering housemaster. On 17 May 1964, he virtually turns the whole affair upside down by writing: 'You need not have worries about my housemaster Tindall's behaviour last term. It has now come to my notice that I am not the only person he finds disagreeable. Last term he had a large row with "R. Evans" (once his staunch supporter). I begin to wonder whom he really does like, if anyone.' A fortnight later, he refers to Tindall as 'my housemaster whom you met last term' and attempts to stir the shit by adding 'By the way, Tindall has been asking questions about *you* via a house monitor.' He also demonised the Head Master, Dr James, at least in his own mind, and did not let go of him, as we know. Two years later, long before he started work on *The Queue*, he would produce a memorandum mimicking the high and mighty pronouncements that sometimes issued from the Head Master's office:

To all Parents who have boys at Harrow School.
DEATH PROPHYLAXIS
In an effort to reduce the enormous amount of work placed on our staff by overcrowding in the boarding houses, the school doctor and myself have decided to arrange to inoculate all boys in the school with "Mixed Rigor Mortis Curranine Vaccine" (Glaxo).

The course involves one injection in the quick of the back and the injectionee is free from all discomfort and death is more or less instantaneous. The injection is safe.

There is NO GUARANTEE that the above dose will produce instant death, but evidence from MRC (Medical Research Council) suggests that the dose will certainly make life much easier for all concerned, especially those in Foss, Leaf Schools, and Workshop 1.

The cost of the inoculation is 7/- and includes GP's fees, Harrow Red Cross Ambulance, Dead Man's Cradle Units, fees to knacker at Kenton etc.

Would you kindly indicate on the enclosed forms whether you wish your son to be killed?
June 1966   R. L. James
                                             Head Master

Does this astounding document indicate extreme morbidity, insight into his own death, or was it simply a delayed letting off of steam after nine years in boarding school? In fairness to Dr James, I should remind the reader that *all* schoolmasters, and headmasters in particular, invite parody and to some extent deserve it.

In other letters that final summer term, Jonathan described a number of school scandals, real and invented, about boys and staff. To my parents he wrote on 7 June about an incident on the sports ground: 'Yesterday there was a thunderstorm while we were playing cricket. An elderly Master (the Revd H. L. Harris . . .) was taken ill while trapped in a pavilion. I am told he is fully recovered now.' Was the intention of this shaggy-doggish invention to amuse my parents, appeal to my father's scatological sense of humour or to settle some score with his form master Mr Harris, who the previous term had written that Jonathan would 'not make a good dilettante'?

To me he began an undated letter with an entirely fictitious story about another member of staff being under close arrest for suspected art theft from the school's War Memorial building. 'He is imprisoned under the Vaughan Library, and I hear him crying every time I pass.' And he has other nonsense to impart about boys. He tells me that a boy named N. has fallen down eight flights of stairs and that police are combing the Bradbys' kitchens. I suspect this item is simply a vehicle for the word *combing*, which he has put in inverted commas.

Towards the end of term, he has a true story to tell about a 'tragic' mass expulsion that occurred at the time – and does so with gusto, concluding with Tindall's comment 'Well you're not involved, thank heaven.' To which Jonathan claims to have replied, quoting from *Truth about Dartmoor*, 'My honeymoon with crime is over'. With or without these excitements, those last few weeks at Harrow appear to have been happy ones. At long last, Jonathan seems to have got Tindall on his side and in a final letter to our parents even plays off father and housemaster by writing: 'Tindall, though always friendly to me now, seems rather displeased with your telephone conversations.' In his last letter to me from Harrow, he quotes his housemaster as advising him, 'Jonathan, before you check out next week, I suggest you toddle along to the Head Prune and say adieu' and wonders about the appropriateness of describing a Doctor of Philosophy as a dried fruit. Then comes a paragraph headlined QUOTE FROM J. H. B.s AUTOBIOGRAPHY and again inspired by the Dartmoor book: 'On my last night at Harrow, the housemaster Tindall looked in through my judas-hole, but now his intentions are purely friendly. He chats, jokes and spews, asking your plans.'

Jonathan left Harrow for good on Monday, 20 July 1964. On his final weekend he had dinner with the art master Treffgarne on the Saturday and with his somewhat maligned form master H. L. Harris on the Sunday, both of whom would later write favourable end-of-term reports. 'He writes with a poise and understanding that are rare in this form not common in the block,' declared H. L. Harris. 'Unfortunately his answers are often irrelevant.' 'He has been very active indeed and produced a quantity of admirable paintings in a comparatively short period,' wrote Treffgarne. Tindall is also positive, complimenting Jonathan on 'a sensible and productive final term' and ending the sequence of Harrovian brothers with 'dignity and common sense'. In his usual neat, typewritten summary, the Head Master of Harrow ignores the bad maths report and declares that Jonathan has finished 'on a good note.'

CHAPTER TEN

Show Business

The doorman at the strip-tease club seemed to know Mary and he lets us in for half-price. It was about 2.30 in the morning and the place was full of men. There was a piano and a low stage. A girl was dancing with no clothes on and she was doing unprintable things with a hedgehog and two slugs. We sat right at the back for fear of being seen.

Mr Jusse the manager brought a bottle of fizzy-pop to our table and a plate of currant buns. Suddenly Mary jumped off my knee and ran, by way of a ramp, onto the stage. She stood up on her back legs and showed off her parts to the audience of 47. They were furious and booed. Many eggs were thrown and Mary fell to her knees twice. But, undeterred, she continued with her routine. It was revolting, obscene and indescribable.

The Queue, Chapter Six

STILL MARKING TIME at Turleigh Combe after sitting my A levels again, I hurried up to London to meet Jonathan the day he left Harrow. We spent the night of 20 July 1964 at Julian's studio at 48 Tite Street – our older brother was always generous in this way – and the following day had an extravagant lunch together at the Coq d'Or in Stratton Street. Seated together on the banquette, we drank a carafe of red wine, ate *coq au vin* and ended the meal with cigars.

Later that afternoon I accompanied Jonathan to the Royal National Orthopaedic Hospital in Bolsover Street off Euston Road, where he was to have the long-awaited operation on his bunion. He had a private room and took along a notebook. In this he recorded the following conversation with a nurse at 7 p.m.:

N: Your flowers go out at night.
J: Yes and why.
N: Those roses are killers.
J: So I believe.

Jonathan's responses have a fictional nonchalance. So does a remark attributed to the surgeon, David Trevor, who popped in to see his foot half an hour later – 'That's the chap' – which has a ring of truth to it, but when my brother asked him if the operation would go well, the same man can surely not have replied, as Jonathan claims, 'Not if my knife slips.' In his hospital notebook, he then records a visit at 8 p.m. from an 'anglo–polynesian orderly offering coffee, Horlicks, stewed milk, poached water, boiled egg juice,' and that the nurse giving him the anaesthetic mutters: 'This will knock you out like a bottle of gin.' He also jots down a remark by the nurse who had watched the TV news with him earlier and responded to an item about John Bloom's washing-machine empire going into liquidation – 'Yes my auntie had a John Bloom but it never worked.'

Anyway, the surgeon's knife did not slip – David Trevor went on to become President of the orthopaedic section of the Royal Society of Medicine – but when I visited Jonathan after the operation I found him drowsy from it and momentarily withdrawn, no longer my intimate friend. His foot would remain in plaster for the next eight weeks and his future – and my future – unresolved. We would spend several weeks together at Turig, reabsorbing the world of dogs and our parents. The house and garden had changed little over the past ten years. The Aga still gave off fumes and there was now a dishwashing machine, the lid of which was held up by a stone suspended by a string and wrapped in cloth. On the way to the kitchen was the 'egg table' on which eggs were marked by the day of the week they were laid. All this was utterly familiar to me. I had been based at Turig since returning from Italy in February. For Jonathan, too, this was the world where he had grown up and spent every holiday for the past ten years. Our joint aspirations to abandon this ultra-homely place for some starry, largely imaginary show-business world strengthened the curious conspiracy between us.

Yet here at Turig was the raw material that Jonathan was already turning into his particular kind of art. At the heart and hearth of it all were the surviving dachshunds, still presided over by Gilda, now eight years old and as bad, naughty and greedy as ever. Of her three litters we had kept Candy, who had died recently at the vet's, Tiger, whom we also knew as Wibby, and a further offspring called Tom. These increasingly conventional names reflected their diminishing characters and lovability. Gilda remained utterly tenacious, gruffly announcing her presence outside the door of one's bedroom but then refusing to be shifted from inside one's bed – and losing her temper if anyone other than our mother attempted to do so. To avoid being bitten in these circumstances, it was necessary to bundle up *all* the sheets and blankets and lift up the whole caboodle at once with Gilda inside, growling ferociously and snapping at one from inside her nest.

Gilda's sex life remained an issue and the dog family was utterly disrupted when she was on heat. 'Oh, it *is* a curse having mixed sexes in a house. I don't know why I did it,' said my mother, protesting not so much about the effect of Gilda's heats on dogs in the village – 'Get out, you great brute!' she shouted on finding Dog Plenty in the back kitchen – but also on Gilda's poor little red-blooded grandson Tom. My mother now responded despairingly to the onset of Gilda's heats. 'Wretched old woman! I could shake her!' she said on one occasion. And on another, more mercifully, 'Oh by the way, Gilda's definitely on heat. She spilt in my bed. Naughty gal.' At these times Tom would be locked up – 'Let prisoner out!' my mother commanded when the coast was clear – and would lose weight. 'Poor little Tom, he's worn to a razzle,' said my mother. 'Tommy's forbidden fruit,' she said on another occasion. And when the two dogs were together, Tommy showed his amorousness by licking up Gilda's urine with such reckless zest that my mother – she had a black sense of humour of her own – declared that he would do so even if the urine had been sprinkled with sulphuric acid. When the heat was over and my mother announced, 'Gilda gave him a real snarl this morning. Which usually means shop's shut,' it was a great relief for us all.

I drag in this slightly smutty material because Jonathan has so much to say in *The Queue* about the libidinous nature of the dog Mary and the endless trouble it brings upon herself and the narrator. And also because this was, of course, a time of sexual awakening for both of us. And because such intensely doggy domesticity was in stark contrast to the theatrical dreams we both laboured under. And because, of course, it illustrates my mother's character.

★

My mother's life revolved around the dogs, the kitchen, the garden – 'I'm worried about the hens,' she once declared, and, 'My roses are my children' – and the few local characters who had entered her consciousness. She talked affectionately of seeing 'Old Sweetie Dagger' at the village bus stop and joined in our old jokes about the Hen-Without-Feathers, often incorporating these people in the elaborate drawing games we still played after supper. The world beyond the garden and the reservoirs where she sometimes went fishing was of limited interest to her. Though she enjoyed television, she had no interest in grand restaurants like the Coq d'Or – Port Salut was the only mildly exotic cheese she registered – and more than once she expressed her disapproval of some of the 'towny' effects Harrow had had upon her sons.

Meanwhile my father's character was blossoming into its full eccentricity. Had all this washed over us in the past? Or had he only recently begun to talk about senior police officers, serious vice charges, cemetery clerks and strangulated hernias? In recent years my father's particular stand-point had been greatly strengthened, underpinned and lent authority by his serving on the West of England Hospital Board, to which he had been appointed by Enoch Powell, Minister of Health, in the early 1960s. During the long journey north to visit our grandmother, my father had once commented on the blankets hanging on some suburban washing line: 'Always a bad sign. Means a man's bowels have come out during the night . . .' And sometimes from his seat at the head of the dining-room table at Turig, he would mimic a judge giving sentence, employing similar words and the kind of ferocity Jonathan would later give to a judge in *The Queue*: 'You are the most despicable human being to ever enter my court. I shall punish you with the utmost severity.'

To be fair, my father could also be extremely lighthearted, even skittish, about court proceedings and even began one grandiose account with a reference to a famous comedy double act. 'We have Mr Jewell and Mr Warriss here. Their appearance in court today is rather extraordinary. They're both wearing cockatoo feathers in their hats.' All of which fed into Jonathan's storehouse mind, along with the names of my father's local heroes, such as Mr Scrine who ran the chemist's shop in Bradford-on-Avon and Mr Self, who ran the village garage.

During this period Jonathan was an avid reader of the *Bath and Wilts Chronicle and Herald* which contained on almost every page of every issue stories about car crashes and court cases and small-town events. Two winters earlier, Jonathan had written a joke letter to this paper protesting that the main road between Bath and Limpley Stoke had not been cleared during a recent icy spell and blaming the uncleared snow for an accident on the B34. This had been published as the lead letter on 15 January 1963, under the headline 'Why was trunk road not cleared?' and generated further letters including one from a Mr Wibby Gulliver of Theo Street, Warminster, referring to 'rutted strips of ice' on the Bath–Warminster road. Wibby Gulliver was of course another of Jonathan's pseudonyms and Theo Street gets its name from my grandmother's long-time secretary-companion, Theo Fox, by then living alone in a Cornish caravan.

Now, on 21 August 1964, Jonathan submitted another spoof item to the Bath paper, which under the headline 'Thank you Bath and the Kindly Constable' again became the lead letter:

My husband and I have recently spent a delightful holiday in Bath, and I would like to mention a small incident which occurred last week.

My husband, a heavy and arthritic man, tripped on the kerb in the centre of Bath, and fell to the roadside. The behaviour of a police constable was an example to us all. Not only did he insist on assisting my husband to his feet, but he also very kindly drove us back to our hotel, and en route showed us the Royal Crescent and the Circus.

This was one of those many examples of kindness that we, an elderly and retiring couple, received during our visit. Our hotel was most comfortable, and we think your city outshines any other provincial town or city for its situation and beauty. We give thanks to the city of Bath for making our holiday, perhaps the last one my husband will ever have, for he is almost bedridden now, the happiest one we have ever had.

The letter, signed Gilda Bigobos (Mrs) and purporting to come from an address in Boston, Lincolnshire, contains the same kind of illogic and non sequitur that abound in *The Queue*. How could any visitor to Bath *not* see the Royal Crescent or the Circus? Has the accident in the Bath street rendered Mr Bigobos 'almost bedridden' or was he already in this condition? If so, why was an 'almost bedridden' man from Lincolnshire tottering around the centre of Bath? Jonathan's final *coup de théâtre* is in getting away with such an absurd name. Whether or not it is in the OED, the phrase *big obo* to him meant faeces. The letter shows how, at only seventeen, Jonathan had a sharp ear for cliché – and a complete mastery of a kind of snivelling provincial vernacular.

Astonishingly, this letter – we later published versions of it in the *Penrith Herald* and *Manchester Evening News* – was followed in that very column the same day by another equally grovelling letter in Jonathan's pen:

> After patronizing the Theatre Royal, Bath, for more than 40 years, I would like to express my sincere yet inadequate gratitude to Mr Maddox and the Theatre staff. The pleasure that the plays, ballet and pantomime has given us is surely incalculable. The annual Christmas pantomime never fails to delight my grandchildren, and I myself would like to thank those two artistes Jimmy Mac and Norman Meadowes. Let us all hope that the theatre will continue to flourish and in order to do so, let us all pledge to support this lovely old theatre.

This letter is signed Jake Jasinski (Mrs) with an address in Devizes. Jasinski was the name of a boy at Clifton which we had occasionally used for comic effect at Harrow. As presiding sixth-former at Bradbys, I had once announced that a boy of this name should come and see me after house prayers. As well as mentioning Frank Maddox, already firmly entrenched in our gallery of local characters, the letter makes fun of Jimmy Mac and Norman Meadowes, who were hardened small-town professionals, and points the way forward to our own show-business venture.

The penning of these letters perhaps shows how empty our lives were. Anyway, I see from my father's engagement diary that we drove up to Cumberland on 24 August: one of those long pre-motorway car journeys that had featured throughout our childhood, involving on this occasion a stop for breakfast at Wellington in Shropshire. From Dacre,

Jonathan and I set off together for the Isle of Eigg in the Inner Hebrides. I had visited this island three years earlier with Mike d'Abo and made friends with a local figure named Fergus Gowans, a mildly eccentric Old Harrovian now in his late twenties, who lived alone in the Old Manse and would eventually commit suicide. I had arranged that Jonathan and I should stay with Gowans for a few days. My mind is blank about what happened there, or how curtailed our explorations were made by Jonathan's foot being in plaster. I only recall Jonathan's remark about 'good living', a subject of increasing interest to us, and something we had decided had eluded our parents and older brothers. 'Fergus gets it. Simon doesn't,' Jonathan snapped when the topic came up on Eigg. And I also remember seeing the writer Tom Stacey and his young family on the boat to the island. Naturally enough both Stacey and Gowans were soon added to Jonathan's ever-expanding cabinet of curiosities, both in their own right and as yardsticks by which to judge others.

I remember the journey south better: we stayed at the grandest hotel in Glasgow, and eventually, our money all gone, stumbled to our grandmother's village on foot. On Sunday, 6 September, we attended evening prayers in Dacre church and were convulsed with suppressed laughter as the Vicar, Mr Smith, preached to a tiny congregation about St Augustine of Hippo and intoned in a singsong voice that, as a young man, St Augustine 'stole from his mother, goods and money'. Did we know this was something both of us were capable of doing if circumstances demanded it?

On 16 September, Jonathan returned to London to have his foot removed from what he called its 'plaster prison', and at 4 o'clock the following afternoon he returned to Scotland, taking a train from King's Cross to Edinburgh, where my father had arranged for him to attend Basil Patterson's tutorial establishment and have another go at his O levels. From here the letters began again, twelve of them during the next two months, giving his address as 'Fort Nell, Edinburgh', 'Arrol Territory, N.T.', 'Steel Castle', 'Double Bed Ford', 'The Castle "Esplanade"' and even 'On the Clipper Packet Boat to Stranraer, S.S. BIGOBO.' In them, I am sometimes addressed as 'Andrew' but more often given a fanciful name with ancient resonances. In one letter I am 'Tommy Tucker', in others 'Miss Clegg', the name of one of the teachers at Morecambe, and 'Axel Burrough', the name of a boy at Clifton I had given no thought to since leaving the school. Jonathan sometimes signs these letters John or Johnny, but more often resorts to some emotive pseudonym, as often as not derived from Clifton, like 'Jarrett-Kerr' or the more comically long-winded 'Kahil & Caish & Dobson & Gas' mentioned earlier. One letter comes from 'The Most Infuriating Man in the World', a label we had given to a man on a bus, and another is signed off with that catchy, guilt-inducing phrase from the Revd Smith's sermon in Dacre church: 'Stole from his mother, goods and money'.

The first of these letters reached me when I was still at Turig and, as so often in the past, took the form of a folded enclosure inside a letter to my parents. In fact, Jonathan's letters to our parents were often as offbeat as his ones to me. On 24 September 1964, he gave his address as 'The Plainest House in the Town', and began with the line 'All goes well here as far as one can possibly tell', which readers will remember was how Tindall had begun a postcard to our father earlier that summer. A subsequent paragraph continues: 'I don't think it's anything really to worry about but as far as I can see Patterson's is a dead end, mouldy, dirty fleapit.' He completes his attack on the crammers by stating 'Nobody can teach backward pupils,' and then arguing, 'Most of the people there are not stupid, but they are there because they have been expelled from minor public schools, for one reason or another.' The letter ends more brightly with the news that he is having a sports jacket made at a local tailors called Anderson for about £18 – this is in my possession today – finally asking for a 'sweet' little suitcase currently in his room at Turig which he needs for carrying 'text' books.

He is also merciless about his lodgings, run by a woman he calls Mrs Essbug. 'I will not attempt to describe either the accommodation or the food in this "house". It might make you sick.' In a letter to me, he describes coming down to dinner at his lodgings at 5.30 p.m. and hearing a fellow lodger remark, 'THESE <u>SPUDS</u> NEED A SHAVE!!' He claims that Pattersons is 'one big source of laughter' and expands upon his earlier theme that its inmates are all outcasts and misfits from other schools. 'At Patterson's there are 8 rape merchants, 16 electro-lesbians, 12 "someone's been in there", and 14 Knellerists (Sexual Offences Act 1956).' Employing the third person and apeing an imaginary older brother, he continues, 'It is all very well for Johnny to go from a sexily dry public school to a co-ed "Vice Palace". I hope he doesn't get too much the other way.'

In another letter he claims there are two Old Cliftonians at Pattersons, called 'Paper, J. C. and Full, P. Z.' – both names were, of course, invented – and adds an illustration of the way the 'grotesques and tiresomes' signed their names in the daily register. On a cheerier note, he mentions that he has had lunch in 'a delightful little club' with a fellow student called Georgie Douglas-Home, omitting the information that his friend's uncle had been serving as Prime Minster for the last twelve months.

During this transitory period, it suited Jonathan to present himself, at least in letters to me, and even then partly as a joke, as sexually ambiguous if not actually queer. Or is it all part of his intention to shock? 'All the best queers go to Edinburgh's Café Royal Restaurant,' he tells me in one letter, and in another: 'I am sending you a book, under plain cover, about Croft-Cooke's and Lord Beaulieu's imprisonment for various offences.' No such book arrived but some months later I remember Jonathan reading Peter Wildeblood's *Against the Law*, which was perhaps the volume he meant. More complex are the occasions when Jonathan presents himself as a sexual victim, being preyed upon. In one of his first letters from Edinburgh he claims that he had been approached by a man named 'Mary', and refers to 'an Old Don Juan' at Mrs Essbug's who peeps through keyholes.

Jonathan was not to suffer in this 'quite vile' household much longer. After only a week or two, he moved to a lodging house at 12 Corbiehill Grove run by a lady called Bella Cunningham. Here he was far happier. An oblique footnote in a subsequent letter – 'Mrs Cunningham has red blood' – suggests that she was a warm-hearted figure, who probably took Jonathan under her wing. This impression was confirmed when I telephoned my brother at this address and was met with his landlady's gushing, exuberant friendliness. Looking back on Mrs Cunningham, I think it's possible that she provided Jonathan with the kind of *carte de visite a l'humanité* we all need during our formative years.

While at Edinburgh Jonathan also found some respite in spending a weekend or two out of the city. In early October he had spent a few days at Aviemore with friends of our brother Julian called Grant. He had done a drawing of Colonel Grant pouring Julian a glass of gin and our older brother primly protesting, 'That's far too much.' He also glee-fully reported – or invented – that Lady Katherine Grant had spent July on Eigg, staying with the island's owner, Lord Runciman, and 'had neither seen or heard of Fergus'. He also spent a weekend or two in Cumberland, writing to me from Dacre and heading his letter, 'Castle of the Fowls, Hill o'the Brae Fort, Cumberland,' and praising Tommy Cooper whom he had seen on television at Beauthorn – 'It's that fabulous snuffling and grunting' – and suggesting that we might have 'overlooked' Aunt Betty's brother, William Loftie, whom he describes as 'very like Tom Stacey'.

Meanwhile, past interests exerted their usual hold over him. His letters still contained references to Christie – had I seen the picture of the mass-murderer at the RADA Diamond Jubilee Ball? – and at least one to Frere. 'An incred-ible thing,' he wrote after his Aviemore weekend. 'On the train up to Inverness last Friday, I saw sitting in a 1st Class carriage a splitting image of Frere, including OE tie, checky cap, boxer overcoat. However, thoughts were shattered – the imposter had a broad Durham accent.'

Many of his letters still involved show business in various forms. There was a passing reference to Mike d'Abo – 'The Band of Angels' new record is heading for the tops. A "sell-out" here in Scot-bug-land' – and mention of the film *From Russia with Love* – had I spotted Eigg in the closing 'chase' sequences? – and the urgent recommendation that I see Joan Crawford in *Strait-Jacket*. 'It is brilliant in parts and more macabre than Baby J.', he enthused. 'One misses Betty Davis's old custard face peeping about but I think it is a greater picture.' Show business was still the world into which osten-sibly we were both heading. In his letters, Jonathan claims that Edinburgh is 'full of song & dance men' who are all most 'friendly' and 'helpful' and makes out that he has visited 'a certain Mme. Louvoisier' looking for 'suitable 2nd hand comedy clothes,' and had his suitcase constructed to fly open for comedy effects.

By now I was in London. On 12 October 1964, I had started a Christmas job working at the Shipwrecked Mariners Association in Victoria and taken a room in Ebury Street. I had continued to seek an agent and made some headway with a ginger-haired Australian named Eddie Jarrett who worked for the Grade Organisation and whose writing paper proclaimed that he was also the European Representative of the Tivoli Circuit. I had alerted Jonathan to this progress and his letters now contained remarks like 'Good luck next week with Eddie', 'I will be thinking of you in Eddie's office' and 'I hope "Operation Eddie" is OK?'

The outcome of all this was that I had been booked to do an unpaid audition appearance at the Nuffield Centre on 28 October. This was a serviceman's club behind Trafalgar Square which put on a showcase variety show each Wednesday for old faithfuls and young hopefuls. Jonathan's first reaction to this news was ecstatic. After a sly reference to the Nuffield Centre being 'the end of the run' he continued gushingly, 'Really this is marvellous and OF COURSE I shall fly down for the performance, hoping that this will lead to the BIG TIME for both of us. We are back to the "beginning" again.' A further letter expressed his bitter regrets that he would not be able to make the midweek booking but explained that he was saving up money to visit London before the performance.

On Saturday, 24 October, I met Jonathan off the *Flying Scotsman* at King's Cross station. He wore his new check jacket, had painted his shoes white and carried the tiny attaché case mentioned earlier. I can remember almost nothing about the weekend, not even where we stayed. During that autumn I moved between Ebury Street and the Oxford Hotel, Cromwell Road. The only incident I remember was that while wandering down Piccadilly towards Hyde Park Corner, Jonathan and I spotted the genuine and unmistakable figure of James Frere. Pausing beside the porter's rest structure still standing at this windswept spot we talked briefly to the ex-herald and learnt that his second book, *Now – the Duchesses,* had come out. He also declared, 'I have a house in Devonshire, near Bideford.'* Weird though this third surprise encounter was, Frere was no longer quite the same object of fascination for either of us he had once been. We had, I suppose, other fish to fry.

The following Wednesday, I made my Nuffield Centre debut, witnessed by Eddie Jarrett and one of his colleagues. I heard nothing afterwards but wrote cheerfully and boastfully to my younger brother, whose reply was dampeningly insincere. 'Thank you for your delightful letter,' he began. 'What a marvellous description of the show! Perhaps it might be appropriate to quote Disraeli who said:"London is a town".' In the meantime, Jonathan had telephoned the Stork Room and spoken to its legendary proprietor Al Burnett about doing an audition there himself. He now reported, 'This could come about sometime in December.' In his final days at Edinburgh he said nothing at all about his academic struggles or the O level exams he was due to sit at Harrow, but instead filled his letters with arrangements for his arrival in London. 'Longing to see you on Saturday,' he wrote on 19 November. 'I don't think it will be too much difficulty composing a

* This was Orleigh Court, Buckland Brewer, a Tudor house described by Pevsner as 'in a bad state of repair and recently rather slummified.'

double act. I have a dozen or so ideas it will be just great to discuss with you away from the grievous burden of a London/Edinburgh phone call.'

On Saturday, 21 November, he arrived in London and for the next fortnight commuted between Turig, London and Harrow where he sat his exams, including French oral and English language. I begged him to remain after these were over and, like me, take a temporary job. On 4 November, he had sent a flattering card from Edinburgh saying on it 'Oh to be in London now that Andrew's there,' and in one of his last letters from Edinburgh he wrote, 'I agree, NOTHING can be gained from swimming about the chilly and misty corridors of T. Combe.'

Jonathan was soon up to new metropolitan tricks, one of which needs explaining. By now I was working at Fortnum & Mason, at first as a porter in the confectionery department – I was tipped sixpence when I carried a customer's goods to the front door – and then as a clerk taking Christmas grocery orders. In this latter role, I handled a call from the actor Richard Attenborough, and then from a customer whose name I did not catch, enquiring about the 'chocolate politicians' in the store's window. Testily informed by my supervisor that there was nothing of that sort in the store, I expressed my apologies to the caller. That evening Jonathan asked me if I had had any odd calls that day and then revealed that it was *he* who had enquired about the chocolate politicians.

On 8 December, Jonathan started working at Swan & Edgar, being paid for a week what a cleaning lady now earns in an hour. Grim though this sounds, Jonathan was now in the heart of the West End, in a corner of Mayfair and in a part of London where he would find a stronger and stronger foothold and which would eventually feature prominently in *The Queue*. This was the world of crowded underground platforms, pickpockets and Rolls-Royces driven by dodgy bachelors wearing silk underwear. It was here in London's West End that innumerable crimes took place, leading to *Queue*-like court cases, and occasionally savage sentences.

But I am jumping ahead. In December 1964, Jonathan and I still thought only of our future as showbiz stars and revved ourselves up that month by joining the crowds at the premieres of films like *The Yellow Rolls-Royce*. Failure

of our audition the previous April at the Talk of the Town had put neither of us off. I had already had a go at the Nuffield Centre and been offered a second appearance there with my name again in *The Stage*. Now it was Jonathan's turn. One Sunday night just before or just after Christmas 1964, and still only seventeen, Jonathan appeared at the basement club in Swallow Street, known as the Stork Room.

Introduced by veteran clubman Al Burnett, and using the name John Le Don, he attempted to entertain the small live audience of hostesses and their clients with an imitation of his Harrow housemaster, Mark Tindall.

CHAPTER ELEVEN

The Dorchester

The first day that I worked there I wore my ordinary trousers under my chef's uniform. I got terribly
hot and Kurt said I shouldn't wear them. Ours was
a very hot kitchen. The reason for wearing the
trousers underneath was because I was too shy to
undress. I think I looked an idiot in the clothes.
Notebook 1965.

I WILL LEAVE the reader in suspense about how Jonathan
fared at the Stork Room and begin this chapter by writing
briefly about myself. Some years earlier, I had spent part
of the summer holidays staying with a couple my father
knew in Cornwall. Mary and Ivan Napier lived in a large
seaside house carpeted throughout in purple. Here, I had
a glimpse of an alternative world and different standards to
those represented by my parents and older brothers. The
Napiers had a live-in servant and a Rolls-Royce, in which
I remember being driven through the narrow streets of St
Ives. Ivan Napier collected antique glass. One night, Mrs
Napier's sister materialised at my bedside with a tumbler
of milk. The tumbler was no ordinary tumbler. It was made
of shimmeringly embossed antique glass yet taken
completely for granted by my hosts. At Turig, my father
had a few interesting old glasses but these were rarely in

evidence and would certainly never have been used for a routine nightcap.

One afternoon, during this visit, I was told some people were coming to tea, a Mr and Mrs Harding, who were on a bicycling honeymoon tour of Cornwall. David Harding, Mrs Napier quickly informed me, worked as banqueting manager at the Dorchester Hotel in London and long, long ago had worked at Claridge's and often helped the Napiers out, getting them a room there during the war. I was riveted by this link with luxury and good living. I remember sitting on a sofa with Harding and asking about day-to-day life in a great hotel. I also remember how the hotelier had gone to pay his respects to the Napier's cook, tapping on the pantry door with a self-confident, theatrical playfulness that deeply impressed me. Did he have dyed hair? I wouldn't have known. Did I expect to see him again? I doubt it.

Shortly after Christmas 1964 and his lukewarm reception at the Stork Room, Jonathan had decided fairly firmly that he no longer wished to pursue our double bid for showbiz success – I had always been the prime mover in that direction – and was now considering the hotel trade as another, more realistic option, and the next best thing. The reader will remember that a love of domestic life was deeply ingrained in Jonathan's nature. Feeding the hens or bantams and collecting their eggs had been an early pleasure, making cakes in the Aga had often occupied him during the holidays and, during his darkest hours at prep school he had, as we know, often asked, 'Matron, can I do the handkerchiefs, please?'

Some time back, I had no doubt told him about David Harding and may have even tried to build him up into legendary status. Now, for the first time since that meeting in Cornwall, I telephoned the Dorchester Hotel and asked to speak to its banqueting manager. I forget Harding's exact response but see from my diary that on Saturday, 2 January 1965, Jonathan and I duly presented ourselves in the lounge of the famous Park Lane hotel. Harding had suggested we had tea there and he would then take us to meet an up-and-coming new hotelier he knew called Kenneth Slatter, who had once worked at the Dorchester and was now development manager of a new chain of hotels opening up in London. All this was already a far cry from the dear old Napiers, but such far-flung links must exist in everyone's private and professional lives.

To start with, anyway, the Dorchester's sofa was not far removed from the plushness of the house near St Ives. And I was further impressed when David Harding emerged through a side door, greeted us and sat down beside us. I can't remember if Harding wore striped trousers and black jacket. I do remember him as a Hanoverian figure; jowelly, white-faced, sombre and grand. That afternoon he explained the meaning of the phrase *millefeuille*, escorted Jonathan and me on a brief tour of the Dorchester – I remember, in particular, the Oliver Messel suite where Elizabeth Taylor and Richard Burton often stayed – and then I suppose, we must have taken a taxi to the office in Bayswater where Harding's friend Ken Slatter worked.

What was the initial impact of this dynamic young man? On that first afternoon I recall only that Jonathan and I were both overawed by Slatter's slickness – he answered the telephone with only his surname – and by some press cuttings on the office wall saluting his role in opening one new hotel after another.* Anyway, very soon after that first meeting, a

---

* We learnt later that Slatter had also worked at the Plaza Athenee, Paris, the Normandie, Deauville, and for four years in America.

friendship between Jonathan and Slatter sprang up which did not include me.

Of course, I now had my own weird preoccupations. The following Wednesday I appeared again at the Nuffield Centre where my antics – 'D'you like this suit? It suits me doesn't it?' – were witnessed by all three older brothers, Simon, Julian and Martin. The next day I rang Keith Devon at the Delfont Agency and announced – I had only just made the decision – that I was going to try my luck in Manchester and was not too discouraged by his advice that it was very *'Eee boi gum'* up there. A few days later, on Tuesday, 12 January, I took the train to Manchester, and got my first professional booking the same afternoon.

From notes Jonathan kept at the time I see that within a few days of my departure to the land of our early upbringing, he began a round of visits, set up by his new friend Slatter, to leading London hotel managers. In a fat exercise book he describes these encounters in a remarkably straight-faced and non-satirical manner. At the Europa, he notes 'the single bedrooms were compact but not cramped but Mr Wurtz was troubled by traces of damp on all the ceilings'. At the Hertford, Mr and Mrs Moore showed him parts of the hotel they felt other managers wouldn't, such as the linen room, housekeeper's office and wine cellars. Mr Alastair Fraser at the Stratford Court Hotel offered him advice about training – 'You could do a lot worse than Lausanne' – and claimed that ability to handle staff and guests was far more important than a wide knowledge of catering. Mr Lund Hansen at Claridge's disagreed, explaining that a manager of a hotel like his would have to have an expert knowledge of cookery. At the Westbury, a hotel Jonathan and I had sometimes lounged in, Mr de la Rue suggested that instead of going straight to a hotel school, he should spend at least a year working in various departments of a hotel like the Savoy.

These jottings have a quite different tone to the letters that Jonathan had already begun to send me in Manchester, which made the usual long, imaginative references to our past and said very little about his new life in London. He does not mention joining the crowds outside Winston Churchill's house in Hyde Park Gate where the statesman was dying in a blaze of publicity – years later I spotted Jonathan in the background of a photograph of Lord Moran on Sir Winston's doorstep – but provides a fragmentary account of his dealings with Slatter and other topical material, however comically tinged, distorted or even actually invented.

At the end of January 1965 he wrote to me at Dacre, where I was briefly licking my wounds after my first few paid appearances as a stand-up comic. 'Dearest, How is Granny I expect she is well. Slatter is well; poor little chap, he caught 'flu last week but is alright now.' He goes on to describe a meeting he had arranged between Slatter and our oldest brother Simon, who had begun his married life in a terraced house under the shadow of Campden Hill Towers, where Slatter had a small duplex flat on the ninth and tenth floors. 'He thought Simon was pompous and not down to earth enough. He said "Don't ever get like Simon".' He then insensitively repeated Slatter's comments about me – 'He left me stone cold' – which would have been depressing had I not had bigger problems on my lap. He also states that he has had 'numerous tea and dinner parties' with the hotelier and concludes: 'Slatter has shown me photographs of the most luxurious country weekender cottage I have ever seen. He bought it in 1963.'

On Friday, 5 February, thanks to Slatter or Harding,

Jonathan began work in the kitchens of the Dorchester Hotel. In my father's engagement diary for this day, I find this fact noted and the name of the head chef 'EUGENE KAUFELER' in capital letters. In Jonathan's padded red book, he describes his first day there:

> Start Dorchester 10 am. Waited two hours for the security officer to arrive, not until 12.30 pm did work begin. Immediately started to clean a large pan of potatoes but the other chefs became bored of this and threw the remainder away. Worked until 5.30 on onions, leeks, sprouts and peas with six other lads.

The next day he is shown how to prepare *pomme purée* with butter, milk, cream, salt and nutmeg. He finds the heat of the stoves very great – and is still unable to understand the order amplifier. He also claims that he was told by a 'man' to 'cut the bleedin' beans in half' or he would 'slit me up the crutch with a jackknife and leave my guts to set in the ice house.' On Sunday, 7 February, he helps 'the rabbis' clean their private utensils and carries these on a trolley – there we go again – to their private cupboard. When several saucepans are knocked off this vehicle, the rabbi in charge tells him, 'Stop mucking it about.' The following week he cleans out the cold room – 'full of mess and fungus' – and arranges asparagus for a banquet, boils chestnuts for a stuffing and attempts to 'shape' potatoes before roasting. He mentions that he has bought a potato peeler and a kitchen knife for his own use – he was now living in Julian's studio at 48 Tite Street – and is advised by a young man working on the pastry section, 'Us public school boys are sought after at the moment.' He also notes the head chef Kaufeler's occasional appearances – 'He cut me dead' – and that David Harding drops in from time to time, on one occasion confiding 'Don't tell Ken too much about the kitchens – things aren't perfect down here.' On Thursday, 11 February, he receives his wages of £6.18s, less deductions.

In another notebook which Jonathan kept at this time, he has written about the Dorchester with a curious detachment and pseudo-sociological, almost Orwellian authority,

perhaps partly picked up from Slatter. He vulgarly refers to Monsieur Kaufeler as 'London's premier chef' and quotes from another senior figure: 'Many of the boys come in here at fifteen thinking they will get a good training and then move on to another hotel or possibly restaurant.' A few years later, after he had left the hotel business altogether, Jonathan wrote a longer and rather wistful account of his life in the Dorchester kitchens – he would remain there only until the middle of May – which glorifies the life, luxury, extravagance and eccentricities of a grand hotel, and embroiders his account with imaginary detail, technical jargon, fake facts and murkier material invested with a sort of spoof authority. Jonathan's 'knowingness' was by now a well-established aspect of his character – so was his inventiveness. Claiming that he had seen the Dorchester's pastry chef, Lefevre, undressing in the staff changing room, he writes, 'He had these strange underpants. They were very short but made in queer grey wool. I once looked inside them when he was in the shower house. They were made in Belgium and didn't seem to have any elastic.'

Looking back on this time, he praises and perhaps exaggerates the *esprit de corps* in those basement kitchens: 'There was no question of anybody not turning up or being late,' he recalled. 'In other businesses, people had innumerable excuses for unpunctuality. Most of them totally unbelievable. But here these people were devoted to their work and the strange hours the business demanded.' He also writes several gushing paragraphs about the huge but speedily consumed breakfast the kitchen staff laid on for themselves each morning, and then plunges into a long description of the plongeurs:

> There were dozens of these men. Their job involved keeping the kitchen clean and washing up the heavy recasting and boiling pans. They all had huge hooks to drag the stuff to the plonge. It would have been too heavy to carry alone. They used to throw down sawdust to mop up spills. The plonge was in a corner and was extraordinary. There was only one man who worked there. The place had an enormous trough. He just stood there all day scrubbing at the pans. He was called Mario. He wore strange protective clothes. Black 'home-made' rubber boots – like waders. Then a sort of plastic frock with string as a belt. Then a rubber cape which went right over his neck – rather like

131

a thing that a cardinal wears at mass. He really needed every bit of it – he sloshed water all over himself. I understand he slept in the plonge on old sacks. He had started in 1924 as a silver room aide – one of the lowest jobs in hotel hierarchy – and was now in charge of all the plongeurs. It is a tradition in hotels that plongeurs always do their own cooking. As most of them were Pakistani, their fare was largely Indian. One would be appointed cook and he would go round the kitchens early in the morning with a sort of pan collecting bits for lunch. They favoured chicken; the old poultrier (there was only one now – most hotels buy ready plucked fowls direct from the markets nowadays) gave them stinking pieces almost green with age. I understand that in fact they turned out some quite nice stuff. They ate in the plonge of course. With their fingers. Once, when a very wealthy Indian prince stayed in the hotel, he sent down some very rare curry essence which we were to make up into something for him. Now curry is considered rather infradig in haute cuisine so none of the chefs, not even M. Kaufeler, knew how to do it. Someone suggested the plongeurs. So they were called in and amidst a large crowd of chefs they made up what I later heard was a very acceptable dish.

Over the next three months, Jonathan built up a considerable knowledge of kitchen affairs, not least the glossary, some of which he would eventually use in *The Queue*. Although grand hotels hardly feature in the book, there are passing references to the fashionable sort of restaurants that popped up in London in the 1960s, and many incidents involving kitchens, catering equipment and food, some of them deeply sinister, which may owe something to his first job. Take the moment when the narrator discovers a strange joint of meat in a station cafeteria's roasting ovens, looks closely at it and decides it is the remains of a human hand: 'Feeling sick and faint I run out onto the platform and throw this foul joint down onto the lines. In a few moments, I see the guard hoist up the hand by means of a long hook: he returns to his office, and after flavouring with salt, pepper, mustard and horseradish, he proceeds to eat the hand. I notice him spitting out some of the tougher sinews. Later, he vomits into his little bowl.'

And of course he was also learning a lot from Slatter, whose knowledge and know-how he seems to have assimilated. From his letters we learn a bit more about Slatter – at one point Jonathan claims his benefactor looks 'not unlike

a church sidesman' – and a certain amount about the rest of his life during this period. He continued to live at Tite Street – Julian was away much of the time and liked to have the place occupied and some of his rent covered – and used our brother's bike to get to work. In an undated letter he describes bumping into Mike d'Abo and makes out that my old friend's career and domestic arrangements were in the balance:

> About Michael: as I was cycling up Sloane St and waiting at the 'lights', I realised he was there, on the pavement, and that he had been smiling at me, and that he was still smiling. I crossed towards him and after greetings he said, 'Why didn't Andrew ring? He must buck up and make up his mind if he wants to share with me, otherwise I shall find someone else.' We went into a pub where he had minced beef and myself a beer, which he also ordered for himself. Suddenly he said, 'I may be doing a cabaret act with Julian Holloway . . . Possibly in Manchester etc . . . etc.'
>
> I left her settled down with all the morning papers to look at. I said, 'What are you going to do next?' 'Probably buy some picture books and sit in Victoria Station' & 'I like your hair very much . . . & your coat.'

This sounds fairly genuine – I have no memory of the flat-sharing plan – but is invested with the same comic patronising tone he often used when describing Slatter. Even with the highly sophisticated pronoun reversal, for those days, Mike d'Abo was one of our heroes and soon afterwards became a real pop star. Here Jonathan suggests he is in limbo, with time on his hands. The reference to Manchester where I was suffering frightful setbacks – pennies were now being thrown at me on the stage – was probably a tease. As were his various expressions of regret that he could not be there himself struggling beside me.

In fact Jonathan did take the trouble to visit my northern

stronghold; flying up to 'Manchester Aerodrome' one Saturday morning in March and returning slowly by rail. 'An insufferable train journey followed my departure yesterday,' he wrote on his return. 'At Derby an old slug called Mr B. Edge got in and asked if I wanted to buy a hen. (He turned out to be Norah Bradley's brother!)' I have forgotten who Norah Bradley was but Mr B. Edge gives us another foretaste of the names in *The Queue*. Hens, as we know only too well, were an almost perpetual presence in Jonathan's mind and writings.

Once or twice that spring, I visited London, where Jonathan had more to say about Slatter. I learnt that, like my father, Slatter had his suits made at Kilgour & French in Savile Row – 'I wonder when he reached the Kilgour & French stage,' Jonathan mused later – and, more interestingly, had taken my brother off to Eton one weekend, photographed him in the college precincts and then booked into the Hind's Head Hotel, Bray, where they had spent the night in a twin-bedded room. Making fun of this eyebrow-raising development, Jonathan told me that getting dressed the next morning he had accidentally put on Slatter's underpants.

Back in Manchester, I received further letters in which he addresses me under various false names including 'Mr Tindalle' and signs off on one occasion 'Christian'. A letter dated 22 April 1965 starts off with a parody of our mother – 'Oh my darling, it is so hot here I can hardly keep alive, I long for Autumn' – but also includes some serious stuff about Slatter. On a recent visit to Turig – I still occasionally fled home from Manchester – my father had raged against my brother's friend. 'I know those busy little men,' he had snarled as he drove me to the station. 'They do you ten little good turns and then one *bloody big bad turn*!' In his next letter Jonathan included a paragraph headed 'K. Slatter':

This man wasn't mentioned when I was home yesterday and I hope Erskinette will never ruin your weekend again. Whether S is or isn't is quite irrelevant. The important thing is that he has a huge influence in the hotel business and may be useful later on. His sexual life is really no concern of mine and he has shown no interest in *mine*. However, one must, as D.V. Proctor says, keep an eye.

Erskinette was a silly new nickname for our father and the final reference to D.V. Proctor, a master at Clifton College Preparatory School I had not thought of for many years, was included to give me a frisson of recognition. Jonathan had a huge cast of half-forgotten names and place names at his fingertips and employed them more or less at random. 'Keep an eye' is what Mark Tindall had said he would do after the scandal that overtook Jonathan during his penultimate term at Harrow.

In another letter, Jonathan mentions being shown around 52 Tite Street by Felix Hope-Nicholson, a bachelor dandy who lived with his mother in a large house two doors away from our brother's studio. 'To Fergus Gowans, he must be the RSM★ of the work shys,' commented Jonathan. Such revelations were relatively rare. Most of Jonathan's letters, even when signed off 'More when we meet' and 'Missing you', contained nothing but fantasy stuff. One letter written from Turig ends with this succulent little question-and-answer: 'D'you remember the "awful thing" you couldn't tell me about on the telephone? I have found its birth certificate.' Another letter from this period, which arrived soon after I

★ Some readers may need reminding that RSM stands for regimental sergeant major.

had made a tenuous connection with a comedy writer working for ABC Television, is cast in the form of a dire warning about me from the Head Master of Harrow to my father:

The Head Master's Lodge
HARROW

Dear Erskine,

I had quite a lengthy conversation with Andrew last night and he made it clear to me that he was aiming for a stage career. In my mind, and I think in his housemaster's too, it is quite unacceptable that he should attempt a show career without full university degrees. It would be foolish to say that in the harsh times up at the university places can be earned by anything but hard work. He clearly has the ability. But whether it is a matter of conceit or crash stupidity, he does not, on the present showing, look like succeeding.

Under my instructions Mr Newby Robson of the Public Schools Appointments Bureau wrote to ABC Television. In these hard times up at Parrs Wood, any eccentricity as far as a comedy career is concerned is in my view wholly unacceptable.

His housemaster's report makes interesting reading. I hope he is mature enough to take advice.

It is proper to remind him that the producers up there give short shrift to a man who does dull things like failing comedy prelims.

It is suggested in these reports that he might be capable of it, so he had better get down to it.

Believe me,

Yours,

R. L. James.

Here, past and present are intermingled. Whole phrases are lifted from the chilling appraisals the Head Master had sometimes added to each bunch of school reports. Jonathan and I had begun to view these well-meant summaries as haunting character assassinations and in this particular spoof he pretends that Dr James is not only still breathing down our necks, interfering with our lives by applying rigid academic rules to our current careers, but is also a complete and utter nincompoop.

With or without subconscious restraints – or encouragements – Jonathan was already moving on. In the middle of May, he announced that he had decided to take a holiday job at the Yellowstone National Park in Wyoming and would be flying out there the following month. Slatter, who had obviously played some part in this development, advised him to go on working at the Dorchester until the eve of his departure but, on this occasion, Jonathan ignored his advice, left the hotel on 20 May and spent some of the intervening time in my grandmother's house in Cumberland. From here he wrote to me in Manchester, saying that he had had tea with Teddy and Gertie Hasell, describing Dacre's longstanding squire and his wife 'as the new couple at Dalemain'. During this encounter the name of Major Hasell's former tenant James Frere had come up, prompting Mrs Hasell to declare, 'Of course he was the most *unutterable* snob.' Jonathan signs the letter 'Moor Divock', which as I mentioned earlier, is the name of a Cumbrian fell, and adds a rather lethal postscript or 'rush repro' from a recent letter to our grandmother from my new sister-in-law Caroline: 'Rumour has it that Andrew is not as keen on the stage as he was, which must please every member of the family.'

There was no truth in this. I was still as mad keen on show business as ever. Thanks to my slender connection with

ABC TV's Ronnie Taylor, I had shared a car with Jimmy Clitheroe and Mollie Sugden, spoken to Harry Worth on the telephone and even met the agreeably patrician Eric Morecambe in the flesh.

CHAPTER TWELVE

Yellowstone

> Mom wrote at last about your work. She says you
> only send back £2.15 a week for keep. Mom says
> this isn't enough but knows you have to buy
> uniform, tools, etc. You can never make a fortune
> out of being a fitter's mate, have you got in touch
> with the TUC branch, Elmer says there's one at
> Fishponds (take a 41 or an 18 from the Centre).
>
> *Letter, 12 August 1965*

THE YELLOWSTONE NATIONAL Park in Wyoming has been
described in official literature as 'an awesome natural monument'. Famous for its wondrous hot springs and bountiful
wildlife, it was designated the world's first natural reservation
as long ago as 1872 and is today marketed with the phrase
'Don't just see it, experience it.' Jonathan arrived on this
sacred ground on 21 June 1965 and would spend two months
working at the park's historic Lake Hotel. Although he sent
me nine long letters from this address, and one from the
nearby Hotel General Custer at Billings, Montana, they
revealed almost nothing of his life there. Instead, he offered
further flashbacks to our childhood, mutual schooling and
fantasy material about our parents, Gilda, etc. Although I find
these things as funny forty years later as I did at the time, I
now wonder if they were partly designed as a smokescreen,

to keep me at my distance, even to conceal the real facts of his life.

My other brothers may have shared these suspicions. On 8 July 1965, Martin, now prospering in his job at Matheson & Co. in Lombard Street and scheduled to go east later in the year, wrote to Jonathan at the Lake Hotel protesting about his 'uncommunicative' letters and urging him to travel around the world and get out of the 'Slatter hotel clique'. From Italy, Julian wrote to me: 'Nothing would make me more happy than to see Jonathan travel abroad for three years.' The mild tension at this time between Jonathan and these older brothers is apparent in the curious paragraph about Simon written in a particular tense – past conditional? – with which he ends his first letter dated 12 July from Yellowstone:

> Simon had been complaining about me buying Truslove & Hanson writing paper, about the extra cost of going home by Pullman, and about the cost of your Moss Bros. Coat compared to his Lazy Boy Sweaters he had when 18. Suddenly one realized that Simon, if he had been born into another world, would have made a very good cash register.

And he would employ a more vicious but equally comical tone when planning his return to England two months later. He insisted that I be present to meet him at London Airport on 8 September. If not, he might fly direct to Manchester from London. 'I "dread" seeing Julian's rat's arse face staring at me as I toil up the awkward green Tite Street stairs carrying my blue Globetrotter,' he wrote. 'IT IS IMPERATIVE YOU BE IN LONDON.' Such rudeness or openness was, as I have said, extremely rare in these letters so that I know next to nothing about Jonathan's feelings on all fronts, his attitude to America, the work he did, and, more importantly, the girls he met. Questions from me on various topics usually fell on stony ground. When I asked him what colour TV was like, he replied dismissively – even getting the date wrong – 'The last time I watched TV was *Panorama* on BBC1 on June 23rd. As this place is about 100 times the height of "Mell-Fell"* it is impossible to receive either TV or sound. So life is a misery.' But then a few paragraphs later, he contradicts himself: 'Incidentally talking about TV shows I saw one colour TV variety show starring Sid Caesar and Jimmy Durrante. Colour added very little.' And then he adds confidently, 'Danny Kaye's red hair often overawes viewers.' How did he know such things? Or did he invent them? He would strike this knowledgeable note often during the next few years and does so again a few days later: 'Yes, I have bought a car. But wait – do you remember that superb black American Ford at the *Yellow R-Royce* premiere. It is just like that but second-hand.' And then comes the knowledgeable bit: 'The American Ford is a very poor car but looks good.'

A serious straightforward note also attends some but not all of his remarks about Slatter. On 22 July, he starts flat-teringly – and insincerely? – regretting that I could not be with him in America – 'It would have been fabulous' – and then continues, 'However Slatter may be here next month . . . so he is some substitute.' He quickly follows this informa-tion with manipulative, joke stuff about who I could release this information to – and plays with his older brothers' names at the same time. 'Tell Daddy and Mar-Tin . . . I would rather you didn't tell "Si-Mon" . . . but by all means tell Jul-Ian

* Readers may need reminding that Mell Fell (height 1675 ft) was near my grandmother's house in Cumberland.

142

(sic).' In another letter, he wonders if I have seen recent press cuttings about Slatter — 'In case not, see *Hotel & Catering Review*, August (New photograph) and *Financial Times*, August 2nd (Nude photograph)' — then asks me if I knew that Slatter's parents are both dead. 'Rumour has it,' he continues, 'that Mother is going to adopt Slatter. He will muck in with us all, do the stove & the hods, shut up, open up, fetch the milk and run errands for Erskine. He will have my little room. This means me moving out.' Jonathan had never, incidentally, had a 'little room' of his own at Turig. He had usually shared my room at the back of the house.

The same mixture of truth and fiction is present in Jonathan's remarks about show business. I was still up to my neck in my struggles and dreams and still in Manchester and still telling Jonathan — and everyone else — that I was on the verge of a breakthrough. A letter claiming that I was soon to have my own radio series generated a response on 3 August, incorporating comments by both Mark Tindall and my first Harrow housemaster, Jan Thompson: 'I hope he will accept the responsibility of being a comedian next term; he now wears spectacles.' And on 24 August a reference to a comedian I'd got to know called Reg Gray parodies an end-of-term report in which Tindall had made light of my work in the Art School by pointing out how little I'd been on the playing fields: 'Three rousing cheers for Regez Gray. Really excellent, but I notice Reg has been on the off-eccer list. So he has had plenty of time to rehearse.'

By this stage I had left Manchester and sought work in other parts of England. On Saturday, 7 August 1965, I had appeared at the Bedwas Working Men's Club near Caerphilly and been paid off once again. On 11 August Jonathan wrote, saying, 'Looking forward to hearing how your S. Wales tour went', adding the information, 'Pontypool Road YMCA is quite good, they say, but so is the Cardiff Hilton.' In the same letter he says he has had a letter from our mother making no mention of my radio show and concluding, 'For all I know you could still be a punch card operator at a furniture factory near Brislington, Bristol.'

And there the serious content entirely evaporates. Many of the remaining letters from Yellowstone contain sentences lifted from our mother. These included a reference to the dentist in Bath we also saw. – 'I have been to see odious little Clifford this morning' – a spoof invitation – 'Can you make drinks tomorrow night about 6 pm? The Copland-Griffiths will be here' – and one of my mother's most commonplace laments about Jonathan or me: 'You can never believe what he says.' There is also the paragraph quoted at the start of this chapter about an imaginary mother, based in a Bristol suburb, which gently undermines my claims about the radio series.

In the midst of all this fantasy, Jonathan repeats verbatim but does not comment on a grim piece of real news from our real mother about the son of my grandmother's handyman, Bob Ferguson. 'Alan Ferguson has been in a ghastly motorbike accident & is at death's door.'

It is odd that the delights of the Yellowstone National Park, the fellow hotel staff and being in America for the first and, as it happened, only time in his life did not stop him dwelling on old family events, especially those in which Gilda had played a central role. In a letter dated 14 August, he described the hotel where we sometimes stopped for break-fast during the long drive from Wiltshire to Cumberland. 'They have an excellent b&b + pub, where they serve gallons of Wilson's Manchester beer. The place is called the "Open Road". Old Gili, now rotting in a Warminster funeral home, used to do her business in that very yard.' As a deceased

144

fictional character rather than as a living beloved family pet, Gilda was never far from his mind and the same letter contains further details of her incontinence, and variations on her

name. Though not employed in *The Queue* itself, the deliberate misspelling of familiar names was already one of Jonathan's devices – 'How is MIKEL D'ARBO' he asks in a Yellowstone letter – and he tops and tails his correspondence with an ever more elaborate range of names from the distant past. I am 'Grandmama', 'Wing Commander Thomas' (a Wiltshire neighbour) and 'Mrs Ned Richardson' (a character in Dacre), and he signs off, variously, 'Daffi Fothergill' (a popular Harrow beak), 'Samuel Whiskers' and 'Jon Le Don', the name under which he had appeared at the Stork Room and to which he now added the phrase – 'ill-fated'.

I repeat that Jonathan had nothing else to reveal in these letters – I never knew if Slatter had visited him and he said not a word about Yellowstone's habitat – but the flood of reminiscence certainly kept him freshly in my mind during this period. On 8 September 1965, he returned to London via Montreal, where he stayed at the Sheraton Mount Royal

Hotel. My brother Martin and I met him that day at the air terminal near Victoria Station. In the coffee bar there, Jonathan quickly revealed, more to Martin than to me, that he had had a serious fling – I forget which words he used – with one of the waitresses at the Lake Hotel. He never supplied any details of this first encounter with the opposite sex, nor did I seek them, but quite a long time afterwards he claimed that this was 'all part of Slatter's plan'.

CHAPTER THIRTEEN

Hotel School

The chef fills a forcing-bag with pomme duchesse and inserts a half inch star tube to the nozzle. Holding the bag in his right hand, he rapidly marbles around the perimeter of the dish. This is then put under a very hot salamander grill with just time enough for the surface to brown. The dish is then tidied, placed on a silver platter and sent to the table.

Notebook, 1966

AT 8.45 A.M. on Monday, 13 September 1965, only five days after his return from America, Jonathan was enrolled as a full-time student at the hotel school in Vincent Square. The building, officially known as the Westminster Technical College and dating from the 1930s, has trained many generations of catering students and is still in operation today. During his first few weeks here he lodged in a flat in Ashley Gardens, only a few yards away.

I saw Jonathan from time to time during this phase. I borrowed money from him and he enraged me at one moment by demanding a cheque in return, which bounced. I fear I spent a lot of time at Turig. From there, I made visits to Bristol and appeared at the Palm Court Theatre Club near

the city centre. On 3 October, I went to London to see my brother Martin off at Liverpool Street Station from where he would travel slowly via Moscow to Hong Kong. The same week, I appeared at the Peacock Club in Streatham and one lunchtime at the Hirondelle Club in Swallow Street – unpaid experimental appearances which hardly justify my subsequent claim that I spent this phase of my life working as a professional stand-up comedian.

On several occasions when in London, I also lunched at the hotel school where a formal but inexpensive three-course lunch was available to members of the public and where people joked, 'They say the students eat the mistakes in another room.' Jonathan was often in evidence wearing a long white apron, casting sidelong glances, and armed with a little card listing that day's choice of desserts. A surviving aide-memoire from this time carries the scribbled words *Gateau Jamaique*, *Lintzer Torte*, *Peche Rose Cherie*, *Ananas Creole* and *Souffle Vanille*.

By now, Jonathan was immersed in this exotic world. He had already acquired significant recipe books, like Joseph Donon's *The Classic French Cuisine* – his copy bore Slatter's name and one-time address at Mount Carmel, California – and more peripheral works like *The Pleasures of the Table* by Sir Francis Colchester-Wemyss. The hotel business suited Jonathan's intensely practical nature – he had instantly passed his driving test – and the luxury end of the trade would be reflected and distorted in *The Queue,* not least in a tasteless story about a Mr K. P. Lotte choosing *truite au bleu* at the Riscini Restaurant in Buller Road, only to fall in love with the poor fish and take it home in a jam jar in his Rolls-Royce. As every pantomime dame knows, there is a slapstick side to kitchen life and Jonathan was alert to the comic possibilities of people going mad in kitchens – or, for that matter, in food shops. I still have a press cutting he tore from a catering magazine around this time which describes the havoc caused by vandals in a shop in Market Harborough. 'One cake was thrown at a television set, cream horns were rammed among the till keys, two chairs were smashed and about 20lb. of cooked meat was thrown about.' In *The Queue,* Jonathan writes calmly enough about Mary entering a bread shop and stealing two eclairs and a Maid of Honour, but goes right over the top when describing a man being sick out of the window of a bus – and into a gale-force wind: 'There is a throw-back and I get the whole lot in my face. It is the most extraordinary vomit. He must have a digestive disorder. In it there are whole cutlets, rashers, burgers, sandwiches, sausages, pies and offal. Nothing is chewed . . .'

At the hotel school, everything was of course orderly and under control. Students, some of whom had scars and cuts as if they'd been in fights, were gently told to get their hair cut – 'Snip, snip, perhaps?' suggested an instructor – and Jonathan was reprimanded for adding dark glasses and black boots to a drawing of a sheep carcass divided up into neck, best end, saddle and so on. Some years later, Jonathan recalled

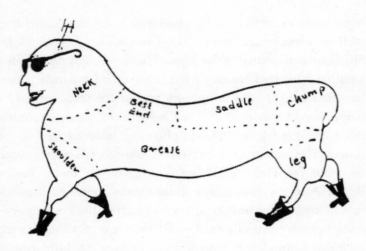

lunchtime instructions at the school: 'Barrow, you haven't done cheese service before,' he remembered being told. 'Maxwell, show Barrow how we do cheese service. For one person. Go to the kitchen and get two hors d'oeuvres plates and a carving knife for the turkey on table four.'

Of course Jonathan learnt lots of other things at Westminster besides cheese service for one, how to carve a turkey and serve Omelet Arnold Bennett. He wrote essays on economics, monopolies and the Bank of England. He learnt how to translate '*The old gent has ordered a brandy*' into French. And he struggled, as always, with elementary maths.

While Jonathan was forging ahead in various ways – he had now formed a close attachment to a girl called Rosemary Leventon, whose parents lived in Wiltshire – my own life was petering out. Or at least my career as a comedian. On 5 November 1965 I turned twenty, though the event is not listed in my father's engagement diary and nor do I know where I was this day. We spent Christmas as a family – those of us who were not abroad or, as in Simon's case, married

— at Scorrier in Cornwall, where my mother's cousin Meg Williams lived and one of the highlights was a visit from a high camp member of the family called Peter Williams, then editing *Dance and Dancers*. Early the next year, I made a final appearance at the Webbington Country Club★ near Weston-Super-Mare, was paid £3 and sat up half the night at the seaside railway station. At Turig, tensions between my father and me mounted as I entered a tricky final phase living under his roof.

Here I received regular communications from Jonathan whose new term had started on 3 January 1966. On a post-card signed 'Gilda, Cotta & the Belgae', he told me he had called at Campden Hill Towers and found an Old Harrovian we both knew there named C., who was apparently an old friend of Slatter. A few days later, Jonathan made clear his continuing interest in Harrow and its headmaster by writing the 'DEATH PROPHYLAXIS' memo quoted earlier, and by inventing a long, wild speech from the headmaster paro-dying the orations he gave to parents and boys on Speech Day, praising 'much beloved masters' who had died and other departing members of staff, one of whom was apparently the possessor of 'a really lovely tenor voice'. The speech eventu-ally disintegrated, and was followed by a mind-bendingly scatological account of other events that day at Harrow resulting in severe traffic congestion.

Jonathan's erratically kept engagement diary for this period records dinners with Rosemary Leventon at the Casse Croute, the Sans Souci and the Spot and the fact that on Sunday, 13 March, he started working on a part-time basis at the Hyde Park Hotel's Buttery Bar. This was an ancient and slightly dingy haunt of my father — never mind the mural

★ The club is still in operation and visible from the M5 motorway.

by Roland Pym – where we had dined on the evening of Simon's wedding in June 1964. The head barman, Billy Bone, was a crony of my father and soon became a friend of Jonathan – and the source of various anecdotes and *bon mots*. Talking later that year, during a heatwave, Billy Bone would say of a longstanding customer, the overweight baronet Sir Anthony Tichborne, 'A man of that build really gets kicked in this weather.' He had also amused Jonathan with a story that my telephone acquaintance, the comedian Harry Worth, had once hired a taxi simply to cross the busy road outside the hotel.

Jonathan's diary also records that, on Monday, 28 February, he had taken a room in the Hope-Nicholson house in Tite Street, across the road from the new studio our brother Julian had now acquired, and where he still lives and works five decades later. From his new humbler abode, Jonathan would write on 9 March describing an 'incredibly impressive' dinner given by his bachelor landlord the previous night, enriched by the presence of the fashionable publisher Anthony Blond. A few days later, in a letter signed 'A. J. P. Taylor (down from Oxford)', he announced spurious plans for Gilda's burial – 'Gilda, sociologist & dog of letters, will be buried in a banana-sealed vault three hundred feet below the Polish Embassy in Cadogan Lane' – but soon returned to his landlord's dinner party: 'Macmillan's grandson was there, and Marlon Brando was supposed to come but didn't. Dozens of brilliant remarks. You will hear them on Monday week when I return to Turegess.'

The exchange of 'brilliant remarks' had long been part of the basis of our relationship – as it still is between me and some of my friends today. Anyway, I did not have to wait until 'Monday week' to hear Felix Hope-Nicholson's announcement about the sudden death of Bill Astor, a key figure in the recent Profumo Crisis. In a letter dated 12 March, Jonathan wrote that Gilda – 'firm on her rump' – had heard this news from a man she'd met while wandering in the Turig garden.

On 31 March the General Election strengthened Harold Wilson's position as prime minister and marked the beginning of the end for me at Turleigh Combe. A few days before my departure, Jonathan arrived home – he had a fortnight's holiday from the hotel school – and cooked a special meal that night in spite of pleas from our mother not to 'mess up the meat'. During those last few days together at Turig, we sent samples of Jonathan's drawings to various eminent figures in the art world, accompanied by a letter drafted by me explaining that Jonathan was only eighteen and that these pictures were meant to be serious and funny at the same time. On 19 April, Ronald Searle would scribble back on Jonathan's own letter: 'Dear Mr Barrow – I wouldn't bother to take it seriously if I were you – if this is as far as you have got in 18 years. Sincerely RS.' During the same period Jonathan would acquire a second-hand 1960 Ford Escort van from a Wiltshire neighbour named Admiral Mills. Tinny and grey coloured, this car had a boxy, purposeful, semi-official look and I, a non-driver until my early thirties, became a regular occupant of the passenger seat.

On 20 April, I left Turig at last – 'It all sounds rather vague' said my mother when I told her my plans – and made my way via Birmingham to London. Here I stayed in Julian's old studio at 48 Tite Street and quickly got in touch with Reg Gray. My comedian friend was now in London trying to break through into television. During one of our meetings in the West End, he introduced me to a showbiz café in the Seven Dials area called the As You Like It. In due course I introduced Jonathan to this place which was used by stage hands, struggling actresses, out-of-work comedians and odder figures in the no-man's-land between the sexes. Quentin Crisp was a regular customer, though I did not meet him there until the following January.

Over the next year or two, Jonathan and I would make many visits to this café. As in other situations, Jonathan observed the scene more beadily than I did. He noticed a tiny darn on Reg Gray's trousers, he observed that the café proprietor Barrie Stacey was 'no fool' and that a cup of coffee cost him 'a farthing'. He became familiar with the café's regular customers, particularly Reg's friend Tommy Deane, a stand-up comic from Australia, and fitted in these new interests with his other commitments. He attended the hotel school five days a week and worked at the Hyde Park Hotel Buttery many weekends. There were also occasional trips to Turig. One Sunday night, he had driven me back from there in a violent thunderstorm. We had a monumental row, God knows what about. Early in July, in desperation and hope, I took a job at the Classic Cinema, Waterloo Station, and with this pitiful feather in my cap was able to risk a slightly longer period at home. While there, I received a letter from Jonathan, dated 13 July, addressing me as 'My Dearest' and beginning in Tindall-style: 'It is a question of "not going quite flat out" . . . and the sixth-formers feel the same. However he remains settled and happy.'

I was neither of these things, but soon returned to London to start the job, and on 15 July took a room for 4 guineas a week at the Hope-Nicholson house. Jonathan had shown me around, pointing out the two adjacent bathrooms on the second floor. 'I always use that bathroom. Keep the tradition up.' In a letter dated 17 July he announced his imminent departure for France – 'I may be voyaging with Rosemary' – and said he would not see me until 6 September.

He went on, 'Suggest you keep a separate notebook for Felix's remarks. Keep me posted. I shall mail you my address.'

Jonathan and Rosemary Leventon left England in the little grey van on 19 July, and headed for Cannes. 'Are they living together? Do they have a double sleeping bag?' our older brother Julian would ask more than once. Meanwhile I had settled into my short life as an assistant cinema manager, hugely enjoying the films on show, particularly *The League of Gentlemen*, starring Jack Hawkins, which I watched over and over again. My few weeks in this job may have had a mild knock-on effect on Jonathan. I have already mentioned a scene in *The Queue* set in a cinema, and a phrase from *The League of Gentlemen* about somebody having 'an almighty hangover' also finds its way into Jonathan's book. Later that year, long after I had been dismissed, Jonathan would visit the Waterloo Classic, do a sketch of its kiosk and quote from a sign in the entrance hall, 'Please obtain admission tickets downstairs.'

During Jonathan's absence I went to the As You Like It on my own. Jonathan had already had enough impact on this little club-like café for its owner to announce in an almost proprietorial way, 'His brother's in the South of France.' I knew very little of what Jonathan and Rosemary were getting up to there. Five letters arrived from Cannes and St Tropez, which revealed practically nothing. 'Of course St Tropez makes King's Road look like Melksham on early closing' begins his first letter, dated 26 July, but then departs into fantasy material about figures from our past like Frere and Hankey, and a Wiltshire neighbour called Canon Padre Williamson. And Clifford the dentist. And Hussey Freke, an acquaintance of our father. Was the main motive for these streams of consciousness simply Jonathan's delight in rescuing obscure names? Subsequent letters from France refer to the viola instructor at Clifton, Miss V. Pryce-Lucas, getting up to mischief with Steen Folke, 'Swedish massage'. Moor Divock gets another two mentions. And contemporary figures like Tommy Deane, his name characteristically reduced to Tomi Dene, and the Puffy Man, our nickname for a regular customer at the hotel school lunches, are thrown in for good measure. As on earlier occasions, Jonathan sometimes mimics our mother's letter-writing style: 'Mrs Hemming has had more bad luck – her shoulder this time – a fall in Derbyshire', but there are only the faintest allusions to Mediterranean glamour, conjured by names like Picasso, Frank Sinatra and Rudolf Lancia – 'one of the world's richest men'. On 26 August, he mocks my powers of observation and then offers a joke observation of his own:

> Your two basic observations about France:
> 1. Café owner polishing glasses.
> 2. Patisseries filled with fancies.
> are of course still true. Also French policemen preening themselves. Blue silk shirts with tiny rats embroidered on the cuffs.

He also claims to have met various Old Harrovians. One of them was a boy called Adda – 'Do you remember he had a slightly good talc that smelt like the inside of Dacre Church?' Another was Serge Beddington-Behrens who'd been a friend of mine at Harrow and would not re-enter my life until several years after Jonathan's death: 'He mistook me for you & said "Are you still reading history" – which seems a pretty curious starter' – then adds a sartorial detail: 'BB has a little beard & a navy blue polo neck (with little buttons running down one side like a dentist).' And as always these letters incorporate biro-and-ink drawings. Though he included a sketch of Barrie Stacey with a tray of teas destined for the Saville Theatre, his style was now more fluid and abstract. A portrait of our brother Martin doing the stoves gives him thirteen fingers on one hand. Tight brief underwear also features in several portraits.

My only other sources of information about this six-week holiday are things like the dinner menu at the Hotel Martinez – *Aspic Mousse de Foie Gras* was one of the first courses – and Jonathan's irregularly kept engagement diary. The entry for Monday, 25 July, reads 'Ro very ill. Car damaged.' And for the next day, 'Ro in hospital all day.' Knowing Jonathan, it is possible these were jokes put in to amuse Rosemary Leventon at the time. Ditto some of the comments he made later to me. Perhaps in an attempt to make her appear more interesting Jonathan had a lot of tales to tell about his girlfriend, some of them too good to be true. One of his less outrageous claims was that she had washed her hair in the ladies' loo at the Carlton Hotel, Cannes – a minor enough offence but one which nevertheless elevates Rosemary to the status of the naughty dog in *The Queue*.

Jonathan's diary also tells us that he and his girlfriend left St Tropez on 2 September and made their way to Calais, spending nights in Lyon, Langres (Haute Marie) and St Omer. They left Calais at 9.30 a.m. on 5 September and on arrival in England drove straight to Wiltshire. That night, Jonathan dropped Rosemary off with her parents at Steeple Ashton and eventually reached Turig at 10 p.m. A few days later, he was back at the hotel school and living in Julian's new studio at 33 Tite Street. By now, I had been sacked by the Classic Cinema and was working at Selfridge's – and had moved into a downstairs room at 52 Tite Street with its own bathroom. Thanks to reading David Ogilvy's book about advertising,

Confessions of an Advertising Man, I had suddenly decided that this was the career I wanted. Jonathan's position was in some ways equally uncertain, but he continued to spend weekends at Turig while I hung around in London.

On Sunday, 2 October, Jonathan memorably and significantly returned from one of these weekends with Gilda, the focal point of our childhood, beside him in the van. It was not her first big journey – she had accompanied us on holidays in Cumberland and Cornwall – but it was her one and only visit to London. This five-day excursion is very important in light of *The Queue*, which describes a boy and his dog's adventures in and out of London. Gilda was now quite old, a bit grey around the chops, not as battered as Mary but quite a veteran; bearing scars, a ripped ear and signs of her hernia. There are many instances in *The Queue* which could have been applied to Gilda during that brief autumnal visit to the city.

Fanciful entries in Jonathan's diary make the most of this episode. For Monday 3 October, he has written 'Gilda's abortion Dr Grant-Cohen 283 Baker Street 3rd Floor 2 rings.' On Wednesday, 'Gilda to Vet 31 Wigmore Steet, 5 pm' and on the Friday, 'Gilda to Battersea DH for 2 weeks.' He also records meetings between Gilda, Rosemary and a girl called Diana who lived at 67 Moor Park Road, which probably took place. I seem to remember that Gilda was then taken to the As You Like It or at least to the Seven Dials area. I certainly remember that she relieved herself in Shaftesbury Avenue.

Was it all too much for her? A lot of time was spent sitting in Jonathan's grey van near the hotel school in Vincent Square. And here there is another area for speculation. Jonathan reported at the time that his car had been towed away by the police, and indeed his diary tells us this has happened on 3 October. But was it really true that he eventually found Gilda in the police station house being befriended by police officers? I still do not believe it, but the idea obviously appealed enormously to him. And the encounters between the police and the dachshund in *The Queue* are drawn with passion.

The following weekend Jonathan returned Gilda to Turig, and our mother noticed the dog hung well back from his car when he set off again for London on the Sunday night. A dramatic fortnight lay ahead. On Wednesday, 12 October, he failed his accounts exam at the hotel school and was duly summoned by the school's principal Mr Lee. His diary entry for Tuesday, 18 October, reads, 'Lee said, "You will have to leave Westminster".' On the Thursday he had dinner with Kenneth Slatter and describes the experience as 'interesting'. He told me with confidence, 'It makes no difference at all whether I was at the Hotel School or not,' but begged me not to mention this matter to our father. Within a day or two, partly thanks to Mr Lee, he had got a job at Claridge's Hotel.

CHAPTER FOURTEEN

Claridge's: Part One

I find it best to walk to Claridge's each day. The
cold air and brittle of the pavements puts me right
for the day. I walked back yesterday and found the
sensation not as good as the morning. It may have
been because I saw a woman feeding hens in Sloane
Street. The feed was arsenic. All were dying. A bus
conductor was stealing eggs. Two in his mouth,
one in his pocket. The driver had the rest. The
meal was all over the road and the poor hens were
dropping like shoe polish. It was really nasty, I mean
this, Andrew. Tomorrow I shall walk up by
Beauchamp Place and avoid the scene. The old
hens have gone now, the remainder are in an
Ipswich convent.

Letter, 28 November 1966

CLARIDGE'S WAS AND perhaps still is the grandest hotel in
London. Built in the 1890s in Brook Street, Mayfair, it had
soon become a home from home for low-profile aristocrats
and publicity-shy multimillionaires. It also had a flourishing
banqueting side. The marriage of my brother Simon and
Caroline Peto-Bennett – they were now expecting their first
child – had been celebrated there in June 1964 and more
than forty years later Claridge's still features in my life. Not

so long ago, I telephoned the American writer Dominick Dunne at the hotel and learnt that he had had his nails mani-cured that morning in Claridge's barber's shop beside the beleaguered Lord Black of Crossharbour.

To give a flavour of the hotel's prestige when Jonathan worked there I need only quote from the List of Visitors in Residence on Tuesday, 13 December 1966, which Jonathan brought home. Several such documents eventually reached my attention, including a fascinating blacklist of dodgy customers which then circulated the top London hotels. The most common complaint was BNP (Bill Not Paid) and culprits in this connection included bogus clergymen and men masquerading as naval officers – one offender was even said to 'wear a cap to prove it'.

Among the highly respectable and unflashy characters staying or arriving at Claridge's that December day were the Earl and Countess of Dudley, Lord and Lady Halifax, the Duchess of Roxburgh, HG the Duke of Northumberland, Mr and Mrs A. Weinstock, Baron Guy de Rothschild, Mr and Mrs H. J. Heinz and Dr and Mrs A. Plesch along with various maids and valets. The List of Visitors reveals that a certain Mrs Tozer Moreno is also known as Miss Ivy Holloway but does not disclose that Miss Harriet Brown, staying in room 224, was the famous pseudonym of the great Greta Garbo. Nor, of course, does it explain that Lady Honor Svejdar, staying in room 242, was the former wife of diarist Chips Channon. Stitched on to the end of this fascinating list are the names of Mr and Mrs S. Niarchos and the hotel's chairman Hugh Wontner who kept permanent penthouse suites throughout this period.

This is all very wonderful – the showbiz element to some of these names would not have been lost on either of us – but Jonathan would waste no time in reminding me

Luigi, Maître d'Hôtel
Claridges

that Mrs Godwin, our cleaning lady at Turig, had also been to Claridge's, as a guest at our brother's wedding reception. And, amused and impressed though he was by his youngest son's new job, my father soon pronounced that his surviving mother-in-law, Granny Dacre, would look upon Claridge's as 'the haunt of sin'.

Anyway, Jonathan had begun work at this famous establishment on Monday, 24 October 1966, and been given a job in the hotel's Control Office. Here he would meet and observe senior staff like Ernst Van Thyne, Harry Lund Hansen, whom he had already met, and Evangelo Brioni, who had changed his name from Brian Evans. Among senior waiters, his eye was caught by a totally bald-headed man named Larry Tubman and Luigi, the elderly maître d'hôtel. He soon sketched these characters for me in black and white and repeated their boasts, like, 'I have half the crowned heads of Europe staying here next week. All incognito.' He also mentioned the ribbed pink tablecloths in the Causerie and the man who came in every morning with a tray containing twenty pots of paints to touch up nicks in doors, chairs and skirting boards.

While Jonathan found his feet in this exotic new environment, I had at last made progress towards getting a job in advertising. On 4 November, on the eve of my twenty-first birthday, I was offered a job at the London Press Exchange as a trainee copywriter. Later that day Jonathan and I drove down to Wiltshire and on our arrival I was struck by the way my father said nothing about my job but instead made a beeline for my younger brother. During the feeble birthday celebrations the following night Jonathan remained slightly detached, refusing my father's offer of a cigar after dinner.

I was not due to start the job until the New Year, and decided I would let Jonathan have my room at 52 Tite Street and spend part of this interlude with my grandmother and aunt in Cumberland. Here the letters came in a thicker flood than ever from my brother. Written as often as not on Claridge's writing paper, contained in Claridge's envelopes, they offered the usual mixture of fact and fantasy. His first, dated Sunday, 13 November, is more serious than usual, or at least strikes several serious notes. In fits and starts he describes visiting London Airport the previous day with Kenneth Slatter, who was opening a new hotel there. Driving through Shepherd's Bush, Slatter is critical of another motorist – 'OK, take it easy, buster' – and in a cafeteria at the airport, Slatter orders 'Number 6, please, with the gherkin' and asks, 'Do you like gherkin, Jonathan?' He then touches lightly on Slatter's campaign that my brother should see a psychotherapist, a big topic which had already been mentioned more than once. There is also a playful passing reference to a Cumbrian village – 'When you are tired of Blencow, you are tired of life' – and a surrealist claim that in the cinema the previous night he had found himself sitting next to the Isle of Wight. The letter ends with an off-beat reference to a forgotten West End character: 'I think the long white haired man who walks about the West End near the Palladium is the funniest man/thing in the World,' he suddenly claims. 'With his terrifically long white hair he strides about the corridors of W1 – with an umbrella, stopping and turning like as if in some military display. I have tried to draw him but it is not a likeness.'

His next letter, written on about 21 November, begins with a description of the Royal Variety Show, which he had seen the previous weekend with Rosemary Leventon – 'I think you will agree that Gene Pitney really was top of the show' – and continues, 'Rosemary struck new ground by sitting on the floor at the back of the stalls.' Then comes the rather ominous sentence in capitals, 'THE SOUND OF CAUTIOUS TYRES ON THE GRAVEL AT TURLEIGH INDICATED THE ARRIVAL OF A SCHOOLMASTER TO TEA.' Details of another fictional misfortune for the luckless Mrs Hemming follow: 'Near the Aust Ferry Mrs Hemming got out of her car . . . and a horrible helicopter passing overhead from RAF Melksham sprayed her with some full scab.' This long letter concludes with a real sounding quotation from Mrs Hope-Nicholson – 'Oh, the cold, I feel quite idiotic' – and a fictionalised, oversimplified and non-sensical lament from one of the other lodgers, a nonagenarian named Lilla Phillips: 'Would you be so kind as to lift this tap. Mr Hope-NICKERSON will leave it off.'

Jonathan's letters have nothing whatsoever to say about Claridge's, and in fact the only time he mentioned the hotel in this correspondence was in the hen-oriented paragraph quoted earlier. He is more down-to-earth when describing another ITV gala show which he had seen, again with Rosemary, at the Palladium the previous night. The Tiller Girls, he tells me, were 'by far the best', Ted Rogers was 'disgusting', Peter Cook 'poor and under-rehearsed', David Frost 'fat and amateurish', Morecambe and Wise 'not too good' and Bob Monkhouse 'very homosexual'. He concludes this vicious rundown with the words, 'YOU MUST WATCH THIS BAD SHOW'.

The other great subject on which he wrote that autumn, at length and with few obvious divergences from the truth, was his treatment by Edward Griffith, an eminent doctor whom Slatter had been gently persuading him to see for some months. On 16 November, he told me an appointment had now been fixed – 'Slatter says he is quite anxious' – and from his diary I learn that he duly reported at Griffith's at 6 p.m. on Friday, 25 November, after presumably spending the day working at Claridge's. The following morning, Jonathan described the experience in a remarkably frank, open and only slightly embroidered letter sent to me at Dacre:

I have made careful detailed notes on last night and this has been filed away under G in my private fan file. Anyhow here is a shortened version.

Dr Griffith has rooms in Bickenhall Mansions,

about two minutes walk from Baker Street Underground Train. The approach to the mansion block is similar to Ashley Gardens. His rooms are on the third floor and there is a good lift.

Dr Griffith opened the door quickly; I had been wondering about him during tea in the ABC in Baker Street and I say he looks a cross between a very slim version of Mr Black★ and a version of old Mr Scrine the chemist at home. Not a particularly imposing figure, the sort of man that Daddy could invite to tea at Turleigh and pass by un-noticed. He looks medical of course but when he takes off his more or less rimless spectacles he looks rather like a schoolmaster. In fact he was once; he taught for three years at a prep school in Broadstairs.

The entrance hall is not really impressive, the sort of place one would reject while looking for flats. Griffith took me to an inner room about the size of the spare room at Turleigh. Slatter said Griffith had taken pains to lay out his room in a soothing and relaxing manner and how well he has done it. Three walls are concealed with the most interesting library I have ever seen. Books on every possible subject. There was a low green armchair which Griffith asked me to sit in. Griffith sat in an identical low green armchair opposite me. Above a rather common electric fire is Poiski's 'Staircase': you will not know about this picture but analysts all over the world agree that this is the finest picture of its kind for the soothing of diffi-cult and uneasy patients. Griffith has the original.

★ An old fishing friend of my parents from the Lune Valley.

Griffith had a page of glossy file paper on his lap and he pencilled in my details. He used this page throughout the talk. Obviously Griffith had to find out as much as possible about me to discover just what the trouble is. By the way Griffith is a psychoanalyst. It is common knowledge that the best way to get information is to give some away yourself. Griffith did this; he told me about his past.

Griffith hated school so his mother sent him to Lausanne. Here, among the snow and rocks, he found his true happiness. His interest in rock-climbing and mountaineering has never dwindled since, and he is grateful to his mother for sending him to Lausanne. He joined St Marks Hospital as a medical student when he was about my age and, after graduating, specialized in gynaecology. It was about this time that he became interested in sex education and also became a founder member of the Family Planning Association. He has studied contraception and in 1932 went to Zurich to study under Dr Jung at the Jung Institute. He has written over 43 books, his volume 'Marriage Guidance' is universally regarded as a standard classic work. It has had sixteen re-prints. Under Jung's influence Griffith went to Prague and under Solomon Rooland did a thesis for Prague University on marriage problems. Since then, he has devoted his time to solving the difficulties that set to in nearly all marriages. Slatter said Griffith is the best in London and it is probably true.

Griffith then started to probe my past. At that

time Griffith knew nothing of my problems, this is standard practice with analysts. Slatter told him nothing. Youngest of five brothers is important, schools, academical trouble, dislike of games, relationship with parents, relationship with brothers. Sexual trouble at Harrow, present day sexual Hetero/Homo relations, he questioned Rosemary carefully. Many other things were covered. What did I do in the holidays? This is very important. All the time Griffith was pencilling his sheet and being gentle. Poiski's 'Staircase' looked even better than before.

Griffith pretended that he could not understand what the trouble was. Of course he knows very well what it is and it may be something that you or I would not think of even in our wildest dreams. Griffith probably earns five figures and is very busy. He would not waste time with me if he thought nothing was wrong. He is going to talk to Slatter about me. All Griffith said was that I am a late developer (Griffith was too) and that I am very introverted. Dr Jung classifies all persons into the extrovert personality or the introvert. In the latter, the personality is directed inwards in fantasy, daydreaming and thoughts about oneself rather than thoughts about the outside world. There is more than this but Griffith would not give it.

Griffith is a frightfully nice man and it is interesting to examine Slatter's relationship with Griffith. How much does G know about Slatter's problems. An interesting thing is that Slatter has been under a psychologist not since, say, before the war but in the last five years. I told G that Kenneth was concerned about my constant movement from rooms to rooms. G. replied 'Well, I have known Ken since he was younger than you and goodness he has lived in enough places.' Throughout the meeting there was a hint that G. was slightly teasing, perhaps critical of Ken. It was very slight but definitely there.

Griffith has his own flat off his consulting room and a humour point is that latched to the consulting room is a huge thick green baize door. Terrifying. Obviously to conceal noise from someone who might be in the flat.

I was with him an hour and see him again next Friday. He saw me out and closed his outer door very, very quickly as I waited for the lift.

Love JHB.

How much of this makes sense? Was there really such a person as Solomon Rooland or a painter called Poiski? Is Griffith's analysis of Jonathan's personality any good?* Perhaps not – but the process was only beginning and Jonathan's report on their next discussion was terser, gleefully concentrating on Griffith's criticisms of our father and the suggestion that he had ignored Jonathan's difficulties at school and, above all, never showed him how to express emotions. 'A child at that age is a great imitator,' Jonathan intoned, 'and I would soon have followed his example, but he never set one. Good or bad. He just said, "Oh you'll be alright one day. No, I don't want to talk about it".'

Whatever one makes of these remarks, there's no doubt

---

* On learning that there was a lot of celtic blood in Jonathan's background, can Griffith really have tut-tutted, 'So bad, psychologically'?

that Edward F. Griffith certainly had been – and perhaps still was – a very eminent doctor. His book *Modern Marriage,* first published in 1935, had, according to Jonathan, sold a quarter-of-a-million copies and been translated into several languages. Just how brilliant he still was isn't easy to judge from Jonathan's account, but earlier that year, he had published a new book, *Ups and Downs in Married Life*, which I still find gripping today. Anyway, Jonathan would see Griffith for several months and he would feature in our conversations and make appearances in other letters, sometimes fictional – 'G studied under Pernot at the Pernot Institue in Leipzig' – and sometimes fairly flatly straightforward. On my return to Turig around 9 December, he wrote claiming that Griffith had now asked, 'Why did your Father retire so early – or was he sacked?' and urging me to go to the Bath library and read all I could about Dr Jung. 'Griffith is very expensive,' he added. 'It costs £5 an hour and I shall have to see him at least once a week for three months.'

Jonathan's finances, always better than mine, were good in part because he had already started to undertake freelance work as a waiter. I see from his engagement diary that on 17 November he worked at a banquet at the Savoy Hotel and was paid £2 for four-and-a-half hours work. The following day, he worked at the Royal Garden Hotel from 5 p.m. to 1 a.m. and was paid £3. Even considering inflation these sums seem pitifully small, but the experiences widened his world and the Savoy in particular became a great source of inspiration. A few months later he wrote a semi-imaginary piece about a chauffeur's life at this hotel: the 'notoriously slow lights' at the junction of the Strand and Savoy Yard, the roaring limousines and 'grey army' of attendants in tunics and 'flap jackets'. He compares the atmosphere behind the spinning doors of the Savoy Grill – the dense emerald pile carpet, best orchids and *foie gras* on thick toast ('crisp out, cushiony soft inside') – with that of the café where the chauffeurs sit and grumble: 'I'm driving Sir Horace King to Exeter but my car's playing up', 'Ascot job tomorrow. Parking is the bastard thing,' and 'Fuck this rain'.

Outside the hotel world, his life was also expanding. Diary entries suggest ups and downs with Rosemary Leventon. On 31 October, he had noted 'No sign of Ro at pub,' but had then attended those two gala performances with her, taken her to Nick's Diner, sent her flowers, received telephone calls from her and had her back to 52 Tite Street for the night. He also attends parties given by the Bonham-Christies and the Buxtons and meets up with hotel school cronies. And visits the As You Like It on his own. In the street he also spotted people I had met during my showbiz struggles like Robert Wace, incredibly tall, thin, trendy manager of a pop group called the Kinks.*

He also looked after his car carefully, notes its flat tyres and need for a new piston, records his bank balance at regular intervals and makes a stab at at least one moneymaking scheme. On 3 November 1966 he bought a 'patrol' coat at the catering outfitters Denny's in Soho, and on 9 December placed an advertisement in *Private Eye*'s Buy & Sell column, offering 'genuine Nazi officers' jackets' for £4 each. The only punter who had taken up this offer had duly returned the amateurishly dyed waiter's jacket to *Private Eye*'s editor, Richard Ingrams, saying that the garment enclosed bore no resemblance whatsoever to an officer's kit, let alone a Nazi officer's.

Other letters that Jonathan sent to me at Turig – I now had only a week or two to go before starting my job in advertising – were politely adjusted to reflect the fact that I

---

* Their record 'Sunny Afternoon' had gone to the top of the hit parade earlier that year.

had now left Cumberland and was back on home ground in Wiltshire. One letter on Claridge's paper kicks off with a breathless paragraph about the gravelled area beside Turleigh Combe's front door which we knew as the 'forecourt': 'I have just heard that the forecourt's mother has been killed in a collision on the A34. Poor forecourt, it sank to its knees in horror. The beech trees have been wonderful and have helped forecourt with food & driving the twins to Freshford Station (circle line).' But that is not the end of the matter. Had I heard, he wonders a few days later, that the beech trees have been 'forging cheques and have all four been remanded in custody at Coombe Down constabulary under the Forgery Act 1958'? There was also fanciful material about events in our own combe, the rough area sloping down towards the village of Turleigh. Our mother, Jonathan informs me, has found Agatha Christie 'wandering aimlessly' here, and he also tells me that an O level, which lived in this wasteland, had died. 'Her throat was quite parched and lots of creepy crawlies were on her. Poor thing.' He also reports that our father has been apprehended in a nearby village called Haugh Potticks – 'Apparently totally blind and wandering in the direction of the Holy Land. When questioned he said "Let my people go – I quest the star of Bethlehem".' He also slips in that our new Potterton 'Diplomat' gas boiler was becoming interested in the study of Greek – 'Tutors come from Colerne' – and that the local vicar, the Revd Homer Hill, had been 'gutted by fire'. He then offers an incomprehensible story about a neighbour called Mr Wright and the disappearance of 'Donatello's wooden "Magdalene" from the baptistery in Florence's Piazzo Duomo . . .'

In the midst of this nonsense, Jonathan does not mention that on Dr Griffith's advice, he has attended two meetings with the Vocational Guidance Association, but does report that Lilla Phillips, the ancient fellow lodger at Tite Street, has just said, 'I've had a perfectly glorious day. I feel so happy . . .' and that he has dined with our older brother Simon, who 'scored points' by asking him up to the bathroom to talk – 'I was interested in his enlarged scrotum and scaly neck'. In a paragraph headed IMPORTANT he also promises to visit Turnbull & Asser to buy a Christmas present for me. 'Please state, BY RETURN OF POST, what you require,' he writes bossily. 'Huge made up bow ties? Checkered socks? If you do not state your requirements then I shall purchase one of the above. Satisfaction guaranteed.'

I forget which, if any, of these items I chose but I see from Jonathan's diary that he skated lightly through the festivities, working all day at Claridge's on Christmas Eve, driving home late that night, and returning to London on Boxing Day. On 30 December I followed him there, reclaimed my bedsit at 52 Tite Street, while Jonathan moved upstairs to what he soon called the Jasmine Room, facing the street on the third floor. I was dismayed by the mess, disorder and broken glass – the gas fire left on and a sleeping bag unfurled – which I found in my room but on Monday, 2 January 1967, I turned up for my first day's work at the London Press Exchange feeling reasonably cool, calm and collected.

Subsequently, I have often wondered if getting this job had to some extent reinstated me into my younger brother's good books. In fact, this was a tense time between us – and had been for many months. Much of the time, I now found Jonathan sly and sluggish and even felt that Dr Griffith had done him great harm. I was annoyed that he sometimes refused to co-operate with me or go along with my proposals. Our meetings were sometimes marked by his monosyllabic responses. He would say, 'Yes?' and 'What?' and 'Drink up please. I'm feeling very tired.' In a pub he might disappoint me by ordering orange juice instead of beer. Outside 52 Tite Street one day I had even asked him about the odd way he walked, that slightly sissy or foppish gait which might owe something to the bunion problem of the past. 'I have to, Andrew. Don't ask stupid questions,' was his lofty reply. Another dispute had ended with him telling me, 'You always were very silly and annoying . . .' Looking back, I now see that he was far busier than me and had a life to lead whereas I was often at a loose end. When I'd tried to involve him in the rather personal question of what new spectacle frames I should choose, he replied dismissively, '*You'd look super in National Health specs . . .*' And when I tried to exploit the menial nature of his work at Claridge's by asking if he still had to 'clock in', he retorted woodenly, 'Everybody clocks in except for managers. And you know I'm not a manager.'

In spite of these hiccups, there were still precious bonds between us. I loved his sense of humour and gained strength from his authoritative, knowledgeable pronouncements. During a rather painful supper at the Chelsea Kitchen in the Kings Road – Jonathan was all elbows in such places – he redeemed the atmosphere by muttering 'Cook's got a headache,' and commenting on another customer: 'Somerset Maugham over there and he knows it.' With hindsight it is easy to see in his jokes a macabre hint of things to come. One Sunday on our way to see Tony Bridge preaching at Lancaster Gate – this controversial clergyman had had a considerable impact on Jonathan when he gave the Lenten addresses at Harrow – he remarked, 'It's very important that I go to church today because tomorrow I plan to crawl across Park Lane during the rush hour.'

Though his life seemed increasingly busy we still did things together, and still had interests in common. We had watched with amusement Mike d'Abo's progress in the pop world. The previous year, my old school friend had become the lead singer with Manfred Mann, already had two hit records – 'Michael's had song-writing tuition,' Jonathan commented drily – and would soon get married in a blaze of publicity. We still went on West End excursions. We still went to the As You Like It together – alas, Jonathan was not present when I met Quentin Crisp there for the first time on 16 January 1967 – and occasionally visited art galleries. At the National Gallery, Jonathan delighted me by pausing in front of *Flatford Mill* and declaring '*It's frightfully bad!*' And one weekend that spring we visited Lilla Phillips in hospital. As we approached the old lady's bedside, Jonathan remarked, 'She thinks she's a teapot now. She has a huge identification disc round her neck,' and afterwards struck an all too familiar note, by confessing, 'I'm pretty scared of hospitals. I think I'll end up in one.'

I also remember companionable drives home together in the grey van. The M4 had yet to be built and we followed an old-fashioned route through Marlborough, passing a sinister signpost to Baltic Farm. Our father was now a figure of increasing interest to us both and we sometimes interpreted his behaviour in light of what Jonathan had learnt from Dr Griffith, who was now part of our shared life. Spotting a man with his children outside Buckingham Palace, Jonathan had remarked, 'That man probably kisses his children three or four times a day.'

Jonathan's actual dealings with Griffith had become more private, and one does not trust his claim that during one session he had burst out laughing and been asked by the doctor, 'What's the matter, old chap? You seem to like laughing.' Anyway, my involvement with the whole Griffith experience had been cemented when on 31 January that year I had gone along to see Griffith on my own, ostensibly to talk about Jonathan and my father. As with other people, I found Jonathan had done 'an extremely good PR job' – his own expression – for the seventy-year-old therapist. Though I had already gained a lot from Griffith's books, I was a little disappointed by the man himself, who seemed forgetful and confused. Perhaps Slatter was right when he said later that I had only gone to 'gape' at him. And perhaps our older brother Simon was right when he argued that Jonathan should have seen a psychiatrist unconnected with Slatter. Simon's view of Jonathan was anyway wide of the mark. During one of several discussions about family matters Simon had pronounced Jonathan to be 'unambitious' and Caroline had declared that her brother-in-law had 'no character' and was 'easily influenced'.

Though his work with Griffith had not yet reached its climax, Jonathan's character, or inner life, was in many ways impenetrable. His writings and jokes and letters and the lethal weight of *The Queue* do not give one the full picture. Knowing next to nothing about his unconscious mind may make a dream he recorded on 22 February 1967 of some interest, though one inevitably wonders how much he embroidered it:

> There were distinctive markings in the sky. My Mother said, 'Oh, it won't rain.' She is so often wrong on things that I nowadays do the opposite to what she says. So I went into the Triumph and got out my mac and rushed back to catch her up. She said, 'You fool, it won't rain'. Sure enough, about 10 minutes later, the rain began. Another case of I know best. Poor thing, she was soaked. I was crowing at her, inside me. Then I thought she

looked so pathetic. There was some heavy thunder now. The lightning was starting and it was rather as if someone had stuck a torch down the inside of her brassiere. It sort of glowed inside. The pink elastic was sodden. She had to run, and her stockings were soaked through. I thought of lending her my mac. But I said to myself no, serve her right. She was running a good hundred yards in front of me now. I saw her disappear beyond a bank. At least I thought I did. Coming closer I saw that she had fallen into some sort of culvert/ditch. Drat her. The rain was gushing over her. She looked like a dead fish in a river bed. The lightning was getting thicker too. It was meshy lightning; all over the sky. I saw my Mother gradually disappear into the mud. Her garments were trapping some air and this kept her afloat. I thought I would finish her off. So I picked a nearby boulder and chucked it on her. She still did not go down. So I jumped on to her. I felt her go down at last. Then I got off. But I couldn't – my foot was caught in one of her garments. She was sinking fast now. It was raining worse than ever. Floods of it came over her and I felt I must get out of it, but I couldn't. I was stuck like her. Only she was drowned and I wasn't. I knew what was happening, she was dead. I was yelling. I was going in with her. There seemed some vice on my foot. I had toppled face down into the mud and was dying.

Though this dream, the only one Jonathan ever recorded, gives us a foretaste of *The Queue* and may tell us something about Jonathan's inner life – one night at 52 Tite Street I had visited his room at the top of the house and found him talking loudly in his sleep – it tells us nothing about our mother. In many respects she was equally inaccessible. In letters to us at this time, she still wrote about Gilda 'hunting manfully' and other animal and gardening matters, but gave little else away.

Throughout the spring of 1967, Jonathan carried on his free-lance bar work in the evenings and at weekends. On 28 February he started 'cellar control' at Claridge's and took responsibility, it seems, for the soap on the hotel's first, second and third floors. His diary tells us that on 10 February he spent the night in Room 250. And that he had started having his hair cut by a man called Kurt who had premises in Aldford House, Park Lane. Also that on 13 February he went to see a man called Cullen at Griffith's publishers, Methuen. Around the same time he saw *The Apartment* at the Chelsea Classic, and Charles Aznavour live at the Albert Hall. On 10 March, he was taken to a stag show in the East End by Tommy Deane, the stand-up comic we knew. His social life was expanding in other ways. He continued to have dates with Ken Slatter, but his engagement diary mentions a party given by Richard Gurney, a telephone call from Margaret De Pelet, drinks in St Loo Mansions, Chelsea, with Isobel Cazenove, and a cancelled appointment with a girl called Diana Keith Neal. The name of Rosemary Leventon occurs occasionally but not regularly, though Jonathan was on hand to share in the excitement on 22 March when it was wrongly announced in *The Times* that Rosemary's mother, now married to Wiltshire landowner Sir Gerard Fuller, had died. This odd story, which made front-page news but was never fully explained, was Jonathan's first brush with vulgar publicity.

Is it also worth describing a tour of the docklands

which Jonathan undertook on 5 April? Driving my father around the Isle of Dogs that night they were stopped by a policeman. Fearing that his relationship with Jonathan might be misconstrued, my father had apparently taken control of the situation – 'Officer, this is my son . . .' – but, on learning that they had been driving on private property, he seemed slightly disappointed that there would be no 'proceedings' against them.

By this stage, Jonathan and I had given serious thought to our accommodation plans. We could both afford to move out of our bedsitters and, though the idea filled me with foreboding, we began to look around for a flat we might share. We saw various properties and rejected them. 'One flat was ideal,' Jonathan remarked later, 'except for the main room which was only a quarter of an inch high.'* We eventually settled on an unfurnished flat in Knightsbridge, which had two tiny bedrooms and looked onto a mews. In preparation for the move, my brother cleared out his room at 52 Tite Street and to my surprise and annoyance threw a box of pictures and writings into the Thames.

---

* Barry Humphries reminded me recently that the best jokes are often understood by only one other person.

CHAPTER FIFTEEN

Claridge's: Part Two

Again I enter the lavatory. In there, wearing only
knickers, was the girl. We shake hands and I place
the sex book, open at the correct page, on a ledge.
I stand beside her, place my hand on her garment
and lower. I am astonished. She has the Private
Parts of a man. I am bitterly disappointed and am
just about to leave when I notice a small object
on the floor. It is covered by a cotton handkerchief and is roughly the size of a sausage. It is a
man's penis. The girl blushes. I grab her arm and
beat her about the face. After further torture, she
admits that her 'penis' is a polythene 'Screw-on'
bought last week at a Holborn joke shop. I run
from the room in total confusion.

The Queue, Chapter Nine

JONATHAN AND I moved into the rear ground-floor flat at
32 Lennox Gardens on 14 April 1967. It was the first time
I had set up house with anyone in the sense of sharing
domestic utensils and sorting out laundry together, yet it was
something we had wanted to do for a long time. Though
only twenty-one and twenty respectively, we had sometimes
pretended to be much older than we were. When, shortly
before moving in, Jonathan claimed he would be getting up

at six each morning to bake cinnamon rolls, I half hoped this would be true. I was certainly delighted when Jonathan went to Elizabeth David's new shop off Sloane Square and bought for a total of £1.16s. 0d, the butter board and chopping board which I still possess today.

I also possess the hardbound notebook marked 'FOOD AND RUNNING EXPENSES' which we started the moment we moved into Lennox Gardens, the three columns per page neatly headed DATE, GOODS and AMOUNT. One of the earliest entries, dated 18 April, is for 'Starch' for 4/6d. At the bottom of the first page, a chicken is recorded costing 8/-. I also see that a dinner for 'Ken' on 3 May cost £2. 0s. 0d. and one for Simon and Caroline the next day cost £2. 4s. 0d. I also see that we bought a sofa for £7.10s. 0d. and a brass lamp, inspired by the lamps at Turig, which cost a massive £8.10s. 0d. Beds had already arrived from Wiltshire and for a while we sat on packing cases and ate off – some readers may be shocked to hear – crockery Jonathan had pinched from Claridge's.*

The charms of having a secluded flat of our own soon began to wear off. 'This is the sort of flat where you'd get a Wildeblood arrest,' Jonathan remarked almost the moment we got the keys – a reference to the famous homosexual case he often talked about. From the kitchen skylight came the nervous flutter of pigeon wings, and equally unhappy noises reached us from the cobbled alley between the house and Lennox Garden Mews. And from the basement of our building came the ugly laughter and voice of the building's caretaker, her complaining tones reminding us of the Mrs Bates figure in *Psycho*.

---

* A stolen Claridge's egg cup later found its way to Turig and was regularly used by our uncomprehending father at breakfast time.

The flimsiness of the internal partitioning also bore in upon us. From my bedroom I would hear Jonathan preparing supper, his shoes squeaking on the lino, water pouring from a tap, the thud of the fridge door closing. On one memorable occasion I heard a piece of crockery smashing but delayed my reaction by several seconds. 'Hello, what went?' I asked eventually. Jonathan reciprocated with a further delay and then said, simply, 'Mug.' The food he cooked, however, was often superb. I remember brilliant chicken dishes and a Turin Loaf and, accompanied by a crash of thunder, a shrimp omelette being prepared. Jonathan was interestingly frugal. He took his own shirts to a launderette and starched them at home. At night he had his special routines. He cleaned his shoes, filled a hot water bottle, offered me a slightly phoney James Bond-like good-night, clicked light switches, then fiddled with his alarm clocks, often activating one or both in the process. In the morning they rang loud enough to wake up the entire mews.

Our conversations were vigorous and variable. By moving into this independent flat we had to some extent completed the conspiracy against our parents and three older brothers. Across a photograph of our brother Martin, Jonathan had scrawled, 'I cannot help looking so pathetic,' and of Julian, our benefactor for many years, he said, 'He deserves to be absolutely flown at.' Our sister-in-law Caroline had inspired even fiercer rebuke. 'She deserves a damn good whipping,' he said after a mildly catty remark of hers had reached our attention. And, of course, Jonathan could be equally spiky about *me*. Returning early that summer from working at a showbiz party at Claridge's, Jonathan rubbed in my lack-lustre personality by telling me, 'You must have your hair tinted, waved, dyed and spectacles changed immediately.' On another wilder occasion, he would flair up and say, '*Madness! You're on the road to it!*'

I had enough doubts about myself in all areas without this sort of broadside dismissal, and indeed would soon take myself off to a series of shrinks. Jonathan's time with Dr Griffith was meanwhile drawing to a close. The Vocational Guidance report which had arrived earlier in the year had proved singularly uninteresting, uninspired and platitudinous. In April 1967, Dr Griffith wrote Jonathan a longish letter, stressing the importance of getting 'understanding and encouragement' from his father and urging him to 'go and see him and tell him all about coming here, all about your aims and ideas and indeed, try and make as positive a relationship with him as possible.' The letter, typed in medical blue, concludes with the sentence: 'From what you have told me about him, I should think he would be only too pleased to hear about all this.'

As far as I know, Jonathan never discussed these matters with our father and, anyway, his relationship with Dr Griffith now came to an end. An appointment scheduled for 7 p.m. on 8 May was cancelled by Griffith, and it is probable that they met for the last time on 24 May. Griffith's name does not appear in Jonathan's diary after this date, though Jonathan may have kept in touch with him indirectly via Slatter. He knew that Griffith had a holiday home on the Cornish coast, and Slatter had already reported that Griffith had been marginally involved in the Torrey Canyon disaster: 'G's been down on the beach helping the birds,' Slatter said. 'Mrs G made G put on gym shoes.' Though Jonathan had talked at length about his therapist, lending him a comic greatness, it may have been something of a camouflage for what was really going on behind the green baize door. In one of his angrier moments at Lennox Gardens, Jonathan declared, '*I've hardly told you a thing about Griffith and I never will!*'

★

Though the Vocational Guidance people and Griffith had suggested Jonathan should try to get a job, like me, in advertising, or scriptwriting, he remained at Claridge's, though in a different role. During the summer of 1967, he was moved from the Control Office to the Dispense Bar where drinks were prepared for the hotel's bars and restaurants. Here he was closer to the action and the recipient of a good deal of hotel gossip, expanding his knowledge of colloquial talk and sharpening his powers of observation — encouraging him to put pen to paper. Soon he had come up with the following diatribe by one of the barmen about a regular customer:

That fuckin' woman has come in every day this week. You know she's got millions — American, to do with the autos. Well, everytime she's been in she's always had the same. Bloody Mary with *no* lemon. What, she must have had it like that fuckin' hundreds of times. Well today she orders that, then says 'John, why no lemon?' After she's had no lemon for fuckin' years. Well I've learnt over the years that it's best not to argue with her so I just said 'Oh I'm so sorry I forgot it. I'm <u>awfully</u> sorry . . .' But she's an awkward fucker — always was — Doug, do you remember that thing over her room? She'd lost her key somewhere and she was sure that her daughter was in the room having a quick screw with one of the waiters. Well everyone knew the daughter <u>was</u> a screwy type. Anyhow she made Van Thyne open it for her, but it just happened that VT had missed the 112 keys. So what he did was to send Romeny up the inside well and let him get in with a ladder. Well, Romeny got the ladder, went up and got in through a window. Oh, no,

Romeny didn't look into the bedroom. Oh, no, that wasn't Romeny's job. He just went down the passage and let VT into the suite . . . No, I wouldn't mind her but for her complaining all the time. No, it would be alright if she complained about <u>big</u> things like, er – lipstick on a glass, snowy ice or er – say a piece of cork in a glass or something. But she complains about fuckin' <u>small</u> things like – saying there's a door open somewhere or that the carpet isn't straight or that she hears noises.

And Jonathan clearly egged on his colleagues for more, asking later whether the lady in question had been in the hotel the previous weekend and being told, 'No, she fucked off to the coast.' He also recorded – or invented – a rather flatter monologue about fruit juices and someone's apron being 'thick with tomato piff and pips', and another describing an incident in a café behind the hotel, frequented by Red Cross theatre attendants. One of the women spills the contents of her bag and goes down on her knees to retrieve a pair of scissors. Her skirts are rucked up and Jonathan looks closely at her underwear. He notes she is wearing white pants made of 'a gauze similar to her dressings', 'a sloppy girdle made of pink flannel' and 'a sort of petticoat stitched into her uniform'. Eventually a little gasp tells him she has found her scissors and finally he hears a tiny click as she shuts the eye and tooth clip on her satchel.

Was this a real story or does it show that Jonathan was aching to write a slightly salacious form of fiction? He certainly had much to regale me with from Claridge's and other hotels. He told me that when barmen offered each other a drink they would ask – I occasionally employ the phrase today – 'Large or very large?' When dinner is announced at a small private party at the Dorchester he hears the oil millionaire Paul Getty remark, 'What happens now? Do I take somebody's arm?' and at a medical conference at the Savoy he sees doctors *running* for the bar when the speeches are over. Or so he says. He is staggered by how wet the Earl of Snowdon's voice sounded and hears Claridge's senior floor waiter Larry Tubman boasting that he had told the elderly Duke of Windsor, in London to unveil a statue of his mother, 'If I may say so, Your Royal Highness is

looking *not a day older* than when you first stayed here forty years ago.'

Jonathan shared these anecdotes and experiences with me willingly. He was much more guarded about other aspects of his life. He continued to see Slatter and have what I thought of as soppy, sloppy evenings alone with him. Slatter also telephoned from time to time, sometimes rather late at night – and Jonathan would speak to him for fifteen minutes. During the summer of 1967 he also became increasingly involved with what could be described as the 'deb scene'. New names now appear in his diaries, like Bridget Doyne, Miranda Seymour and Margaret Peile. Rosemary Leventon is now attached to someone called Tony and he occasionally has dates with them. On 17 July, he attends a performance of *A Man For All Seasons* with Ro, Tony and Margaret Peile, also known as Peanuts. There are lots of parties. A dance given by the Fullers at their Wiltshire stately home on 22 April gets only a passing mention but at Bridget Doyne's dance on 21 June he meets a girl called Sara Pilkington. Sometimes I was included in the invitation. On 1 July 1967 we drove together to Norfolk. I forget the dance but we stayed on that occasion at Barningham Hall with Sir Charles Mott-Radclyffe, whose late night announcement 'Breakfast is a moveable feast. It's there on the hot plates' is later uttered by the hospitable Sparrow in *The Queue*. Our older brother Simon tried to rev me up about these events – 'I want you to get five names and addresses at each dance, even if they look like the back end of a bus' – but Jonathan was more dismissive, describing our fellow guests as a 'load of duds' and claiming that we were only invited because they were short of single men. Getting back to Lennox Gardens one Sunday night, Jonathan had completed the dampening-down process by refusing to go out to dinner. 'If you'd just driven a hundred and fifty miles you'd be tired too.'

This is all a bit grim but the 'deb world' crops up more amusingly during the train journey in *The Queue*. Following a particularly disgusting encounter with two homosexuals in a lavatory, the narrator staggers, stark naked, into a compartment where four debutantes, all aged seventeen, are writing out invitations to a dance they are sharing in Worcestershire. The encounter starts badly – 'They have never seen a naked man before and hide their eyes' – but the boy soon puts them at their ease and something of an orgy begins. Then one of the girls' mothers bursts in, white with rage: 'You must never see my daughter again. How dare you. Where are your clothes? Get out. How dare you.'

But the incident does not end there. As he leaves the compartment, one of the girls slips the boy an invitation to meet 'in the first-class lavatory in twenty minutes' time'. He then begins to shake with fear – 'You see I have never taken a woman and doubt my powers' – and deluges his four-legged friend Mary with questions about 'the actual experience'. Luckily he finds a copy of Gray's *Sex for the Young Man* tucked into his inside pocket – 'I rapidly examine the relevant chapters and carefully study the diagram on page 18' – and then, pulse quickening, hurries to the meeting place where the events described at the beginning of this chapter take place.

Of Jonathan's actual sex life I know very little. I remember a frail-sounding girl called Erika ringing from a callbox, and being thunderstruck when I later found my brother embracing someone on the doorstep of Lennox Gardens. Thunderstruck and depressed on account of the fact that at twenty-one I had made no headway at all in this area, and preferred to see Jonathan as being in more or less the same boat as myself. In literary terms, Jonathan certainly preferred to present himself as sexually inexperienced. Early on in *The Queue* the narrator boasts that he has 'an astonishingly small penis', and there are no happy descriptions of heterosexual sex in the pages that follow and indeed more than one account of a heterosexual disaster. During his rooftop adventures with Mary and the Sparrow, the narrator witnesses a couple having intercourse. 'It is most interesting and I halt for a moment to watch.' Urged on by Sparrow, he then sends a slate crashing down. 'The startled couple leap off the bed, fearing they have been discovered. Unfortunately, the male withdraws too quickly and his penis snaps off. He howls with pain and I feel awkward and embarrassed.'

Shocking though such descriptions sound, Jonathan seems less interested in using *The Queue* as a vehicle for sexual revelations or fantasies than as a compendium of sexual jokes – and clichés. Discussing the sordid underground relationship between Mr J. P. Hinne and a badger, the narrator observes that they 'did just about everything, apart from actual intercourse'. When a replacement arrives for a homosexual bus driver, the company 'made certain it was a married man'. And the past history of a swimming instructor who has resorted to teaching children to swim in a sewer is told with an open-eyed innocence which marginally redeems its *News of the World* ingredients. Caught committing 'an obscene act' with a twelve-year-old at a public bath, the instructor has used forged references to get a post at a small public school in Surrey. There he has committed further offences and been given one day's notice by the Head Master, 'himself an active homosexualist'. Three weeks later, with more forged references, he has taken up a post as a shower-room attendant at Medlinton Road Youth Club. On his first Tuesday there, the Administrator catches him trying to bugger a boy who was 'far too young to know what was going on', but again overlooks the matter. Now Scotland Yard are on the case and soon the instructor is in the dock at the Old Bailey. Then comes a twist: Mr Justice Cullum, who is described as a 'kind and sensitive man', forgives the instructor all his sins and gives him an absolute discharge. On the condition that his penis be, there and then, severed at the root. As so often, Jonathan finally goes into comic overdrive. 'Bandages are applied and the instructor is led out of court. That night he returns to the court and methodically searches the disposal bins. He finds his penis and, with amazing skill, re-fits it to his stump. Two years later it falls off in front of a large crowd. He is arrested on a gross indecency charge.'

For some reason, perhaps largely comical, it suited Jonathan to present the narrator as sexually ambiguous, to put it mildly. On almost countless occasions, the boy is preyed upon by homosexuals and even once by the gigantic, car-driving, gay wood pigeon mentioned earlier. Sometimes he reacts violently, jumps to his feet and kicks the interferer in the balls. On other occasions, the boy uses his charms to get favours from men and apparently enjoys himself in the process. When the driver threatens to throw him off a bus, the boy notices 'the frills of women's underwear protruding above his blue serge trousers'. Confident that he is a pervert, he quickly offers to go on the back seat and be 'dirty' with him in lieu of payment. 'He agrees instantly and we pass a pleasant half hour in complete privacy.'

Though Jonathan was fascinated by eccentricity and perversion across the board, his sorties into county society and job at Claridge's exposed him particularly to upper-class dottiness. In *The Queue*, there is a gentle, knowing reference to Lady Ruffas, who dies on a train, a passing reference to 'Lord Dob's place at Skelton' and a longer description of a retired army officer called L. P. Toote, who gets the narrator to do three hours of gardening and then watches him from an upper window, shouting instructions and warnings over a hand megaphone: 'Mind that hydrangea. Watch out, you're going to step on my bietiunium. Take more care. Look, you've missed out one bit . . .' In the shooting-party episode, he offers a savage caricature of the upper classes in Lord 'Arsehole' Drew, Lord Fuck, Nicky Shit and Rory Scott. In the Dog's Home, he is more affectionate about 'the dear old sheepdog that used to work for Sir Ivan Cutt's shepherd' and ponders over the plight of a red setter lying in a vomit-covered bed surrounded by empty spirit bottles. 'Years ago,' he tells us, 'he was owned by the late Lord Focle who drank himself to death. Red Setter was left to fend for himself and now, well into his 90th year, he seems to have adopted the habits of his former owner. He looks forward only to the few drops of alcohol that his miserable pension can afford.' Describing this creature as a sad dog and remarking, 'I wish I could do something,' he reminds me of Chips Channon's concern for the decrepit Lord Alfred Douglas, and elevates himself into the role of would-be philanthropist.

And of course there was a strong metropolitan element to this newly acquired knowledge. As a barman, he had already rubbed shoulders with Paul Getty, Lord Snowdon and someone called Sir Harold Samuel. Later he would fill *The Queue* with London characters like the Rolls-Royce owning, dog-hating bachelor Marcus Peimme. And with satirical allusions to places like the Restorante Quixinto Inmexo where Mary had fallen under the charms of a bulldog named David and the Rescini Restaurant in Buller Road where K. P. Lotte meets the trout of his dreams.

During this period Jonathan was also acquiring what my father might have called a good working knowledge of London, England and the world. *The Queue* resonates with real and imaginary London addresses like Charter Street, SE1, Ely Place, NW8, Cattel Street, N1 and provincial place names like Buckingham, Ancaster, Rochester and Clacton-on-Sea, as well more far-fetched ones like Ratford-on-Avon and Cunterferd. There are curious little places like Little Bickford Station, Woodford Tunnel, Icely Common and pub names range from the common enough Three Crowns to the highly improbable Fox and Vixen. By 1967 the motorways were being built, the M1 has made its presence felt and the Great North Road was now semi-redundant. As an author, Jonathan's geographical knowledge was slapdash – Holborn Station is *not* en route between Euston and Tottenham Court Road – but his eye for sombre detail is sharp. He had grasped the names of the big London hospitals like St Barts and St George's, and started to cut out items from newspapers about gory accidents. One cutting recorded the death of a woman under an approaching train at Gloucester Road Underground station – 'engineers, firemen and ambulance men worked for nearly an hour to free her' – and another described the death of a railway guard who caught his foot in a door and was dragged under a train at Gidea Park, Romford. The latter incident also inspired a horrific pen-and-ink in which the passivity of the ignorant passengers is compared with the agony of the dying man.

Many of his experiences were still shared with me. Sometimes it amused me to accompany him to whichever hotel he was freelancing in. One weekend we drove in heavy rain towards the Savoy. In Belgrave Square, as rain hammered on the roof of the little grey van, Jonathan remarked, 'If only it was *always* like this!' We also went to see Ken Dodd at the Palladium – Jonathan pronounced him 'the absolute master of microphone techniques' – and discovered old restaurants together like Schmidts in Charlotte Street where tail-coated waiters served sauerkraut costing 9d. a portion and dinner for two set us back £1.10s.0d. We ate less well in Knightsbridge cafés – 'These teas for two often end in tears' – and sometimes ran into trouble when walking the streets near our flat. On one such jaunt I had spotted Rosemary Leventon, but Jonathan had shown me how little I knew about his life by walking straight past her. One day in June 1967 we had tea more happily with my new chum Quentin Crisp. As we approached the famous bedsitting room for the first time, Jonathan declared that Quentin Crisp would be 'frantically getting tea ready'. This was a joke. We already knew there was nothing 'frantic' about our host and 'tea' was hardly something he would need to get 'ready'. But the remark certainly reflected the slightly patronising and quizzical way in which we viewed this outstanding outsider.

We also paid fairly regular trips together to the As You Like It. We usually made these visits after midnight, a last-minute idea after an evening at home. Jonathan would prepare carefully for these 'late swoops', emerging from his bedroom heavily scented with his shirt open and causing me to write in the notebook I now kept, 'Poor child, what will become of him?' In the café, he sketched the lively proprietor Barrie Stacey on a napkin – 'Keep still, you bastard!' – and cast a haughty eye on other customers. Of a subsequently successful singer named Al Stewart, he remarked, 'He hasn't eaten properly for over a year, he's just eaten coffees,' and of a newspaper worker engrossed in a copy of the next day's paper, he murmured, 'He's reading *every line*. Which takes some doing. It's probably an article on Russian archaeology. He might as well read it. Why not?' Looking back, I realise the café's regulars made distinctions between the two of us. I recall the occasional reproofs I received from the proprietor – 'You're mad! As mad as a hatter!' – and being set upon by an actress girlfriend of the comedian Tommy Deane, 'You're a great big bullshitter,' she screamed at me. 'You're typical of everything I can't stand. Pseudo-Chelsea! You're so rude. What gives you the right to write things down in your notebook?' Then came the complicated bit. 'I like your brother much more than you. He's charming.'

In spite of such verbal assaults I remained optimistic and arrogant, and was perpetually bucked up by what camaraderie Jonathan still offered, and by my growing respect for his writings and drawings, irritated though I sometimes was by the squeak of his pen on paper from the other room at Lennox Gardens, and offended though I was by the fact that he showed no interest whatsoever in the novel I had begun writing, never asking to read even a page of it.

Our weekend trips to Turleigh Combe, or Turig as we still called it, were another shared experience, though here again I was often aware of my father's preference for Jonathan's company. More than once my father would draw my younger brother into his study and close the door in my face. My father's respect for the practical, semi-manual life Jonathan led at Claridge's was balanced against his suspicion of my semi-intellectual postures. He often accused me of what he called 'Clifton/BBC responses' and when he found I'd left a copy of Freud's *Interpretation of Dreams* in the drawing room – I took a greater interest in such books than Jonathan did – he removed it and put it beside my bed. But grim and restless though my father was – 'Father's doing a Slow Mile downstairs,' Jonathan commented one night as we settled into our shared back bedroom – we had by this time begun to have a certain respect for his quirkiness, his wry sense of humour and originality. Crossing the road on one of their shared outings in London, Jonathan had reported that our father was as 'proud as a peacock', and the time would soon come for Jonathan to pronounce him as 'a concealed yapping genius'.

Our mother has not featured enough in this narrative. She was, I suppose, as passive as my father was active. 'Live and let live is my motto,' she had once declared. She focused on domestic life, still worried about her hens, and when I made pretentious statements about the *Mona Lisa*, boldly retorted, 'I've never liked the *Mona Lisa* very much.' Jonathan had also failed, quite literally, to get through to her. After tapping on the bathroom door one night, he announced: 'Mother was asleep in the bath. *Absolutely sound asleep.*'

And of course the dogs were still a formidable presence

and influence on the scene. Gilda was still fat and greedy and naughty and had outlived, as some dogs do, several of her descendants. By now she was halfway to becoming the fictional 'sociologist and dog of letters' and the inspiration for innumerable speculations by Jonathan. In one piece from this time, he even plans her funeral. Echoing the words that Dr Harland Rees had used three years earlier, he states, 'I have gone over this fairly thoroughly with her,' and then plunges into graphic details: 'Mr Deakin of Windsor and Price has already built the coffin. It is about 3 feet long and is extremely elegant. We had a trial run yesterday. Gilda said it couldn't have been a better fit.' He also raises the question of a memorial service. Our mother thinks this 'rather silly' but has insisted that Pebble, 'the tabby cat who used to be such a pal of Gilda before she married and went off to live in New Zealand,' should be invited to the funeral. He ends this fantasy by saying that, although Gilda is currently 'extremely fit, and couldn't be in better spirits', he feels it's a good thing to plan ahead.

Another much longer piece, reliving Gilda's visit to London the previous October, and the time he claimed she had spent in police custody, is a vehicle for all sorts of other material close to Jonathan's heart:

I moved into a bedsitting room in Chelsea last March. The man showed me up. Unfortunately I was taken ill during my first night there. The man came up the next morning. He saw what I had done. So he showed me down. Ten minutes later I was out on the Embankment with nowhere to go. I rang up Mum from a callbox. I asked her if she would send up our black-and-tan dachshund, Gilda. She would be company in wet London.

Mum said she would put her on the 11.30. I got to Paddington with a few minutes to spare. There was some trouble on the platform. A man had gone berserk. Three transport police were holding him down. I asked if I could help. Apparently he had come from Bridgwater that morning.

I could not find Gilda in the luggage place. A friendly porter said she was with the police. I went up and knocked on the section house door. It flew open and a cross sergeant asked me what my business was. I said I had come to collect Gilda. He began to get very angry and pointed at a sort of packing case. 'There she is', said the rude policeman. I looked at the box and I realized at once that poor Gili was in trouble. She was hand-cuffed about her paws and in a straight-jacket. I looked in the charge-book (while the cross policeman was out getting tea) and saw that my dog had been arrested when she came off the train. I calmed her with chocolates and she told me everything. Apparently she had gone along to the WC somewhere near Didcot. She wanted to have a shave before she got to London. Anyhow she was shaving away when there was a tap on the door. It was the ticket-collector. AND GILDA HAD <u>NO</u> TICKET! Silly Mum forgot to buy her one. And worse still she had been in a first-class carriage. She lied and said she was second-class but the guard checked. He found a compartment that was obviously hers. There was muck and make-up stuff everywhere. She had had an accident on one of the seats and had made pathetic attempts to sponge it off.

I scolded her in the taxi. There was a £25 fine. I remember it well – that journey. It was a wet October morning. Gilda sat on my lap. She looked round and seemed pleased to be back in London. 'That building's gone up quickly' she said. A policeman was being sick in Bayswater Rd. (Seldom seen nowadays). I saw my old headmaster in Mayfair. He was beaten up by 14 thugs. We went into the 'Chelsea Potter.' I was hungry and had a steak sandwich. A man tried to buy Gilda a drink. She asked for a pint. The barman passed it over. I got angry, 'Look, don't be such a fucking idiot. My dog wants a proper floor-level drinking dish. She won't enjoy the bitter out of that.' I was absolutely furious. Now the barman was yelling, 'That dog ought to be in a fucking zoo.' Gilda, a sensitive creature, immediately burst into tears. The barman said, 'Ah! Now the bugger's blubbin'.' Oh dear what a cruel world this is. I tried to comfort Gilda.

The story tails off at this point but is interesting as a precursor of *The Queue* for the savage reference to the Head Master, and other pointed material. The reference to a female dog having a shave is doubly grotesque, and the description of Gilda as 'black and tan' when she was a pure brown colour is typically subversive.

While Jonathan retreated into fantasy, my father remained tenaciously practical and money-minded. During the summer of 1967 he saw the fulfilment of a long-laid plan that, partly to help with Turleigh Combe's running costs, our surviving grandmother, born when Disraeli was prime minister, should abandon her house in Cumberland and come and live with us in Wiltshire as a paying guest. Need I add that Jonathan quickly seized upon the comic aspects of the situation? Within days of her arrival, he was murmuring, 'Granny in drag would make Hitchcock blanch', and during Sunday lunch slipped me a pencil-written note: 'Granny has just put a biscuit in her left hand pocket. It could be the sign of a kleptomaniac.' And when my grandmother elicited an indignant response from me by asking if I was still trying to find work as a comedian, Jonathan muttered in a corner, '*OK, so she goofed. Forget it.*'

With our grandmother came the picture captioned 'By an Unknown Painter of the Latter Part of the Ming Period' and her old maid Barbara Borrowdale, a character with crudely cut hair, whom it amused Jonathan to present as a genius. Left alone in Cumberland was Aunt Jean, who had now moved to a cottage of her own on family land near Carlisle. Here Jonathan and I soon paid her a weekend visit and got a refreshing dose of primeval country life. Our aunt's new home was surrounded by the noises of calves, cows and bullocks – she later kept hens in her small garden – and during the course of the weekend we also relived childhood experiences of walking up a local fell known as Cardonnock Pike, many yards apart from each other, stumbling across shale and bracken. After witnessing a rather ferocious discussion between me and our headstrong aunt, Jonathan commented 'You could argue with Jean for a million years over the most obvious point.'

Throughout the summer of 1967, I struggled away at my job in the London Press Exchange and Jonathan soldiered on at Claridge's. Though neither of us were particularly happy about our prospects, one good thing had come from my advertising job. I had made friends with a fellow copywriter. David Kaye was a would-be author like me and would indeed soon publish two novels, *The Australian* and *The Demise of a Poet*. I have no idea where David Kaye is today but in 1967 he became a regular caller at Lennox Gardens, where he observed us closely – he soon claimed that Jonathan drove his little grey van as if he was 'taking a pig to market' – and flattered us by confessing 'I can only get on with sick people,' and then qualified this remark by adding, 'I don't mean crazy.' He was also an immediate cultural influence on us. He talked of Ozenfant, Rimbaud, Verlaine and Man Ray. He was enthusiastic about my brother's macabre drawings, especially one Jonathan had called 'The Train Accident', and encouraged us to see a film called *Freaks* by Tod Browning, which ends, if I remember rightly, with a half hen/half man being paraded in a circus ring.

David Kaye had his own life in London, and one Saturday in September 1967 had called at the Obelisk Gallery in Crawford Street, off Baker Street. The Obelisk specialised in surrealist works and was run by a robust, heavy-drinking queer called Jimmy McMullan. David had been sufficiently impressed by the paintings and objects on display to suggest that Jonathan should show his pictures to the gallery's proprietor. On Monday, 25 September, Jonathan telephoned McMullan, and was delighted and impressed by the generous response. '*How about right now?*' Within hours or minutes, McMullan had more or less dismissed the work but taken a great liking to Jonathan himself. The following evening Jonathan went to dinner at McMullan's flat round the corner at 6 Porter Street, and did not return that night to Lennox Gardens or contact me the next day.

I have no idea what happened between Jonathan and McMullan. Nor do I care. But at the time I was rattled by this development, not at all satisfied by his explanation – 'Because I like him' – and even said preachily, 'Your friendship with him seems utterly alien to your best interests.' David Kaye was equally indignant about this turn of events and said of the art dealer, 'That man has no interest whatsoever – except sexual. He's a very sick man who needs to have people around him, telephones ringing . . .' But is it surprising that, within a few days, I would become as fascinated by McMullan as Jonathan was? And that, in due course, Jonathan would excite this interest further by doing a drawing of his new friend completely drunk on the floor of his gallery and by writing about the 'thick grey, winter-weight suit' he was wearing, his 'polished up crocodile shoes', 'tie with large oval white spots on a navy blue background', and 'very clean hair slightly oiled and brushed up at the back'.★

Meanwhile, with some encouragement and advice from me, Jonathan had decided to try to get a job in advertising and to do so, partly to avoid confusion with me, under the name Jonathan Head. On 6 September 1967, a few weeks before the McMullan debacle, he had attended an interview with a woman with the curious name Julian Orde at an agency called Ogilvy & Mather, whose offices were off the Strand. Here is his own description of this momentous day:

> I was early. So I walked out on to Waterloo Bridge. I looked back at Brettenham House and wondered if I would ever go to work there. It was built when my Father was a boy. He remembers when it went up. He was working at Somerset House then. I went out halfway across the bridge. I looked over onto the Thames. Then I walked back into the Strand, or rather Lancaster Place. Ogilvy & Mather

★ Jonathan soon discovered that McMullan had once worked as a breakfast chef at The Sphinx Hotel, Leeds.

is difficult to find. I had parked on Savoy Hill and I expected to get a ticket. But it was worth it. I like arriving fresh for interviews. Supposing I had come here by bus or tube. The hot weather would have worn me out. I wore casual clothes on purpose. I didn't know till nearly four months later, when I was working in Julian's group and had time to poke through her files, that she had written a sort of comment on top of her interview report. 'Mr Head had very heavy brogue shoes that looked terribly old-fashioned but suited him . . .' My brother had been to an interview with a man named Maurice Smelt at Ogilvys about a year ago. He warned me to get the right way in. I found the lift and pressed the 4th floor button. This stopped on the Creative Reception. I told the woman on the desk that I had arrived and she rang Miss Orde. I was already doubtful – there was rather an annoying atmosphere in the place. I saw the Savoy through the window of someone's office. I wished I was in there. My interview for the job that I had held over there was so different. Miss Orde's secretary came up and led me past little cheap four-ply doors with writers' names on them. She led me into Miss Orde's office. I was surprised. Here was a smart little woman – like a proud cock. Her hair short like a man and very lacquered and tinted. She had funny clothes which I remembered well. She said 'I'm Julian Orde. Now you are Jonathan Head, aren't you. Oh, do sit down.'

It had taken me dozens of interviews and approaches to almost every major firm before I had secured my job in advertising.

All Jonathan needed to do was to complete a Copy Test – he later reported that Ogilvy's Deputy Chairman, Stanhope Shelton, had scrawled on it 'I detect quite outstanding ability' – before sailing into a job at this fashionable firm. On 13 October 1967, the offer was confirmed in writing. That night he dined with McMullan at 6 Porter Street and the following week he gave in his notice at Claridge's – 'You've always pulled your weight,' said the barman under whom he had worked for the last few months – and with very mixed feelings turned his back for ever on the hotel trade.

CHAPTER SIXTEEN

Office Life

During the morning I suddenly realize that my
pants are back to front. I correct them but Jean,
the typist, comes in just as my trousers are down.
She thinks I am abusing myself and leaves the room.

Rats, 1969

ON THE MORNING of Monday 6 November 1967, my brother
made his way from Lennox Gardens to Brettenham House,
hard by Waterloo Bridge, to start his job as an advertising
copywriter. Now twenty years old, this was his first experience of office life, conversations in lifts and secretaries'
peccadilloes. Soon he was talking about a typist at Ogilvy
& Mather who ate fish and chips at her typewriter – 'She
even gets batter under the rotating spindle' – and soon the
whole agency had become a part of our shared private world.

In *The Queue,* the only direct reference to office life
comes in the form of a remark in the lift at the Home for
Imbeciles – 'Could you press 5 please' – but in his other
writings there are many echoes of the corporate existence.
His first *London Magazine* story, published two years later, also
uses 'Could you press 5 please', adds the words 'Thank you'
and throws in other bits of office chatter like 'Thank God
it's Friday,' 'Well – have a nice weekend' and 'Nice weekend?
You must try to get in earlier.' Then comes the paragraph

quoted above. And the story also ends in an office – or rather with the narrator's dismissal from one: 'A slip of paper is pinned on the typewriter. I read it and am speechless. For I, along with four other middle-management men, have been dismissed. I am to leave immediately with one month's pay.' Stunned and ashamed, our hero takes the lift down for the last time. Out in the street he realises he has left his office hairbrush in his desk.

Is it worth pointing out that a junior copywriter is not a 'middle-management man' and that Ogilvy & Mather was quite a lively and liberal place with unusual people working in its creative department, some of whom, like Jonathan Gathorne-Hardy and Fay Weldon, would go on to greater things? It was anyway now Jonathan's established practice to make his life sound as amusing as possible – and he had a great deal to say during those first few months about the 'lacquered and tinted' Julian Orde, with whom he would share an office for most of his time at the firm. Some of their dealings were factual and flat, like the following telephone conversation:

Orde: Oh – er is that you Jonathan?
Head: Yes . . . it's me.
Orde: Look . . . Jonathan. I've got a mildish
  stomach upset I can't possibly come in
  today. Think I had some rather 'off' duck
  pâté last night. Would you tell Tony?
Head: Yes I will. I hope you feel . . .
Orde: I don't think it's anything more than a
  mild attack. There's some awfully good new
  stuff called Gromoxon which my awfully
  helpful chemist says is far better than
  Kaolin.

He also repeated – largely for my benefit – an even more banal conversation with Miss Orde about steamed puddings. Egged on by me, Jonathan had asked his supervisor if she liked this form of dessert. 'Very much indeed,' she had replied, and then described a special recipe she knew. 'No flour – and you bake it in a very slow oven. It's got a delicious chocolatey taste. My family love it. In fact it shouldn't go in the oven but I misread the recipe when I first read it.'

The following spring, Jonathan would attempt to show how little actual work Julian Orde did; how much she depended on coffee, drinks and private calls. In carefully recording his colleague's timetable for Friday, 1 March 1968, I imagine he was once again trying to amuse me:

9.50 a.m.	Came in – went to Ladies for 10 minutes.
10.00 a.m.	Came back – cigarette – looked through her address book.
10.05 a.m.	Made four telephone calls trying to fix a supper party.
10.15 a.m.	Went out to some other office – saw her walk past the door.
10.30 a.m.	She interviewed somebody for half an hour.
11.00 a.m.	Wrote a report on the applicant.
11.15 a.m.	Made coffee. Drank it for 15 minutes. Another cigarette.
11.30 a.m.	Somebody rang her from outside – long conversation.
12.00 noon	Rang Barnards for a hair appointment.
12.01 p.m.	Went into another office for a chat. Saw her with more coffee.

12.08 p.m.	Went up to see Ellerington about Worthington. Came down and wrote a verse for the pub sequence.
12.30 p.m.	Took vanity bag from drawer – washed in the Ladies. Went out for lunch with JGH.
2.15 p.m.	Returned from lunch – read a book for a bit.
2.25 p.m.	Dispatch brought in Ad–Weekly – she read it cover/cover.
2.50 p.m.	Eve Smith came in – both went out to Henekeys for a drink.
3.00 p.m.	Returned and sat in her office doing nothing.
3.04 p.m.	Rang the vet about her cat.
3.06 p.m.	Went to a Shell meeting then went on to Shell Centre with some executives to see a film about research in Africa.
4.30 p.m.	Returned and read a book.
4.50 p.m.	Read through some stuff on ICI fibres.
5.10 p.m.	Got ready to go.
5.20 p.m.	Left 'Have a nice week-end.'

Ellerington was the firm's creative director and Julian Orde's lunch companion on this busy day was Jonathan Gathorne-Hardy, who was then in his early thirties, already the author of two novels and working at the firm part-time. A close friendship soon blossomed between him and my brother who would regale me with Gathorne-Hardy 'material', not least the claim that his colleague wore the same green suit every day.

A more fanciful piece from this period starts with Jonathan blowing what he describes as his 'first audible fart' in the office and then trying to 'imitate and disguise' the sound by biffing the underside of his desk with a big book. Julian Orde immediately realises what he's doing and laughs. He then launches into a long account of Julian herself farting, with unexpected consequences. 'There was this awful bulge in her stocking. Do you get me? The wind from the fart had floundered into the mesh of her stockings and created a bubble.' Hours later he sees his colleague crouching in reception trying to kick out the fart but it just rolls up and down. Weeks later it is still there. 'Every day I say, "Julian, can I prick your fart?" But she won't let me and it just sticks there rolling up and down like a spirit level.'

Ogilvy & Mather gave Jonathan much more than the mild embarrassments of office life – and the opportunity to fantasise about them. Thanks to his new job, he became better acquainted with an area of the West End he hitherto only knew in the context of the Savoy Hotel. In his *London Magazine* stories, he would mention the Strand Palace Hotel, the Charing Cross Hospital, Adam Street and, of course, Bow Street. The Magistrates' Court was only a few minutes' walk from the office and Jonathan was soon sneaking off to sit on its public benches. Here he picked up a whole vision of humanity, crime and punishment. The hurly-burly of the Magistrates' Court, the coolness or otherwise of the presiding magistrate, the rapid entrances and exits of the defendants and the relative pettiness of their alleged crimes translates even better into comic material than the slow-moving grav- itas of the Old Bailey, or High Court, and the language of the police court dovetailed effortlessly into Jonathan's own voice.

It may have also been at Bow Street that Jonathan got

the idea of the multi-consonanted names mentioned earlier. In the Magistrates' Court scene at the beginning of *The Queue,* defendants include H. L. Kinne who has been found drunk and disorderly in the Strand – 'staggering along the footrailing, shouting fuck off, fuck off to passers-by' – and B. C. Nanne, found exposing himself in a public latrine in Pont Street. Nanne, we're told, earns £6,000 a year as a stockbroker and receives some firm words from the bench: 'You must learn to behave yourself in public. Don't let it happen again. £55 or one month.' In a typical flash-forward, Jonathan adds, 'That night Nanne threw himself from a window in his Cheyne Row mansion block. Dead on arrival.' Finally M. L. Quasse, found pissing from the upper circle at Wyndham's Theatre, is brought into court. 'A revolting crime. You must go to prison for 16 months.'

Many of the Bow Street crimes were probably more run-of-the-mill than the above but even minor traffic cases threw up phrases like 'collision course' which Jonathan seized upon gleefully, and later employed in *The Queue.* The magistrates themselves come in all shapes and sizes. The first paragraph of his first story in the *London Magazine* ends with a Bow Street beak telling the defendant he can go home: 'Allright. Allright you can go home now. Go and see the gaoler. Go home now. You can go home now.' Others are more vicious. 'Never in my 49 years as Head Magistrate have I heard such a despicable charge,' declares a Head Master-like figure in *The Queue.* 'It is odious, unspeakable and so vile that I intend to punish you personally.' And some of these officials are themselves drunken, vomiting, joke figures, soiling their clothes. But there are also tender touches. In an early court scene in *The Queue,* a gaoler listens to 'Woman's Hour' and takes down a recipe. The final court scene is refreshingly gentle and offers some sort of absolution after what has gone before. In the book's penultimate paragraph a normally brutal court attendant is described as 'visibly upset' and even 'takes a napkin to wipe his eyes'.

Jonathan's visits to Bow Street also increased his general worldliness. This was a time of celebrity court cases. Pop stars were often being had up on minor drug offences: Mick Jagger and Keith Richards had been acquitted on such charges the previous summer and their colleague Brian Jones would soon be told by a magistrate, 'You really must watch your step.' Jonathan would watch stars of this calibre being defended by the showbiz solicitor David Jacobs – he quickly added this smooth individual to his gallery of characters – and he would also be present at Bow Street on 10 May 1968 when the Kray Twins and their henchmen appeared to answer charges of murder. Jonathan would waste no time in telephoning me at my own office to describe the gangsters' immaculate blue suits.

Our life together at Lennox Gardens had meanwhile continued along more jerky lines. We had become increasingly disenchanted by the flat, and by the noises from within and without the building. One evening I heard a dog barking its head off and a voice saying 'I'm going to ring the police. They ought to be prosecuted.' I noted the splatter of rain on the kitchen roof and the sounds – or lack of sounds – from Jonathan's room. Then there might come a sudden sneeze. There were still tensions between us. While I scattered clothes about, my brother remained prim and tidy, taking forty minutes to wash and then pampering himself with a hot water bottle. But there were also the rewards of his cooking. Though he was now out of the hotel world for good, he still produced magnificent and ambitious food. Was it at this time he cooked *Bass Regence* and *Cauliflower Colette*?

And what about our visitors? David Kaye remained in attendance with his wife Lise who had now arrived from Rome. When a friend of mine, Diana Birkbeck, was more than forty minutes late for Sunday lunch, Jonathan remarked gloomily, 'Diana arrives five years late and finds two skeletons and the skeleton of a loin of beef.'

Some of our shared interests were harmless enough. One day Jonathan announced a '32 Lennox Gardens General Knowledge Test' and asked me to name the dog that lived upstairs. Pat. We also watched with mixed emotions the growing success of Mike d'Abo who in January 1968 had had his first number one hit, 'Mighty Quinn'. And in February 1968, we were thoroughly bemused by the news from our brother Martin, now working in Tokyo, that he was going to marry a Japanese girl. Other preoccupations were much darker. One evening in March 1968, I found Sloane Square underground station closed after a suicide, and telephoned Jonathan immediately at Lennox Gardens. He appeared on the scene within minutes and together we watched the arrival of a vast red truck marked 'LT URGENT'. And then saw a stretcher being carried from the station bearing the misshapen body of the victim. The following morning, Jonathan went to work from the same station and, when I asked if there was any evidence of the incident, replied, 'A little telltale sand. That's all.' He would later write to the London Transport Board asking about suicide statistics on the Underground and his incorporation of this incident, and the ominous red truck, into his first *London Magazine* story shows how hard it had hit him.

Such events – and interests – diverted me from my own growing problems in several spheres. Compared with Ogilvy & Mather, or Jonathan's picture of it, the London Press Exchange seemed dreary and second-rate and I now lived in constant fear of being sacked. Indeed, I had already been sidelined, demoted to writing pack copy and other menial tasks. It is true I had finished my novel — but it was now getting unqualified rejections from publishers like Jonathan Cape and Chatto & Windus. Attempts to participate in the Swinging Sixties — I had had a suit made at the fashionable Mr Fish — had also flopped. Unknown to Jonathan, though perhaps inspired by his telling me that I was on the road to madness, I had tried to put matters right by consulting two Hampstead psychoanalysts, one of whom, a lady in her sixties, had smoked a cigarette while gloomily pronouncing on my lack of self-knowledge.

This all sounds bad but I still had enough good times with Jonathan to sustain the myth that we were on a sort of magic carpet. Occasional visits to the As You Like It reminded me that there were others worse off than myself — one

The Hole in the Wall

lunchtime I found Jonathan there on his own, passively squeezed in between stagehands and out-of-work actresses – and we also investigated places like the cider house, known as the Hole in the Wall, below Waterloo Station, which was mainly patronised by tramps. On one such visit Jonathan suddenly muttered that we must leave immediately as one of the old gents was becoming too attentive.

We also returned faithfully to Turleigh Combe, paid our respects at the court of Queen Gilda, got our laundry done, noted our grandmother's deterioration, studied Barbara Borrowdale and went trotting or jumping down the hill to get drunk in the private bar at the Cross Guns in Avoncliff. Here is a long and fanciful account by Jonathan of a visit home around this time:

> Andrew got into the van. I left our flat last because I had some bread proving and didn't want it spoilt. The loaves were a gift for Mother who cannot make bread any longer since her fishing accident last Spring. We took the usual route home. There was a collision between two wagons on that long flat road near the Hook of Newbury – we were re-routed by Berkshire Police. There was a lot of traffic on the road and it was a slow run. But we were in Winsley by 6 o'clock. I noticed fresh laurel trimmings on the drive so I drove slow. GEB would be around with his new Wilkinson Sword. Walking up and down the drive snapping at bits here and there. It turned out that he wasn't there. As I did a circle turn in the forecourt I thought I saw his large shape against some trees but it was the water trough. We took out our stuff and opened the front door. The light in the dining room was on and the

supper was laid. Two places so I suppose the others had already eaten. The food was out too. Cold beef brisket, boiled by Barbara that afternoon. Still slightly tepid. It was very salt. So Andrew went into the harness room and got two bottles of beer. Barbara had made a salad. It was a little known Cumberland one – all greens, with herbs from Mother's garden. Carelessly garnished with haphazard dressings made from cheap olive oil. I find it difficult to understand why there was no more food. I could have done with a trifle and I know that Andrew could. He eyed some cheese on the sideboard. But telltale tooth marks warned me that the dachshund probably had been at it. Wretched little dog. She was overgrown and had a poor background. I think she had been cruelly treated by the people who brought her up for now she is rude and snappish. She is called Gilda which is an excellent name. She was in the dining room in fact. Curled before the heater in her number 2 pose. That is the one like a warped log. She has eight other poses. But I have only seen three. Mother has seen them all but one. Of course we were still awfully hungry. We had both seen the tin, round tray on the hotplate. Two cups and there was the Gold Blend. And the greasy thermos jug. It keeps hot water at fridge temperatures. Which is why our parents can't even drink mildly hot coffee when they dine out. They are not accustomed to it – it burns our lips they say. Well we poured out a cup each and put it down. It is quite good in fact. Better than one expects. Though nothing like our lovely Harrods No. 4 that we brew in a yellow coffee bar kitchen in our flat at the oval Lennox Gardens. We really know and appreciate coffee not like our parents who don't care about things. Andrew once bought a lovely burnt Italian blend at the Saverino Parmian in Old Compton Street.

After dinner there was still no sign of anyone so Andrew suggested the Cross Guns. Down we went immediately across the fields. After six pints of dank Trowbridge bitter we talked openly about family matters while we sat at the glossy green bench end table under the elm tree with the coloured lights that you see from the trains. On the way back we talked of 'Dutch Courage' and other matters. I heard Father on the back steps. He shouted at nothing. Though he heard us and was a little frightened knowing him. He clattered about with a dustbin and I heard him break a port bottle. He isn't an impressive man always putting out cases of empty spirit bottles for refuse collection. I should think he drinks about half a bottle of spirits every year. If that. And then off big spenders like the Buxtons and the Bartholomews.

He did annoying sort of usherette movements to get us into (and back into) his house. He made quite a funny remark about the Cross Guns. He didn't come all the way into the house – he seemed to drop off somewhere near the Potterton. He continually fiddles with that boiler. Always altering knobs on it – like an anaesthetist during an important operation. We found that Mother and Granny were in the drawing room. I think they had been there all the time, listening quietly to a concert on

the Third. I should say that Granny dropped off
several times during the piece. She said hello boys.
Lovely to see you. You're in the end room. Johnny's
next to me. Have some Gold Blend – quite honestly,
it's just not worth the bother, brewing proper coffee.
Yes, but Mummy, it's a bit much when we have
GOLD BLEND on Christmas Day. And tinned
orange juice. Could you throw your washing down.
I find Frend's awfully good for cuffs. (A day later
– Oh Andrew's blasted cuff is grubby.)

Like all his writings, this story contains echoes of other
voices, other speech patterns and vocabularies, and switches
in and out of these without the use of inverted commas.
The fact that, once again, it was written to amuse me and
not for publication is not the only evidence of the surviving
bond between us. On 10 April Jonathan celebrated his
twenty-first birthday with me and a lively Old Harrovian
friend, Jim Vakeel – why haven't I mentioned him before?
– at Bloom's restaurant in the East End, and one weekend
at the end of that month Jonathan and I suddenly decided,
within fifteen seconds, to go to Paris for the night. It was
my first trip abroad for four years and the only foreign trip
that he and I ever made together. We travelled without suitcases of any sort and very little money. Jonathan carried a
folding hairbrush which I borrowed. At Victoria Station he
strolled around, I noted, like a man at a point-to-point.
When our train eventually approached its destination,
Jonathan dramatised the issue by fantasising: 'There's been
a terrible train crash in Paris. All dead.' We stayed that night,
27 April 1968, in a big tall room in the Hotel du Pax in
the Rue St André des Arts and my first visit to Paris ended
the following lunchtime when we took the Flèche d'Or

back to Calais. During the return journey, Jonathan was reprimanded by a railway official for using the first-class

toilet. Opening the door to what he described as violent knocking, he found a small privileged boy waiting to use the facilities.

The next shared experience was the visit Jonathan and I paid to an old writer called Stephen Graham who lived in Frith Street, Soho. I had long owned a book by this man, *London Nights*, published in 1925, and finding the author was alive and his name in the telephone book, had called on him one lunchtime and been welcomed into his drawing room. A few days later I took Jonathan here. Discovering such 'characters' was a sport we had shared since childhood. Recently, I had 'notched up' Quentin Crisp, whose book *The Naked Civil Servant* had been in the bestseller lists earlier that year. Jonathan's latest recruits were Jimmy McMullan, the showbiz solicitor David Jacobs and all those figures at Ogilvy & Mather. As we know, Jonathan made a point of making his colleagues sound more amusing, far-fetched and larger-than-life than my own workmates. Perhaps he was simply more generous than me. He had already 'built up' my colleague David Kaye by referring to his 'Somerset Maugham trousers' and shown an immediate interest in a young, bald-headed copywriter in my firm called Guy Hungerford, nicknaming him 'The Stage Solicitor'.*

This was all good fun but there was much about Jonathan's life he did not share, or at least embarked upon without consulting me. I remember his interest in an American book called *Health Via Food* by William Howard Hay and I see from his diary that under the guidance of this book, he had started a fast on 8 January 1968 which had run for several days. Inspired by the same manual, he had also given himself an enema. This revelation may be of interest to psychologists or others interested in the jubilantly scato-logical content of his writings, but I do not know how successful the experiment was. It took place in my absence at Lennox Gardens and Jonathan told me later he had taken the precaution of stretching the telephone as close as possible to the lavatory in case he needed to call the emergency services.

And then of course there was his so-called 'private life', his independent social activities. Since leaving Claridge's his freelance bar work had ceased. From his engagement diaries, I see he had dates with dozens of different girls, among them Bridget Doyne, Angela Fulford, Margaret de Pelet, Caroline Richardson, Sara Pilkington, Peanuts and 'Ro'. Back in December 1967, he had attended a Cowdray wedding, and his fast notwithstanding, had begun the New Year with a mass of lunches and dinners. On 27 February 1968, he had

* Guy Hungerford did indeed go on to become a lawyer and now sits as a part-time judge in the Crown Court.

met up with Andrew Leeman★ at the hotel school and two days later he had lunch with another fellow student, Jon Callow, at the Cole Hole in the Strand. On Saturday, 20 April, he had a dinner date with Jimmy McMullan. In the early summer of 1968 the new name of Rebecca Pretyman often appears. I do not know what these entries mean or how thoroughly he kept his diary. Perhaps the 'Names and Addresses' section at the back is the most interesting bit of these books, or the drawings he scribbled in them, the mysterious underlinings, the different colours of ink, the faded pencil entries.

I suppose he was, to some extent, playing the field. I am sure he slept with some of these girls and I know he spent at least the one mysterious night with McMullan. He also began to show his writings and drawings to some of these people. Encouraged by me, he had even submitted two pictures to the Royal Academy Summer Exhibition of 1968 and had them flatly rejected – and had then done a drawing of the pictures being carried past the horrified selection committee.

Was I still his principal admirer? Was I deluded about his talents? The readers of this book will by now have seen enough of his work to make up their own mind. The fact that I have quoted so much of his writings and mentioned his drawings so often must imply that I believe these things to have some value. Certainly Jonathan knew how much I admired and enjoyed his artistic efforts. Were they still too much of an 'in' joke? And what, I sometimes wonder, does it tell you about me, that I find even some of the grimmest, most tasteless descriptions in *The Queue,* like

★ Andrew Leeman (d. 2007) later became the head waiter at Langan's Brasserie and went on to become one of England's most successful hoteliers and restaurateurs.

the hospital on fire, or events in the sewer, almost trans-
fixingly funny?

During our last few months in that gimcrack flat in Lennox
Gardens – it was now the early summer of 1968 – Jonathan
completed a number of longer pieces which once again
seemed to be written entirely for his and my private pleasure,
with no thought of their literary worth. Versions of these,
and many of the actual original phrases eventually found
their way into *The Queue*. He wrote about taking a certain
Jane Rudde out to dinner and being violently sick on the
nice pink tablecloth. He wrote about going pub crawling
with Ogilvy & Mather's vice-chairman and the evening
ending in the sort of sexual scene that occurs so often in
The Queue. A fight starts and the vice-chairman exposes his
crutch. 'I saw it all,' he tells us excitedly. 'NO PANTS! Instead,
a curious sort of silk cape was sewn into his trousers.'
    He wrote about opening a dirty bookshop which was
another idea he developed in *The Queue*. He wrote about
rats taking over his Chelsea flatlet – 'I <u>know</u> it sounds mad
but all of this is gospel' – and goes to town describing their
clothes. One rodent, he tells us, wears a miniskirt. Another
is dressed in an odd pair of crêpe skiing tights, which remind
him of the 'trouserings' worn by the film director Val Guest
whom, several years earlier, we had watched making a film
in Bath. A third rat wears a tracksuit 'like Frampton's' –
further evidence of how he kept prep-school names on the
boil. He also produced early versions of those unseemly incidents on the Underground which later find their way into
his book – a man vomiting and shitting at the same time –
and above all, of course, he fantasises about Gilda's final days,
and the idea that she might spend these in London.
    In one such piece, he pretends that our grandmother

has died – in fact she would outlive Jonathan by two years – and that Turleigh Combe had been sold and our parents moved to a council flat. And that all the dogs, except Gilda, had been killed in a terrible accident in the village. What, he wonders, was to become of old Gilda, still pegging on but banned from our parents' new home by council by-law? 'Only one thing,' he replies. 'She could come to London and live with us.'

They put her on the Bristolian and it came into Paddington at half past six. We parked the Escort in a bay and went to 'Luggage' to find her. Mother had packed her up splendidly – lots of woollens and some rag bag clothes . . . She appeared relaxed and cheerful. Of course she had been to London before. I lodged her for a week when I was at hotel school in Pimlico. So she's no stranger. I think she had pissed badly on the journey – her dressings smelt acrid, like an old stable. We picked her up and a lot of the sawdust shavings came away with her. I reckon she had crapped on the way up too. She needed a good wash down – but that could wait! We sped her to Lennox Gardens in the van. She bit Andrew which was not a good start. We had fixed bedding for her in the kitchen. The immediate thing she did was to squat in the carpet and do a largish quantity of shit. I noticed a colour change already. A slight purple tint to it. Possibly due to diesel fumes from the train. She appeared ill at ease then. We called in Dr Lacutonpibiti. He came in ten minutes, put Gilda on our kitchen worktop and gave her the most almighty enema. The things that came out. She certainly looked a lot thinner. She stank. Really bad – Andrew suggested putting her in the lavatory overnight. I went round to United Dairies and bought a large Domestos and together we gave her probably the heaviest scrub down she's ever had. Now she's clean, bright, even more intelligent and ready to have some fun.

That was all last Spring. Now she's a real London dog. She's even better than she was at Turleigh. She eats Mick now, a Mather's account. Two tins daily. Andrew once put a bottle of Tabasco in her dinner to kid her. She was so cross she bit Andrew during the night, her molars went right through. All part of the fun. And the glorious tricks she learnt. New ones, not those smutty Turleigh things. We reared her all over again. Eradicating her country ways yet keeping her sweet nature. Things like barking completely stopped. We bought a device called a fortubountonop, which is a kind of halter. She soon learnt. Though we kept her barking at some things. When we were out during the day, she would guard our place. Once the caretaker came in without a permit. Gilda flew at her battering the woman against the door. I under-stood she broke something.

Those must have been the happiest days of her life. That time at Lennox Gdns. Of course it had to end. We noticed that she ailed during the winter. I know she always ate too much. Now she was ravenously hungry. She would open fridge doors to get at stuff. Cod fries, milk, eggs, cheese, yoghurt. There was something wrong with her. We took her to Dr Lacutonpibiti who said that she was dying and that there was nothing we could do. We took her back to LG to spend the last few days quietly. One night Gilda woke Andrew to say she was worse. It was around 4 a.m. We both got out of bed and lit all the lights. This was a definite scare. We put her up on the yellow worktop. She was dull eyed and her flesh limp and toneless. She must have been moulting . Hairs came away from her neck. I picked her up and took her to my bed to comfort her. But while I was passing through the drawing room there was a little twist in my arms. I looked down and she was dead.

The expression 'drawing room' hugely flattered the sitting area between our two tiny bedrooms and on re-reading this piece I had to think twice what Jonathan meant by it. By May 1968, our dissatisfaction with Lennox Gardens knew no bounds. 'You couldn't give a party here,' Jonathan claimed. 'You couldn't even give a tea party here. It would be a mad hatter's tea party.' He then claimed that all our visitors had crossed the threshold overcome with mirth, holding their hips, shrieking and reeling.

Earlier that year, Jonathan had written me a memo headed 'THE PRICELESS AGONY OF GOING TO BED,' which referred to the flat's '4-ply walls' and the fact that I could hear every noise made by him and vice versa. He had outlined the various alternatives now open to us, which included finding another flat which this time would have 'castle-thick' walls or beating a bass drum and playing thunderous music all night so that we soon wouldn't notice those tiresome little noises that irritated us both, especially me.

By a lucky chance, the flat belonging to our brother Julian's studio at 33 Tite Street now suddenly became available. Julian still spent a lot of his time abroad and had decided that we would be better tenants of the place — easier to push around — than people he knew less well. We quickly snapped up this offer and agreed terms. With the end of Lennox Gardens in sight, Jonathan declared, 'Let's treat the place with a little respect these last few days.'

CHAPTER SEVENTEEN

Return to Tite Street

I had a homosexual affair with Lord Fuck at school
and know him well enough to telephone. Yes, that's
right. We're going to blast those fucking rooks to
pieces next weekend. I've got a big party coming.
There's Nick Shit, Lord 'Arsehole' Drew, Rory
Scott . . . bring a gun and join us. Come in time
for dinner.

The Queue, Chapter Nineteen

ON SATURDAY, 22 June 1968, Jonathan and I moved our
possessions from Lennox Gardens to Tite Street in a hired
van costing £4.11s. 0d. Dripping with sweat, we then carried
our beds, chairs, books and kitchen equipment up to the
second-floor flat below our brother's studio. I later heard the
empty van roaring up the street as Jonathan returned the
vehicle to its depot.

Our new home did not have 'castle-thick walls', at least
not in the Dacre Castle sense, but it was a great improvement
on our previous abode. A purpose-built flat in a purpose-
built block of artists' studios built in 1888, it was solidly
constructed – I particularly liked the brass door 'furniture'
– and had extremely glamorous associations. Augustus John
and John Sargent had both worked here and the ground-
floor studio and flat were now occupied by the fashionable

interior designer David Mlinaric, whose circle encompassed the Rolling Stones. Across the landing lived a painter called Guy Roddon who Jonathan soon pronounced was 'interested in everything' and had 'standards' – in other words had never worked in advertising. On the opposite side of the street was the labyrinthine mansion of the Hope-Nicholson family where Jonathan and I had lodged only fourteen months earlier. From the back of our building there was, and still is, a splendid view of the domes and turrets of Wren's Royal Hospital. And we were scarcely a minute's walk from the Thames, that tidal arm of the sea which would feature often in Jonathan's imagination.

In this semi-stronghold, we began the final stage of our shared domestic life.* In spite of the secure surroundings it was often a rough, uncomfortable ride. There were outside interferences or excitements, like the housekeeper in the basement telephoning early in the morning to say that Jonathan's bath was overflowing, and doorstep encounters with Mlinaric's white faced, drug-taking, velvet-dressed friends as they piled in and out of Rolls-Royces and other chauffeur-driven vehicles. Inside the flat there were the usual tensions between us. I heard Jonathan's kettle coming up to the boil and then battled with him over the one and only hot water bottle. '*Here she is!*' he said one night, flinging the disputed object onto my bed. There was also a cold war over a heavy brown overcoat which had once belonged to our father and which we both liked to use to supplement our blankets.

There were even tensions over food. Once or twice,

* Jonathan later claimed that one morning, soon after our return to Tite Street, we had put out an order for six hundred million pints of milk. 'The milkman just collapsed on the spot.'

Jonathan dampened my enthusiasm by saying, 'I'm not hungry.' And when I claimed the right to eat my share of some sausages he was cooking, he responded, 'Eat the lot. I'm not terribly keen on them.' In the FOOD AND RUNNING EXPENSES book which we had brought with us from Lennox Gardens, I see that Jonathan had responded to some petty entry on my part by charging me '1/28 d.' for a 'grain' of rice and added the phrase, 'Oh, Jesus wept.' And, as at Lennox Gardens, I noticed that my brother began to hide foodstuffs under his bed – oranges, eggs, apples and probably alcohol too – part of a pattern of self-preservation which showed in the way he tidied his room, told me my breath smelled and, after accusing me of listening to his private calls, argued in favour of the telephone extension being cut off.

"Mick Jagger" and chauffeur

On a more positive note, we set up two armchairs and our sofa beside the gas fire in the front room, where I also had my bed. Here, partly inspired by the 'settlements' our mother had perfected at Turig, we sometimes sat with drinks in our hands, or real coffee (from Harrods), and discussed exhilarating subjects, like the Rolling Stones and Richard

227

Burton and Elizabeth Taylor. Today, our respect for smiling film stars like Burton or Sean Connery seems slightly pathetic and indeed I have already noted how Jonathan's James Bond-ish smiles and slickness annoyed me at Lennox Gardens. But Jonathan would talk of such figures with a spoof or spurious authority which appealed to me immensely. Of the current Archbishop of Canterbury, he jokingly pronounced, 'The big thing about Dr Ramsey is that he is terribly bad tempered, waspish and intolerant.' And we also talked, often, about our past. About our father. And about Clifton College Preparatory School. One favourite line of questioning, or area of con-sideration, being the number of times per day, per week or per year each of us thought about certain figures from this distant time. 'Seriously though,' he began one evening, 'how often do you think about Frampton?'

Even today, I might answer such a question, 'Sur-prisingly often, at least twice a week', but in Jonathan's case, the answer must have been a great many more times. He carried Frampton, Hankey and other key formative, yard-stick personalities with him at all times and dipped into this well of exotic past associations at random with the confidence that his audience – me – would understand the reference.

We talked deliriously about life and its ultimate purpose, our goals and codes of behaviour. We avoided anything straightforward about sex but touched often on psychological matters. The confidence with which Jonathan seemed to accept that the healthiest people could suffer from what he called 'depressive fits', and his belief that it was almost an asset to display 'vulnerable strangeness' was a comfort to me at this time, feeling as I did both vulnerable and strange. Though only twenty-two, I was acutely aware of my failure as an advertising man and what I perceived to be Jonathan's growing success in the same field and, even though I some-times averted my eyes with a dull gaze, these fireside chats helped to redress the balance.

We also talked often and vaguely about 'creativity' and the virtues of a 'creative atmosphere'. Though Jonathan continued to show no interest in my writings — another area of failure — and indeed almost turned up his nose at them, he occasionally wished me well in this context. In a note, scribbled as he set off for some house party in the shires, leaving me alone at Tite Street, he wrote: 'Have a good, solid, creative weekend. Regards Jonathan.' At this stage and for a long while afterwards, I alas squandered most of my opportunities.

Not so Jonathan. Within seconds of returning to the flat he was in his room at work on his latest drawing. He never dawdled or was listless. I heard only his sniffs and the squeak of his pen. I remember he once worked through the night on a picture. I am less aware of his writing, I do not recall the tap of his typewriter and wonder if perhaps most of the things he showed me were done actually in his office.

The pieces he wrote at this time struck me then as works of genius. The topics he tackled were, by contrast, utterly down-to-earth — and domestic. Gilda, who had been around since he was eight years old, was still a source of inspiration and would, as we know, become an even greater one. At this time he was still preparing himself, as it were, for her death or disappearance from his life. Here is a curious rumination from this period set in an imaginary place:

I shall never know how Gilda ended her days.
One night, at the end of January, she asked to be let out for a little walk. I took her to the back door and gave her a little pat. I returned to

229

my room and saw her walk down the path and squeeze through the broad bit in the wrought iron. That was the last I saw of her. She never returned. I asked the same question everywhere. 'Have you seen my little brown dachshund. She answers to GILDA.'

Three months later I was still searching for her. Police Stations, advertisements, going to Club Row every Sunday, asking everybody in the street.

But no clues. She had vanished without trace.

There were innumerable false hopes. Many times there would be a knock on the door. I would go and open it, and there would be someone holding a dachshund and saying, 'I have just found her. Is she yours?'

I have really just about given up now. But I still lie awake at night wondering about her.

Other scribblings from this time are much odder, less rhapsodic. He was soon writing about finding a live coiled viper in a cigarette dispenser, and goes over the top describing the creature's terrible bad temper and the whoopee cushion sewn into its intestines. He also penned a one-page story entitled 'Panic by Thames River', which he bound in black. Drawing partly from both Tite Street and Ogilvy & Mather's proximity to the Embankment, he imagines the Thames completely dried up, 1,538,535 dead fish on the riverbed and a live vile beast with wings and claws flapping about, threatening people. He also notices, typically enough, 'sewer outlet pipes still excreting faeces and other ancient wreckage from Fleet Tunnel'. Then suddenly, the waters return and 629 men are drowned. End of story. Another tale began with the words, 'Evidence has cropped up that I am a mongrel,' and leads to a description of a special clinic in Switzerland for 'malformed critical cripples'. Closer to home, he describes returning to 33 Tite Street one day and finding jazz record sleeves scattered about, the fridge door open and – here we go again – a huge rat sitting cross-legged on the hearth rug. Later, he watches the intruder having a bath and observes its 'funny twist of pubics'. In another story, he crudely but accurately describes the ordeal of waiting in 'the fucking slow coach queue' at the local post office. All has gone well for a while then the line had got 'bunged up' by 'some bloody little 32 year old stupid fucking nuisance,' who wanted, 'oh I don't know, hundreds of different values of insurance stamp'.

During these early days at Tite Street, Jonathan wrote further stories to which he would return when he came to write *The Queue*, and sometimes lift whole phrases from. In one such piece he describes being picked up while hitch-hiking on the A35 by a homosexual Rolls-Royce driver. They are almost immediately involved in a road accident. The car goes into a rear-wheel spin, skids across two lanes and hits an oncoming British Shoes Corporation Truck. 'Hush-Puppies all over the road,' he tells us. 'The queer beside me dies on the way to hospital I'm afraid.' He then describes lying on a stretcher, the ting-tonging of an ambulance, the setting up of a plasma drip and a man saying, 'Jean, there's a lad lying down there. Don't let the children look.' Soon there are several junior police inspectors on the scene – peaked caps, brilliantly white shirts – one of whom asks, 'Is that lad dead?' Much of this scene and the final heart-rending question reappears near the beginning of *The Queue*, and this early encounter with an 'old queer' is replicated count-less times in the book.

Many of these pieces also contain semi-overheard remarks with no direct relevance to the story being told. For no reason in particular, the narrator states: 'I must write to the papers' and 'Could you book a table at Bianchi's? I haven't been there for donkey's years', and 'Someone will have to clear it up. Me I suppose. Can I have some Daz for that please.' By this stage, not only had he grasped the fun of such dialogue, he had also become aware of things like 'the black box flight recorder' and 'the tall man agency' and other oddly familiar phrases which he would insert into his narratives, sometimes at not particularly appropriate points. And, just occasionally, there were overt signs of the exuberant spirit in which he wrote. In one story, he describes a big 37654 'Hercules' hauling a train out of a station precinct. 'Whisstle!!! Puff! Puff! Puff! Puff! Chuff! Chuff! Chuff!' he writes, then, 'I am like a child really with all these silly noises but I love it all and wouldn't swap it for anything.'

Did a similar *joie de vivre* infect his social life during those early days at Tite Street? His engagement diary for the summer months of 1968 records dates with Rebecca, Caroline, Sara, Christina, Angela, Vicky, Margaret, Jane – and Rosemary. The most dominant name in this long list is Rebecca. He seems to have seen Rebecca Pretyman several days running during this period. Then, on Wednesday, 10 July, comes the entry, doubly circled and boxed in red ink, 'Rebecca The End.' I knew nothing of these dramas in Jonathan's life. His diary also has entries for the Matisse Exhibition, our grandmother's ninetieth birthday, an event at the V&A, and a date – perhaps I was present – with David Kaye. Much more significantly, in terms of his career as an artist, was a meeting on Saturday, 27 July, with – he spells the name wrong – 'John Singe.'

This was John Synge, a great-nephew of the playwright of that name and director of the Redfern Gallery in Cork Street, to whom, possibly on the advice of Jimmy McMullan, he had shown some of his drawings. According to Jonathan, McMullan's brash recipe for success as an artist was contained in his advice, 'Sleep with John Synge and spend all your time in the British Museum.' But at this particular time he was too preoccupied for either activity. On 29 July, Jonathan set off with Julian for a holiday in Italy. I remember watching our artist brother's coffee-coloured van rumble off up the street, savouring the atmosphere left by my departing siblings – the kettle was still hot, the gramophone still warm – and dwelling on the prospect of fourteen days alone at Tite Street. That night, I found a sealed envelope on my pillow marked 'To be opened in the event of my death.' I ignored this disquieting instruction, ripped it open and read the following message: 'In the event of my death. All pictures to go to my brother Andrew Barrow. July 29 1968. Jonathan Barrow.'

Jonathan started his Italian holiday by staying with his new friend Sara Pilkington at Pianone St Liberta near Grosseto on the Ligurian Coast. I have a photograph of him bent over his drawing board there, tousled head facing the camera, but he apparently left this romantic spot earlier than planned and linked up with Julian in Rome, where he had been given various names and addresses by McMullan. On 8 August, he sent me a huge postcard of Pope Paul at his desk in the Vatican and boasting, 'McMullan introductions have been to people of enormous importance – <u>almost</u> on the Cocteau, Henry Miller level . . . I met Jimmy Ernst – Max's son. He paints too.' And then reverting to his old style by adding, 'Remember that we both sell food for all tame animals,' and 'Could you please send me some Cash's name tapes.'

These private jokes were perhaps designed to fend off intimacy, and the stress on the 'enormous importance' of McMullan's friends was certainly an indication of Jonathan's

233

emerging snobbery. Among those he saw in Rome were a sculptor called Assen Peikov and an American artist known simply as Zev, who was indeed a friend of Henry Miller and lived alone in a remarkable studio attic in Trastevere. Though

Americans seeing Rome

McMullan had already introduced him to the artist Scottie Wilson in London, Jonathan knew none of these sort of characters in England.

Jonathan and Julian arrived back in London during the night of 12 August 1968. In his absence I had brightened up my life by wearing Jonathan's blue Billings and Edmunds suit to the office. I had also had a meeting with the psychiatrist Anthony Storr. I mention this because I still sought official confirmation that Jonathan and I were geniuses and I was foolish enough to imagine that the eminent shrink might be able to provide this sort of affirmation. Naturally enough Storr was having none of this and, with this crushing defeat on my mind, I set off from Victoria for a short holiday in the South of France. I travelled first class, armed with a simple sketch map of Cannes, provided by Jonathan, along with the phrases I needed to book a room. It was a self-indulgent and rather miserable holiday, the only excitement being my decision to travel in style both ways. This was a time of slight recklessness on my part. I returned to the London Press Exchange on 3 September in an obstreperous mood. At the end of the week, I was sacked.

I withheld the grim news from Jonathan for a day or two. Did he know what was going on? Anyway, this was not quite such a bad time as it might appear. During that autumn I would be diverted by occasional meetings with a tall, thin, heavy-drinking, curly-haired advertising man some fifteen years my senior called David Gillies. He did not offer me a job, but from time to time took me out to dinner, usually in a group which included some exceptionally pretty girls, older and more sophisticated than those named in Jonathan's diary. On an outing to the Golden Duck in Fulham, I was excited to find my old friend Michael d'Abo having dinner there with his wife. He had given me his telephone number. Still shy, I encouraged Jonathan to call him the next day, rather than me. He duly reported that a maid had answered the telephone – the family were away for the weekend. My old school friend, who now had several hits under his belt,★ did not return our call.

I had more luck with Denis Mitchell, a famous film-maker whose name I had been given by Quentin Crisp. That autumn Mitchell would take me out to lunch at the Braganza in Soho and I soon introduced him to my younger brother. That autumn, both Gillies and Mitchell, the latter accompanied by his wife Linda, dined with us at 33 Tite Street,

★ Mike d'Abo's 'Build Me Up Buttercup', recorded by the Foundations, went to number two in November 1968.

where we both felt far more socially secure than in our flimsy previous abode. During one of Gillies's visits to the lavatory, Jonathan had shown his innate snobbery or class consciousness by muttering, simply, 'Grammar School'.

This was all quite encouraging – Jonathan was soon caricaturing Gillies and Mitchell and raising them to comic greatness – but in career terms I was now in what people then called the 'wilderness'. Some of my acquaintances were supportive: 'Dostoevsky in there somewhere,' a painter friend of my older brother said, prodding me in the stomach. Others put salt in my wounds. 'Are you nutty as ever?' asked Jonathan's friend Slatter.

One of the ways I occupied myself during this period was by promoting Jonathan's writing and drawings as if they were my own. During the summer of 1968, I had sent off a bundle of Jonathan's writings to various publishers and received far more encouraging replies than the stereotype refusals that my own novel had encountered. On 17 September, Michael Levien, Managing Editor at Peter Owen, had described these offerings as 'lively and amusing' and wondered if I had anything else that could be added to it to make it a publishable length. The very same day, Jonathan had returned home with the news that the Redfern Gallery had sold one of his macabre drawings for £30. Though many years would pass before I received any confirmation of my own talents, I was sustained by this affirmation of my own judgement that Jonathan's work was good.

A second bundle of Jonathan's material was rejected by Peter Owen, but over the next few months he and I sent the stuff out again, or samples of it, to find out if publishers would like to see more. We met with many encouraging replies, which I still possess. Mr O'Keefe at MacGibbon & Kee and Aubrey Davis at Secker's said they would certainly like to see more. Michael George at André Deutsch 'rather liked' the submitted piece. George Rapp of Rapp and Whiting found his sample 'intriguing and full of flashes of surrealist wit'. Anthony Blond, whom Jonathan had met with Felix Hope-Nicholson three years earlier, found it 'frisky and fun'. Although, like Peter Owen, all these publishers eventually decided not to pursue the idea of a book, these responses were quite unlike anything my own first attempts at a novel had received.

The language of publishers also added to Jonathan's general worldliness, and would come in useful when he came to describe how *The Queue*'s narrator opens a dirty book-shop. Following the police raid involving the highly trained cod, one of the policemen sheepishly hands the boy a dirty book he's written and wonders if he would like to publish it. 'Too many four-lettered words,' decides the narrator after a quick glance, '"Fuck" came up 350 times in the first paragraph.' And he also notes the crude illustrations that the policeman himself had added. 'Huge penises and vaginas completely out of proportion.'

Meanwhile Jonathan had strengthened his grasp on the art world, and become friends with John Synge at the Redfern Gallery and his assistant Maggie Wales. He had also sold pictures and objects through the Pace Gallery in St Christopher's Place, run by a character called Ralph Turner. On 10 December 1968, Turner issued a receipt accepting four framed drawings on a sale or return basis, one of which was called 'Prison Forms' and priced at 20 guineas. Jonathan had also sent copies of his work to Roland Penrose and Cecil Beaton, both of whom lived in Kensington. Penrose had replied on 15 November, 'Your drawings are probably more inter-esting to you than to others. I have no advice to give except for your own satisfaction, continue.' Beaton's handwritten

237

response was more upbeat. 'Your drawings are very individual,' scrawled the royal photographer on 6 November, '&
this is already an achievement. I certainly think you should
go on developing along these lines though whether you will
make any money is a —???'

The art world soon intrigued Jonathan as much as the
publishing one, and at about this time he wrote a short story
set in a saleroom. He described the atmosphere: 'There seem
to be a lot of continentals about. Danny La Rue hairstyles.
White scarves. Shoes with very soft black leather.' The narrator
soon gets into a violent argument with an official and is
lifted into the air. 'Untold damage' is done to a Picasso. The
narrator then hurls a Matisse ceramic at an elderly Polish
dealer called Zeiss. He is arrested, taken to West End Central
and sentenced next day to twelve months. In prison, he
receives a 'charming letter' from Picasso, who 'doesn't mind
a bit' about the catastrophe and even promises its perpetrator
a drawing when he comes out – 'This arrived yesterday,' he
adds in a typical flash-forward, 'and I'm afraid isn't frightfully good.' He also mentions his sufferings in gaol. 'There
had been a lot in the papers about the incident and I'm
afraid a lot of the prisoners ganged up against me,' he explains.
'Criminals always have good taste in art and many have valu-
able Impressionist and Post Impressionist collections.' On his
release he is unable to pay a taxi fare but, not for the first
time, tells the driver he will be dirty with him on the back
seat.

Writings like these, and the pictures he was doing at
the same time, reflect not only the state of his mind – whatever that was – but also throw light on the world or worlds
he occupied. He still kept a foothold in the mainstream,
attended conventional events like the Fulfords' dance on 12
October that year, went to a party in Eaton Place given by

people called Williams-Wynn, met Princess Anne and Peter Townend, an amusing bachelor figure who 'ran' the deb season, and stayed with Sara Pilkington at Saxmundham in Suffolk. He also began to see more of an American girl called Christina Dolan whose father owned or ran a Mayfair advertising agency.

This was all quite harmless but, however well he may have got on with these people as individuals, he instantly made fun of their worlds. Hearing that a double-barrelled couple in his circle had a baby he asked, 'Hasn't it got a million eyes?' In *The Queue*, he features a character called Sir Roland Humphrey, who swallows a £450,000 brooch in a Mayfair discotheque, fears it has passed through his bowels and hires frogmen to search the sewers. And he goes completely over the top in describing Lord Fuck's shooting party. Unable to avert this event, he explains how the 'meticulously soldiered' rooks practise their defence drills and then finally, armed with shotguns, grenades and other weapons, climb up their trees and take up their positions. Meanwhile, Lord Fuck's guests start arriving. The faces of Nicky Shit and Lord 'Arsehole' Drew are flushed – 'I would guess they have been abusing themselves during the tiring, Friday evening journey' – and dinner ends at 2.45 a.m. with many of those present pissing into their wine glasses.

> Next morning, they set out in the direction of the rookery. Assistant-Rook gives the alarm and all take up their appointed positions. Robins, doves, thrushes and pigeons gather in neighbouring elms. They have heard the news and watch eagerly. Lord Fuck fires the first shot; he is too badly hung-over and misses. Then Nicky Shit raises his shot-gun and sends 400 pellets up into the branches. A junior

239

rook cries, twists and falls 400 feet. The Labrador takes his carcass to the mortuary. Now Head-Rook retaliates. He aims directly at Nicky Shit's heart and fires. He's crumpling and down on his knees. Blood pouring from a deep wound. Labrador drags him away. There's a loud cheer of encouragement from watching birds. Lord Drew's turn. This expert shot scores a direct hit and Assistant-Rook dies instantly. Lord Drew fires again and another junior rook falls. She's not badly hurt, just a broken wing. But she is captured and mercilessly tortured. They want information about the rooks' weapon source. How many other rooks are up there. Which rook was responsible for shooting Nicky Shit. But brave junior rook lowers her head and refuses questions. They are furious and pull her wings. She is in agony and sweat pours off. Then Lord Fuck produces a pen-knife from his pocket and slowly cuts off a claw. This pain will cease if you'll betray your friends. She shook her head. They lose patience, throw her to the ground and stamp on her. Labrador protests. That's awful. You can't behave like this. Immediately Lord Fuck kicks Labrador in the ribs. Whose side are *you* on?

Head-Rook, enraged by this cruelty throws a hand-grenade at Lord Drew. It lands in his pocket. He tries to get at it but too late. He is split in half and his bowels come out.

Head-Rook orders his staff to retreat. They climb further into the trees and try to disguise themselves in the foliage. An assistant throws a hand-grenade at Rory Scott. It lands at his feet and explodes instantly. He is blown to pieces.

Now game-keepers are running to the rookery. They carry heavy rifles and are ordered to shoot all rook dead. Head-Rook is determined not to surrender and orders his rooks to keep their heads down and aim for Lord Fuck. A sharp-eyed junior rook scores a direct hit on one of Lord Fuck's testicles. Sperm pours out and every rook laughs. Lord Fuck is furious and orders his game-keepers to set fire to the tree. There is a pitiful screaming as the poor brave rooks are suffocated by dense smoke. They fall into broad nets held by waiting game-keepers. However, one Senior Rook manages to slip into a mask and remain conscious. Single-handed, he resists for a further twenty minutes and hurls stones, shit and hand-grenades at Lord Fuck and his men. Finally, he collapses with exhaustion and falls to the ground. Lord Fuck, unable to control his anger, kicks at him until the skull cracks in several places.

At four in the afternoon, Lord Fuck's cook, Miss Grieve, is busy preparing an enormous rook pie. Lord Dob is coming over from Skelton with a party of ten: there must be no mistakes. She uses the finest ingredients: expensive hand-ground flour from a local mill, carrots from the home farm and mushrooms flown in from Dijon that morning. Miss Grieve has won many international competitions for her pastry, and her celebrated Coinou de Finne won the Golden Bowl at the Salon Culinaire in Paris last summer.

The estate poulterer has already plucked and gutted the rooks. Eighteen carcasses wait for Miss Grieve's attention on a wooden board. She sets the oven to ratio 6, places rooks, stock and vegetables into a pot and covers with pastry. Then she reads a woman's paper for twenty minutes. She is suddenly disturbed by a moaning from inside the oven. She opens the door and sees a rook trying to push his way through the pastry. He has cleverly avoided the poulterer's deft hands; he carries a pistol and appears to be in a furious temper. Before Miss Grieve has a chance to raise the alarm, he has jumped out of the oven and pointed his gun at her. Stay where you are. Don't move or I'll shoot. Rook jumps to the sink and runs the cold tap: he is trying to get off the gravy that matts his feathers. Rook then leaves the kitchen.

He flies cautiously to the library. Lord Fuck is reading *Country Life* in a deep leather chair. Rook aims, fires and Lord Fuck falls forward. Severe face lacerations, brain haemorrhage and other grievous injuries. He dies in just over a minute. Then Rook gives a signal. Immediately other birds enter through the open French windows. There are giant eagles, carrion-crows, vultures and other large species. In twenty minutes, they have completely dismembered Lord Fuck's body. Every limb is sorted and neatly stacked. Then Rook produces a knife. He shaves off edible flesh from wrists, thighs and chest. This is taken to the kitchen and Miss Grieve is forced, at gun-point, to add it to the pie.

That night, Rook returns alone to his tree. Depression soon sets in. He is desperately lonely without the other rooks and, some time during the night, he throws himself off a branch. He is found by woodsmen and buried in the Animal

242

Graveyard. But when Lord Fuck's heir hears of Rook's foul deeds, he orders the body to be exhumed and thrown to the dogs.

I quote this episode in full because it captures the other side of the Swinging Sixties, when field sports were not endangered and the *Tatler* still featured bluff, Labrador-loving landed gentry and young poker-up-the-arse toffs. And also because, in spite of the narrator's claim to have had an affair with Lord Fuck at school, it offers a counterblast to the more effete world with which Jonathan was now so amused, at least on the superficial or comic level.

As we know, Jonathan's life had long been populated by homosexuals. We have already met a string of bachelor-types and there was a much bigger fish waiting in the wings who would enter Jonathan's life the following spring. In *The Queue* there are homosexuals of every class and hue, even two gay birds. I have already mentioned more than once the gigantic gay wood pigeon who offers our heroes a lift down the Great North Road and gets the narrator's penis in its claw. Another pigeon with 'proclivities' features later in the story, but in this instance the intended victim is another bird, indeed the friendly sparrow who has been such a help to our heroes. Foolishly accepting an invitation to go back to the pigeon's nest in Chapel Street, Sparrow panics when he notices that Pigeon is heavily scented and wearing women's make-up, and that his nest is furnished with effeminate fabrics and features bronze phalluses on all the tabletops. 'Sparrow has never been with a man and doesn't want to begin now,' the narrator tells us. 'Pigeon chuckles and says he will have a lot of fun . . . When Sparrow sees Pigeon's stiff penis, he jumps with fright and flutters to the nearest window. Pigeon lurches at him but it is too late.'

Jonathan's vague vision of homosexual style also comes across in the account, early on in *The Queue*, of a raid on an interior decorator's home in Moss Street. 'The owner of the house, on seeing the police, jumped out of the window and fell into his greenhouse. His body is at the mortuary now and all London mourn.' He goes on to describe fifteen of the dead man's friends being led into a police cell and claims that they have not learnt their lesson. 'For I can hear huffin' and puffin'. Masturbation in progress I should think.' At times, such haughtiness sounds like gay-bashing, but in this instance the extraordinary lenience of the warder, who tells the men to do up their fly buttons or forfeit hot tea and muffins – 'whichever you prefer' – suggests Jonathan was equally indifferent, more amused by the silks and scents and eminent position so many homosexuals occupied in society than in the morality of their behaviour.

Yet *The Queue* also features a much more downmarket type of homosexual, the sort featured in the *News of the World*, a newspaper I sometimes found Jonathan hidden behind at Tite Street. I have already mentioned the bit about the London games master with a terrible criminal record who has resorted to giving swimming lessons in the sewer. Later, the narrator describes buggery and bestiality taking place in the bottom of an empty swimming pool and how the attendant puts an end to it all by filling the pool with boiling water. 'I witness an appalling and memorable scene,' he continues with relish. 'The men rush for the exit steps but the water is entering at 200 gallons a second and they don't stand a chance . . . Only one man escapes. He is hideously burnt and grovels on the duck-boards. A blister runs the whole length of his back and his face is torn and running with puss. I return him to the pool. Much kinder really.'

Another great talking point in the late Sixties was, of

course, drugs. Chatting with me at Tite Street, Jonathan claimed to be 'psycho-thermic' – whatever that means – and then boasted, 'We don't need drugs. We're switched on all the time.' *The Queue*, nevertheless, carries various references to banned substances. In the hospital waiting room, Mary and the boy sit beside a drug addict named G. L. Husse. 'His terrible predicament means that he is no longer able to keep his job as a post office counter clerk,' the boy explains. 'He had an experience with *Methalin* whilst on holiday in Spain and since then has not been able to control his craving. He showed me the dropper-jabs in his arm (like bee stings) and I sympathised.'

Soon afterwards, Mary has her own announcement to make along these lines. Speaking in a hoarse whisper, she confesses that she had been a drug addict for thirty-four years and is now suffering withdrawal symptoms from the killer *Letharine.* The narrator's response is at first none too sympathetic. Finding hundreds of needle-marks on the dog's thighs – 'Blood oozed from many of the punctures and septi-caemia was present' – he hurls her across the room. The incident ends with Mary dragging herself back to the boy, licking his ankles, and begging for kindness, help and under-standing. Her drug addiction is then completely forgotten. Other canine problems and addictions surface with no direct bearing on my brother's life.

With or without these distractions, Jonathan continued to work at Ogilvy & Mather, returning to 33 Tite Street most evenings to change and go out in the second-hand red Mini which had replaced the van, or settle down immedi-ately to drawing. Though we lived together, the lives we led in the winter of 1968 were now largely separate. He still told me a little bit about his life, gushed about McMullan – 'McMullan always comes up trumps' – but mortally offended me by not taking me to the much-publicised Tiny Tim concert at the Albert Hall. On the other hand, I saw a lot of his longstanding friend Margaret Peile and by this stage had formed a separate relationship with her, in which words and ideas flowed more easily, she said, than they did between her and Jonathan. My brother, meanwhile, had formed an independent friendship with David Kaye, now back in London after a spell in Los Angeles, though we did pay one visit together to the Baker Street bedsitter where my old colleague was now hanging out – a visit made memorable by the fact that Kaye changed his clothes in front of us, prompting Jonathan to remark, when all was momentarily revealed, '*David's tool*'. Another evening we went to dinner together with Felix Hope-Nicholson across the road and met for the first time Isobel Strachey, a writer and painter and niece by marriage of Lytton Strachey. Isobel took an immediate interest in us both, and started inviting us to small parties at her house in Oakley Street, where many of our fellow guests were homosexual.

Jonathan pursued his active independent life, especially at weekends and was often halfway across England before I had stirred from my bed. It was on one of these social excursions, perhaps into the land of folk like Lord Fuck, that he met a young man called James Graham, who wore an eyepatch and was a member of an ancient Cumbrian family my father had once known quite well. On 28 October 1968, Jonathan brought this rare bird round to 33 Tite Street and the three of us immediately became close friends.

CHAPTER EIGHTEEN

James Graham and Mr Grant

Today nothing can go right for me: it starts to pelt
with rain and the sky goes a filthy colour. A platoon
of marching infantry pass me. I salute but they
think I am taking the piss and do not acknow-
ledge. Poor men: they must return to cheerless
barracks. A grim evening ahead, for their TV was
stolen on Rogation Sunday and has not yet been
replaced.

The Embankment, 1969

JAMES GRAHAM, WHO was distinguished at this time not only
by his eyepatch — its strap caused his hair to fluff up like a
game bird's — but also by his short sharp corduroy coat, was
twenty-two years old and, like me, had no job. He soon
began to visit me at Tite Street during the day, lunch with
Jonathan in the West End and call on both or either of us
in the evening. James was at this stage deeply philistine but
his conventional, upper-class façade disguised a lively and
rebellious originality he shared with young friends of his like
Richard Wrottesley and Dai Llewellyn, both of whom were
now beginning to establish themselves in the gossip columns.

This new friend appealed to Jonathan and me in different
ways, but he soon got into the habit of bringing round a
bottle of draught port, drawn from a barrel at the Imperial

Wine Stores in King's Road, and the three of us had late-night drinking sessions in the front room at 33 Tite Street. Jonathan was more wary of James than I was, admired his backward-sloping handwriting – 'like a king's' – but also described him as 'MD' – my father's expression for the mentally deficient – and said of his appearance: 'Good though it is, he could easily be considered typical and extremely boring.' One weekend, on one of the now increasingly rare visits together to the As You Like It, Jonathan remarked, 'This is the *only* place in London where we're safe from James Graham.' At Tite Street, Jonathan and I sometimes decided not to let James in – 'unless he makes a very good proposition' – and some evenings James needed to bang on the door handle with the port bottle which Jonathan described as his 'admission ticket'.

I need not describe the outings James and I went on without Jonathan in the West End, our visits to Prunier's, the Moulin d'Or, Annabel's – Sir Roland Humphrey territory? – and a Park Lane gambling club called Le Cercle. Or speculate how I paid for these escapades, now that I was unemployed. Nor will I describe the parties he took me to, where I at last began to find my feet with the opposite sex. Here, I am concerned with his role in our shared life. Within weeks this greatly increased when James moved into a room in the Hope-Nicholson house across the road, and I learnt to distinguish between the noises made by his badly parked bonnet-less Hillman, fitted with an absurd and soon-to-be-illegal horn which one could hear several streets away, and the softer sounds of Jonathan's red Mini as he fitted it snugly into the smallest parking space.

James Graham quickly joined in with some of our jokes, even attempted to do a drawing in Jonathan's style – '*James may be better than Michelangelo,*' Jonathan solemnly intoned – and occasionally played us off against each other. 'You've just missed a superb meal,' James enthused when I got home late to find that the two of them had already reached the port stage. On another occasion, James told Jonathan: 'You just relax, John, and let the big boys talk business.' To which Jonathan had replied, 'Press on!' Early on in the relationship, James had provided some pheasants he'd shot and the wine he'd been given as a twenty-first birthday present, and Jonathan had cooked the three of us a very good dinner, eventually putting our platters on the table with the words, 'Tails up, boys, and away to the woods.' On tasting the Leoville Barton 1963, Jonathan had then ruminated, 'When this wine was being bottled, I was struggling with the intricacies of O level maths, Mr B. gripping me by the shoulders – and sometimes his hand used to wander . . .' At other times, Jonathan only participated half-heartedly in our goings on, taking to his bed in the next room after only one glass of port.

James and Jonathan also had their meetings in the Strand. Jonathan floated along that winter at Ogilvy & Mather and continued to fill me in on the events, personalities and myths of the place – he understandably made much of a story of how a lady copywriter at the firm had not so long ago coshed her babies and then slit her wrists. He also continued his rambles through the West End: I once bumped into him looking ill and untidy in Old Compton Street, saw him shooting out of the Marquis of Granby – but not pursued down Charing Cross Road – and he often had tales to tell of his excursions. One lunch-time he saw my drunken friend David Gillies coming out of a cheap restaurant in New Fetter Lane carrying a file of papers and pronounced him 'the complete professional'. Another day, he entered the London Press Exchange and found his way to the creative floor where

I had worked. Here he cleverly spotted the man who had hired and fired me having a working lunch and accurately described him as looking like a 'bad tempered army dentist'. In a corridor he then passed a bearded and hang-doggish

senior copywriter I had disliked and quickly did a devastatingly accurate caricature of him. On another jaunt, he ran into one of his old colleagues at Claridge's who apparently exclaimed, 'So you're a copywriter now! *That* can't require any intelligence. I should think you could do that without the *slightest* difficulty!'

During this phase and for the remains of his short life, Jonathan looked back nostalgically on his time among the bartenders, plongeurs and commis chefs. He still made knowing references to high cuisine – 'In France, they always use the crackle for the stock' – and in a semi-fictional fragment from this period makes a sharp comparison between the Savoy Hotel's chef, Trompetto, and his current creative boss, Stanhope Shelton:

I worked as a copywriter at Ogilvy & Mather. They are just off Waterloo Bridge. I used to catch a tube every day from Sloane Square to Charing Cross. I walked across Embankment Gardens and then, instead of going directly into the agency, I used to divert round the back of the Savoy. I used to watch staff arriving. I watched Silvino Trompetto, the Chef de Cuisine, arriving. He seemed to walk down from the Strand under some tunnel to the back of the Shell building. He went in by the banqueting entrance. He is an impressive man. The last time I saw him would have been in his office behind the grill kitchens. He said he was sorry I was leaving his kitchens and thanked me for my work.★ He is very smart both in his chef's uniform and in his off-duty clothes. I think he is so much better than Stanhope Shelton. In every way he scores. Shelton has a house that is just so dull. A real fairy place in Bloomsbury – with all his collection of this and that. Trompetto lives in the Savoy – he has a flat right on top. I have never been up but people say it is nice. Trompetto is so good the way he goes into the Savoy. Just wearing a French black overcoat. Enormous respect from every member of staff. None of the 'There goes that f.cker' that one hears so much in hotels.

★ Wishful thinking? Jonathan occasionally worked as a barman at the Savoy, never in the kitchen.

At about the time he comes in, the carriage men would be having tea in their room. Trompetto has to walk through. These smart men in their granite grey uniforms all stand up. The men, who would have had breakfast hours ago, are eating an enormous platter of 'petit hamburgers', a speciality of the hotel – one that is superbly executed. It is about 9.30 a.m. Trompetto jokes at them. 'Eh! This early for eating . . .' The men laugh and change the subject. 'I hear there was a nasty fire in one of the kitchens during the night sir . . .' The Scotch grill chef, covering the early shift – 2 a.m. to dawn – had panicked when a salamander exploded. Scalding fat had sprayed his range. 'Easily done', said Trompetto.

Thanks to his mixed feelings about advertising, his growing self-confidence and disrespect for most of his colleagues, Jonathan encouraged James Graham and me to gatecrash his office party at Christmas. James Graham was at his most outrageous, threw his champagne in the air, shouted 'Fountains!' and then asked the office manager for a job.

Jonathan by this stage was also marginally over the top. At Christmas 1968 he was in a provocative and comically critical mood, bursting with irreverent ideas. On the journey to Turig, he had quickly terminated a discussion about Mike d'Abo, now starring as Gulliver at the Mermaid Theatre, and suggested that a film should be made for our parents' benefit, entitled 'For Those Who Are Out of Touch', featuring Robert Maxwell working – the press tycoon was much in the public eye – and huge close-ups of a dinner table. On arrival home he remarked, 'I should think no Old Harrovian has ever lived in a house as un-stately as this.' He laid into our father in other ways, blaming him for savaging the small pond in front of the house — 'It's the complete opposite of Cecil Beaton's pond' — and accusing him of 'cadging off others' the entire time. 'If only', he fantasised, 'we found Father with a cup of coffee, a cigarette and *Queen*'. His sentiments about our mother also involved cigarettes. 'If only Mother was searching for cigarettes all the time, cheap cigarettes, Embassys, like Mrs Buxton does.' Later, he said more affectionately, 'I suddenly thought she was back to her good old self this morning when she was dealing with an ill Tiger. She's not fit to be married to a concealed yapping genius . . .'

The festive atmosphere at Turleigh Combe was enriched that year by the presence of our brother Martin and his new bride, Noriko, who had got married on 27 November 1968 in Yokohama, with no one in our family present. 'There's so much he's got to be filled in on,' Jonathan had murmured as we'd waited for our brother's aeroplane to touch down at Heathrow. At Turig, Jonathan expressed delight with our tiny new sister-in-law and seeing her clad in padded trousers and pushing a wheelbarrow full of leaves declared that there was 'no sweeter sight'. For Martin, who had avoided the effects of the Swinging Sixties by living abroad, he had another 'If only' response. Seeing Martin drive off somewhere, Jonathan muttered, 'If only he had thirteen thousand pounds worth of cannabis resin in the boot. If only he was going off to a commie gathering in Bath and coming back with a flag on the car . . .'

About our grandmother, now ninety, he had equally mixed views. 'She's had experience,' he acknowledged, but after seeing her in bed, commented, 'She looks very odd actually, as if she is trying to hide something.' Then fantasy took over and he added, 'Granny doesn't go to sleep until the small hours. She stays up tuned to an Italian experimental station.'

This was a reference to the radio-listening habits of his painter friend Zev, whom he'd met that summer in Rome. More obscure in its origins was his subsequent remark, 'She's writing the fifth part of her chronology,' but, as I have pointed out, it amused Jonathan to imagine almost everyone as some sort of Nobel-prize-winning genius, not least my grandmother's old maid, Barbara Borrowdale, who sat in the kitchen studying every word of the *Penrith Herald* which arrived regularly from Cumberland.

For Aunt Jean too, also at Turleigh – it was a full house that Christmas – and helping occasionally with the cooking, he had further superciliousness. 'Congratulations, Jean, on the salad.' Ignoring our aunt's protests, he had continued, 'Did you do a sketch for it first or did it come straight out of your head?' Alone with me he was more down to earth, 'Loose end?' he asked on finding me sauntering around in the back kitchen area of the house. But when I entered my father's study on Christmas Day and found Jonathan on the telephone, he snapped, 'Private call. Please leave the room.'

One afternoon over Christmas I played along with Jonathan's more fanciful side by reading aloud to Jean and our grandmother from Kafka's *In the Penal Colony*, a wildly unsuitable story in the circumstances, recommended to me by David Kaye. Jonathan sat drawing in the corner – our mother later reproved him for doing his 'scribbles' on her best cards – but may have taken in more of this gothic tale than he let on at the time.

It was around this time that Jonathan's own literary activities, simmering away for several years if not most of his life, came to the boil at last. During our recent foray into this field, two publishers, Peter Owen and André Deutsch, had suggested that *The London Magazine* might be interested in publishing one of the shorter pieces. This distinguished, nicely produced literary monthly had an illustrious record and had been edited since 1961 by the poet, cricketing correspondent and racehorse owner, Alan Ross. Sometime the previous autumn, Jonathan had sent the magazine a piece called *Rats*. Ross had returned this with a compliment slip on which he had written that he found it 'v. funny indeed' until halfway, but that it needed 'at least a semblance of coherence & structure to make it work'. He promised to have another look at it if Jonathan could 'cut it & give a bit of narrative to the second half'.

Shortly after Christmas, Jonathan had sent Alan Ross an amended shortened version of the story and on 15 January 1969, with its fate in the balance, had gone off to Paris for a week. Here he stayed part of the time at the Hotel Nouvel in the Rue Monsieur Le Prince, visited galleries and called on the veteran surrealist Man Ray at his studio – David Kaye had furnished him with the address in the rue Ferou. He also sent me, on 17 January, a jokily reproving postcard saying that I was 'a perfect idiot' – an expression of our mother's – not to be over there myself and urging me to 'snap-out-of-it' in London while typically acknowledging, 'Of course many things about Paris are very, very annoying.' His return to 33 Tite Street on 22 January was both annoying, and triumphant. First, his bag of duty-free wines and spirits burst open on the stone staircase, smashing most of its contents. Secondly, I was able to tell him that a postcard had arrived that morning from Alan Ross accepting *Rats* for publication. 'We've made a few cuts,' Ross had scrawled on a postcard featuring his racehorse, Acrovat, with J. Gifford on board, 'but if you don't mind that we'll gladly print it.'

Many months would elapse before the story, along with another he submitted later entitled *The Embankment,* appeared in this esteemed magazine. More unstructured than the *The*

255

Queue, both stories are littered almost at random with odd bits of the vernacular. In *Rats* there is even a sequence of such phrases: 'Bad weather over Biscay. I fear a storm. Drop anchor. Tea's ready,' which reads like modern poetry or could even have come from a Pinter play. Elsewhere single phrases like 'Thank God it's Friday,' and 'I wonder what God's got up his sleeve for me,* or questions like 'What's got into you Billy? Have you gone wee-wee on my carpet?' sit on their own and have no function in the narrative. And of course both stories are also permeated with gloom, foreboding and violent death. Or do I mean the comedy of violent death?

Life at Tite Street continued less ominously. For what it's worth I was now on the dole. And making stabs in different directions like trying to contact the writer Philip O'Connor after hearing his querulous voice on the 'Third Programme'. Jonathan was out and about as usual, lunching one day with his friend Zev, over from Rome, and claiming afterwards that this flamboyant American 'was *heckled* all the way from the flat to the restaurant'. At home, our port sessions continued haltingly. So did our conversations. Once or twice Jonathan called me 'Frederick', an affectation he had picked up from James Graham, which rang the wrong note. Downstairs, in Mlinaric's studio, the parties went on and the tree outside was sometimes illuminated by the festivities long after 3 a.m. And, of course, there were constant, almost daily visits from James Graham, who remained a powerful presence in our lives and an influence on each of us and who was now to play his trump card.

One lunchtime in the middle of February 1969, James

---

* Jonathan first heard this remark from the lips of one of the tramps at the Hole in the Wall.

and Jonathan were lunching together in Yates Wine Bar in the Strand when James suddenly spotted among the other customers an old schoolmaster or private tutor he had once known called Mr Grant. After a fairly brief conversation, James and Jonathan invited this old man to come round to Tite Street that night. Snow had fallen on the day in question – 19 February 1969 – and the old man did not reach the flat until ten o'clock.

Before describing this momentous evening, perhaps I should state the few facts I know about this character. James A. Grant was of Scottish origin, widely known as Jimmy, and claimed to be a little bit younger than the second Lord Leverhulme, who, I see, was born in 1888. I guess Grant was already over seventy. During the 1920s or 30s, he had been part of the entourage of a famous fashion designer whose name I forget. In more recent times, he had worked as a schoolmaster, spent three terms at Downside and a shorter period at Eton. He had also worked as a private residential tutor for various grand families. He had taught everyone from Prince Nicholas of Prussia to Lord Winterbottom's son and had established a particular reputation in Northumberland where he had tutored boys called George Benson and Danny Enderby, and had been spotted by James Graham. He had now fallen on bad times and survived by scratching a living as a freelance guide to London, picking up tourists, rich or poor, in Horse Guards Parade or outside Buckingham Palace. He lived on and off in different hostels, had a severe drinking problem and a criminal record.

That February night at Tite Street, with the snow piling up outside, Grant came across as a small, vintage figure, a little older than my father, better educated, with a courtly foppish manner. He wore a worn tweed jacket, shabby check waistcoat and an overcoat to the collar of which he appeared to have sewn a strip of moth-eaten fur. In spite of these sartorial disadvantages, he was soon talking facetiously over port, handling his cigarette in a dainty, supercilious manner

and announcing, 'I deliberately put on this dirty shirt because I thought it was more Chelsea.'

Jonathan's response to this homeless, friendless, alcoholic old schoolmaster was astonishing and immediate. That first evening he tried his best to persuade me that Mr Grant should spend the night in our flat. I was strongly against the idea and eventually persuaded Jonathan to drive his new friend back to his current lodgings in the East End. James Graham and I travelled in the back of the red Mini for the ride through the snowy streets. At about three in the morning, Grant dismissed us at a street corner, refusing to reveal his precise address, and Jonathan repeated his apologies that we could not let him stay the night. Grant had then glared at me in the back seat and said, 'It was *your* decision and *yours* alone.'

After that first evening, the relationship between Jonathan, still a healthy and active twenty-one-year-old, and the old private tutor progressed rapidly. A few days later, I found a note on my desk at Tite Street, reading *'Met Grant in the Strand – he was superb.'* And though his life was already quite full, Jonathan found time to pursue the old man vigorously. He kept me informed of the progress of the relationship, regaled me with Grant's latest pronouncements and sang his praises. 'He's a shrewd, intelligent man,' he told me. 'Not some silly down-and-out in a dirty mac.' He also paid tribute to James Graham for the initial introduction. 'It's the best thing he's ever done.'

His growing commitment to Mr Grant fitted in with a lot of other activities on many fronts. Though he drew the line at calling again on Quentin Crisp – 'I was bored stiff last time we visited him' – he introduced me to Ward's Irish House, a large bar under Piccadilly Circus serving draught Guinness on a colossal scale. One evening in this place, he murmured, 'There's a very smart man behind me who could be the director of an advertising agency.' Then he added the knowing words, 'Obviously queer.' He also found time to get up to pranks with James Graham and me together. Earlier that spring, the three of us had invaded Danny La Rue's dressing room at the Saville Theatre without having seen the show he was appearing in.

Of course I remained excluded from much of his life. At around this time, he had sat for his portrait by our new

259

friend Isobel Strachey and taken the luscious oil painting home to Turig, where my mother pronounced it 'horrible'. According to his engagement diary, his dates with debs and ex-debs – the names of Caroline Dawnay, Vicky Baden-Powell and Georgina Oliver must now be added to the list – were counterbalanced by appointments with Chris Gosling, John Baldwinson, McMullan's friend Nina Froud and Jim Underwood, an editor at Calder & Boyars, who had now agreed to publish David Kaye's first novel. By now, his relationship with Margaret Peile had been revived but when I asked how she was, he replied, 'Fine,' and, when I tried to press the matter, snapped back, 'I've already said she's fine. Please don't ask the same question again.'

His work at Ogilvy & Mather seems to have been dashed off without difficulty, and he was even confident enough to pursue jobs in other agencies. And he still had time to wander the streets of Covent Garden and beyond. On 24 March he had slipped through the stage door at the Opera House, explored the backstage area and sat in on a rehearsal. Later he would enter the Old Bailey where the Kray Twins and their friends were now squeezed into the dock. He also watched the crowd arriving at a memorial service for General Eisenhower at St Paul's Cathedral. And, while keeping his customary discretion about his private life – he once volunteered, 'It's frightfully rude to use a contraceptive' – he filled me in on these other experiences in rich detail.

He continued his writing and painting. 'Keep going and send us more,' Ross wrote back on receiving Jonathan's second story, *The Embankment*. 'Can you not relate them to make a book?' Under the name of Jonathan Head, or Jonathan Head-Barrow, he also sold several more drawings through John Synge at the Redfern Gallery and other pictures and objects elsewhere.

He had now begun to carve stone and experiment with new materials. According to a Pace Gallery receipt dated 30 April 1969, these latest artefacts included an object called 'Rat Trap' made of wood and iron and something called 'Leg Head' made of wood and plaster.

I had mixed feelings about some of these new artworks, particularly what seemed to me a slightly pretentious, wavy line which had replaced the robust crudity of his earlier drawings. It seemed to me he now had aspirations to be

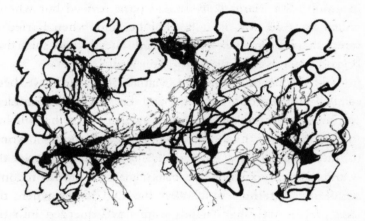

taken seriously. His figures appeared with swollen skulls and many of his pictures were adorned with spilt ink, masquerading as blood and tears. These large new pen-and-inks compared badly with the smaller earlier caricatures, done largely for my amusement, of people like Luigi, the head waiter at Claridge's, and even – wildly inaccurate – of John Synge himself.

At about this time, perhaps thanks to some journalist he had met on the party circuit, Jonathan began to receive some erroneous gossip column publicity. On 21 May 1969 the Charles Greville column of the *Daily Mail* announced that Jonathan Head was starting work on a £200 mural for the roof of John Lennon's Rolls-Royce. Slipping into interviewee style, my brother is reported as saying, 'It will be abstract pen-and-ink under glass panels. The interior of the car is rather dull and I suppose Lennon thought this was a way of cheering it up.'

While Jonathan got involved in these high jinks – there was no truth in this published story – my life ticked over. I had no money at the time, and lived off the odd half-crowns I found under the cushions on the sofa. My minimal private income neatly covered my share of the rent – no more – which we paid our older brother Julian, who occasionally wrote to us from some exotic location. 'My dear brothers,' he had written recently from New York, 'I have not heard from you for about a month. Is all well????' and ended the airmail with the information, 'I am very busy with business and social activities on all levels.'

By this time, I was also aware of Jonathan's vague plans to leave 33 Tite Street. He would prefer to live in a bedsitter – and perhaps not have to cope with my demands, my continuous attempts to climb onto the bandwagon. The idea of James Graham moving into Jonathan's place had also been aired. 'It would be James's greatest pleasure to have a room in the flat,' Jonathan declared when the three of us were together. 'It wouldn't at all,' James quickly retorted.

Even in the face of this impending fracture, there were still bonds between us worth noting. These were emphasised at the beginning of May 1969 when we heard from our mother – the news came in the form of a letter – that Gilda had died at Turig, found dead in her basket by Barbara Borrowdale. Jonathan balked at our mother's description of 'dear Gilda' – he preferred 'magnificent Gilda' – and as we know had already written a great deal of fanciful stuff about her and would fully celebrate her character, her naughtiness, her greed, her bad temper, in *The Queue*. For the time being, all he said was 'I expect Barbara did a fairly professional prod

to make sure she really *was* dead.'

At the end of that month, Jonathan would leave 33 Tite Street for good. During those last days together, there were still some lively moments. One weekend Jonathan went out onto the staircase during lunch and returned with the poet John Betjeman, who was having his portrait painted in Guy Roddon's studio by an artist called Robert Buhler. Betjeman studied a photograph of the Kray Twins on our mantelpiece and made sympathetic gurgles, provoking Jonathan to remark afterwards, 'He was talking to us far closer than Father's ever talked to us.' He also said later, 'Betjeman is an absolutely ace contact man. He must be, to have got so far,' but was equally impressed by the poet's lack of pomposity. 'If we'd offered him a piece of bread,' he explained, 'he'd have settled down and eaten it. The man's got no dignity at all.' I had soon passed on the news of this illustrious visitor to our older brother Simon, whose grudging and strangulated reply – '*Good!*' – prompted Jonathan to declare, 'They're all off their rockers up there.' Such sweeping dismissals reassured and amused me, and the issuing of them added to the fun of being in Jonathan's company. During our next visit to Turleigh Combe, Jonathan remained in a subversive mood. Grilled by our father about his future plans – 'Right, now, who are you sharing a flat with?' – he had playfully replied 'John Smith.' To which our father had snapped back, 'Real name please.'

In fact he had no plans other than to move across the street into yet another room in the Hope-Nicholson house. On 29 May 1969, he accomplished this simple and convenient manoeuvre with the minimum of fuss and was promptly replaced in the back bedroom overlooking the Royal Hospital by James Graham, to whom he issued the warning: 'Be prepared to have your letters opened by Andrew.'

CHAPTER NINETEEN

Living Alone

> At last we arrive at my lodgings and I am once
> more fiddling with the tricky mortice. We climb
> the stairs and find my door (Room 7) has been
> smashed in. I gasp and gaze around. Everything has
> gone. Even the concealed bachelor cooker. The
> place is in smithereens. I immediately dial the
> police: but the desk sergeant on duty is in a foul
> temper and tells me to fuck off.
>
> *The Embankment*, 1969

JONATHAN TOOK VERY little with him to his new room on
the third floor of 52 Tite Street, a few clothes perhaps and
his little attaché case containing resin, chalks, inks, brown
sticky paper and other tools of his trade. Our shared kitchen
equipment, including the chopping and butter boards,
remained in my care. On his first night across the road, I
watched my brother ascend to his bedsitter and then flash
the staircase lights on and off for my benefit.

As always, Jonathan quickly set about glamorising his
new environment. He reported on the opera cloaks he found
slung over the banisters late at night and the Covent Garden
programmes sticking out of their pockets. He also elevated
his fellow lodgers and their most mundane pronouncements.
One of these was Zena Douglas, who had lived in the house

since the 1940s. 'The way she says "Good Morning",' he reported, 'she could be a girl in a country house.' Another was Anna de Wolkoff, with whom he discussed James Graham. When Miss de Wolkoff, who had served a longish prison sentence for relaying information to the Germans during the war, refused to admit there was anything funny about our new friend, Jonathan prompted her, 'Surely his face?'

He made frequent reappearances at 33 Tite Street and cast a beady eye over the life I now shared with James Graham. Quite often, over the next month or two, he would return to cook meals in the flat and join in port sessions. Just occasionally, he also joined James and me on our West End escapades. One hot summer night the three of us dined at Claridge's. Here, he claimed to have heard a hall porter murmur, 'Swaying slightly,' as we entered the hotel he knew so well and when we spotted the infamous Duchess of Argyll at another table in the restaurant, he commented knowingly, 'She only comes here for the music.'

In spite of a continuing intimacy on this level, Jonathan continued his progress away from me. He was on the move, on the march. He often fidgeted in my presence. Or yawned. He spent evenings with Mr Grant without telling me in advance − or afterwards. At 8 o'clock one morning I saw him setting off from the house opposite with a large picture, newspaper sellotaped over it, under his arm. I did not always ask him where he was going. He was now, after all, a free agent. His battered engagement diary for this period is on my desk as I write these words. Scrawled entries in different colours of ink are often difficult to read but I see that he went to a dance for Miranda Seymour on 18 July and dined with his landlord Felix Hope-Nicholson on 21 July. And the following week with Jimmy McMullan. He also has appointments with Alan Ross and Isobel Strachey, and takes his new friend Georgina Oliver to the Hole in the Wall under Waterloo Station. Other new names, sometimes accompanied by telephone numbers, which lie scattered over those pages, include those of Auberon Waugh, Juliet Wrightson, Richard Cork, Alan Parker, Jim Tucker, Ross Hunter, Venetia Murray, Bernie Jacobson and Robin Baird-Smith. All these names will mean something to somebody, and some of these people I would later meet, though in some cases not for many years.

Earlier in the summer Jonathan had begun an intriguing friendship with the painter Patrick Procktor after a lively street encounter, also involving David Hockney, and partly orchestrated by James Graham, who thought nothing of bearding lions, especially those he had never heard of. Jonathan had soon noted Procktor's Manchester Street address in his diary and at 5 p.m. on 18 June had had tea here with the tall, thirty-three-year-old artist who was also a client of the Redfern Gallery. From then on, he seems to have been an habitué at Procktor's tea parties. One day, in these louche surroundings, he would meet Cecil Beaton, who on learning that my brother worked in advertising, apparently cried out, 'Oh you rascal! You mustn't!' Jonathan meanwhile continued to work on his own drawings. He sold two further pictures through the Redfern Gallery and duly received a cheque for £53.6s.8d. – the equivalent of how many thousands today? He also sold two drawings to an amusing market researcher called Daniels, for whom I occasionally did freelance interviewing. His diaries contain scrawled references to Muybridge's *The Human Figure in Motion* and books on 'Keith' Lichtenstein and Jackson Pollock.

I only know these things because after Jonathan's death I had access to all his papers. At the time I only knew what little he told me, and had to content myself with his observation that Francis Bacon was 'a millionaire many times over,' and that a girl called Fiona Phillips lived in a thirty-room flat in Grosvenor Square. I also lapped up his comments on James Graham who was already proving a tricky flatmate. 'That suit ought to be thrown away. The hair is pathetic,' Jonathan told me and, when I criticised my flatmate's finger-nails, responded, 'Have you seen his *toe*nails? They're like *huge wands!*' James Graham, he concluded, should be in a flat with three other men just like him – 'drinking claret the whole time'.

James and I, meanwhile, had mixed feelings about Jonathan's apparent progress. Sometimes, James noted Jonathan's secretiveness: 'He's putting up a smokescreen between us and his soul.' At other times, he chose to adulate Jonathan's social techniques: 'He goes out of his way to be charming.' He also tried to wound me by making unfavourable comparisons between Jonathan and me. 'Jonathan paints pictures which he sells,' James told me. 'You write a whole lot of twot.' These difficulties came to a head after a difficult evening the three of us had spent together. 'Two people with immense charm and one person with a mass of complexes and *no charm at all* inevitably do not get on,' James diagnosed. 'We merely feel a motherly, fatherly affection for you.' He would later reassure me, 'Don't worry. I'm not going to leave a sinking ship' but in fact these attacks washed over me. I was too mad, too cocky, to be much affected by these forays, which were sufficiently witty to make me laugh rather than cry.

Yet my life was fairly dire much of this time. 'It's a wonder you survived,' the playwright Peter Nichols wrote to me many years later after, reading my first autobiograph-ical novel. As Jonathan moved forward with such superlative ease, I remained car-less and lover-less in spite of admirable attempts by James Graham – 'Get that poison out of your system!' – to push me into encounters with the opposite sex. During the summer of 1969, I had finished another book, which had been rejected by Anthony Blond with the words, 'Too much self-pity. Go out and get at 'em!' and I was only too glad to when any diversion came my way. In July 1969, I was summoned to do jury service at the Old Bailey and duly took part in a murder case in Court Number One, where Christie had been tried sixteen years earlier, and on my way there met John Betjeman on a traffic island on Ludgate Hill. Back home in Tite Street, I was diverted by the presence on the staircase of the Archbishop of Canterbury – the man Jonathan had maligned was having his portrait done by Guy Roddon – and by a doorstep encounter with a figure in purple trousers and red shoes, whom I eventually recognised as Mike d'Abo. My old schoolfriend, whose group Manfred Mann had now broken up, had been paying a visit to David Mlinaric in the ground-floor studio. When I immediately telephoned Jonathan with this news – d'Abo had even inspected the flat upstairs – he said, '*Prove it!*'

Perhaps the main remaining link between Jonathan and me was Grant. I don't think I met the old schoolmaster during this period, but Jonathan felt this was an area of his life he could share with me. During that summer he had quickly regaled me with Grant's latest outpourings and made them sound so funny that I, too, had become fascinated by Grant's character. Jonathan presented his new friend as a preposterous bad-luck case who had once been 'the best dressed man in England'. No doubt Grant's grand, Lord Fuckish connections – the old man talked often of his time in various Guinness households – appealed to Jonathan, along with his pluckiness, much of which he would later, together with the alcoholism, apply to Mary in *The Queue*.

Jonathan's high regard for the old tutor continued. He

described him as 'a very well organised, professional free-lance guide' claimed that he was 'not in the least rheumatic' and indeed 'indestructible'. He told me that Grant wore make-up, Leichner and Helena Rubinstein tan, which he claimed was very important for his work as a guide. When I responded doubtfully about Grant and pointed out that he hadn't got a single friend, Jonathan retorted, 'Grant says his friend is his drink,' and lapped up the pub and bar culture in which the old man was immersed. In the Salisbury in St Martin's Lane, Grant had apparently murmured that he would like to talk to Jonathan 'in camera', marched him into a private bar and asked, 'How is the privy purse this morning?' The old man's comments on pub food, the 'excellence' of the shepherd's pie at lunchtime and how 'tired' it looked in the evening, also amused him. Grant talked of pubs he knew across London: the Two Ducks in Holborn, the 'Old Hammer and Hen off Cable Strada,' the Captain's Cabin, with which he had 'evil associations', and of course Yates Wine Bar where they had first met, and which the ex-tutor claimed was popu-lated by 'gargoyles, who've been sitting in the same place for thirty years. They're usually ex-alcoholic, ex-prison, ex-theatre . . .' Such murkiness appealed a great deal to Jonathan – and me – but his relationship with Grant hung on much more than *nostalgie de la boue* and 'good copy'.

The bond between them was made clear when, in August 1969, Grant sent Jonathan a terse postcard, fiercely termi-nating the friendship and blaming my brother for the current crisis in his life. Instead of taking this rejection lying down, Jonathan told me he was not prepared to let the old man 'get away with it' so easily. 'I just want to put my side of it,' he said as he set off immediately for the East End. Still unaware of exactly where Grant lived, he had left letters for him in fourteen different pubs near the spot where we had dropped him off that first night. 'Isn't that rather odd?' I asked nervously, to which Jonathan replied with supreme confidence, '*Grant knows I'm odd.*'

Twenty-four hours later Grant had telephoned Jonathan at his office, professed himself to be 'very touched' by my brother's note, and they met up again that same day. After this incident, Jonathan declared, 'I would *absolutely adore* to see his room stroke cubicle stroke dormitory', but such pleasures would be denied to him. Grant remained elusive, often changed his address and frequently required tracking down. Calling later at the Church Army Hostel in Johnson Street, E1, Jonathan found his friend had left the previous Sunday and was told by the custodian, 'I wouldn't swear to it but he could be in prison. This is typical alcoholic pattern. Yes, we've got some of his things here. Who are *you*, by the way?'

Grant's flightiness is also manifested by Mary in *The Queue*, who often gives her protector a run for his money and, like Grant, becomes extremely difficult if she is not allowed another drink. Here is the scene that follows Mary's discovery that she is in the family way:

> I stop at the first phone box we come to and make a reverse-charge call to the abortionist in London . . . His nurse answers and she takes our particulars. She feels sure that Dr Attel will be able to help and asks us to go straight to his surgery as soon as we arrive in London. I leave the callbox and am annoyed to find that Mary has disappeared. She was there a moment ago; I saw her through the panes. The nearest building is a large pub called the Three Sailors and I enter thinking she might have wandered in accidentally. I am worried and distressed to see her up against the bar, holding a double large whisky

in her hands. She is already tight and as I approach she snarls and tells me to leave. I reason with her. You can't go on like this. You're five months pregnant and drinking this amount will do you no good at all. Doctor Attel in London is willing to help you but we must hurry. Mary tells me to fuck off and she orders herself another double large whisky. The barmaid, realizing Mary has had enough, looks at me for confirmation.

I shake my head and tell her to stop serving. There is a frightful scene and Mary jumps onto the bar. She stamps her paws and howls with rage. The landlord, hearing the noise, runs from his office and orders his Labrador to kick her out. There's a

little dachshund in the saloon bar who's had one too many. Get her out, would you please. Labrador jumps onto the bar with one leap and takes Mary firmly by the scruff of her neck and carries her out. Mary kicks, snaps and demands another drink. I thank the Labrador and apologise.

When we are safely away from the pub, I gave Mary a firm ticking off. She becomes pathetic and lies down on the pavement. A crowd gathers and asks what the matter is. I ask them to go away; it is nothing serious. Then Mary is horribly sick. I try to get her to her feet but each time she stumbles and falls again. Too pissed-up, I'm afraid. Her eyes are terribly bloodshot and she asks constantly for water. Alcoholic dehydration is obviously setting in.

One wonders how often Jonathan had to cope with Grant in such a mood, and how much of Mary's alcoholic symptoms and behaviour, her grunting and burping and clasping of half-bottles of sweet sherry, were taken straight from the old schoolmaster. One also marvels at the generosity of Jonathan's increasing commitment to such a hopeless case.

Whatever the answers to these questions, Jonathan's friendship with Mr Grant should be kept in context, and put alongside other activities and demands on him at this time. In July, a telegram had arrived for him at 33 Tite Street asking him to contact at 'earliest opportunity' a man named John Cox. This young theatre director had been impressed by Jonathan's drawings at the Redfern Gallery and wondered if he would do backcloth material for a production he was mounting at the Edinburgh Festival the following month: an experimental new musical work about the horrors of war written by Iain Hamilton and entitled *Pharsalia*. Jonathan appears to have got going at once, and quickly produced the twenty drawings which proved an integral part of the production. He gave me a detailed account of the preparations and had much to say about the dynamic quality of John Cox. On 27 August, he drove himself to Edinburgh in the red Mini and was present the following evening at the show's first performance at the Freemason's Hall, which was widely and favourably reviewed in the national press.

Judging by what the critics wrote, it seems this project was ideally suited to my brother's tastes. In the *Financial Times*, Ronald Crichton wrote of 'Jonathan Head-Barrow's menacing, disaster-filled drawings'. In *The Times,* Stanley Sadie mentioned 'a harrowing series of drawings by Jonathan Head-Barrow, showing love and violence, death and mutilation . . .' but protested that these screen projections had 'an appeal so loud and coarse as to drown the sense of

Hamilton's score'. In the *Observer*, Peter Heyworth described Jonathan's 'macabre projections' as looking 'as though Bosch were redrawn by Thurber', and claimed they created 'an alarming impression of a human ant heap in the process of disintegration'.

Impressive though these verdicts were, Jonathan seemed far more interested in telling me about the eminent musician he had seen outside his hotel, personally supervising the loading of instruments into the boot of his car: 'Really odd cases. Chauffeur doing it meticulously, probably hoping for a big tip.' He also mentioned that while in Edinburgh he had a drawing accepted by the fashionable Richard Demarco

Gallery in Melville Crescent. I see from a statement dated 29 September 1969 that this picture, entitled *The Arrival Outside Pharsalia*, sold later for five guineas to Mrs Charles Goldman of 781 Fifth Avenue, New York. Jonathan didn't mention if he had also called on his old red-blooded land-lady, Bella Cunningham, under whose roof he had lived only five years earlier.

Jonathan drove back to London via Northumberland, where he visited a family called Charlton at a stately pile called Hesleyside, and then called on Aunt Jean in her humble home in deeply rural Cumberland. He was back in London on the Sunday night and returned to work at Ogilvy & Mather on Monday, 1 September, in a sufficiently buoyant mood that even the theft of the red Mini from outside 52 Tite Street did not unduly annoy him. Or perhaps he vented his spleen on the car itself. 'I'm seriously tempted to sell the *red maggot*, even if the *confounded jalopy* does return,' he soon boasted, employing two antique phrases from the rather pre-war diction used by Mr Grant, whom I see from his diary he had an appointment with on the Wednesday of that week at the Church Army Hostel in Great Peter Street, Westminster. The following Saturday, 6 September, Jonathan and I rebonded – had he now started doing things just to please me? – when we took a day trip to Brighton together. I still have black-and-white photo-graphs of this outing, showing Jonathan in a tweed jacket he'd picked up in a skip, carrying a pint of beer on the pier and being waited upon on the Brighton Belle. Back in London, his diary tells me that he saw Isobel Strachey at Oakley Street on 11 September, had a late lunch with John Cox on 13 September and three days later a drink or two with James Graham.

I mention these appointments only because during

this period, not noted in the diary, he attended a party in Julian's studio – I was not present – where he met for the first time a tall, slim, commandingly attractive girl called Anita Fielding with whom he would spend the rest of his short life.

CHAPTER TWENTY

Anita

I found a quiet corner with Mary and begged her to tell me her own sexual experiences. When she was 16, she went to a cocktail party and met a bulldog called David. That night, after a long drunken dinner at the Ristorante Quixinto Inmexo, he fucked her. I poured out questions about the actual experience, but she grew shy and whined. Since that night, over 46 years ago, she told me she had had a great many dogs and several cats too. And, once, in Dublin, a frog.

The Queue, Chapter Nine

A FEW FACTS or rumours to start with. Anita Fielding was three months older than Jonathan, born on 6 January 1947 at Fleetwood in Lancashire, on the same estuary as the town where we had spent our own early childhood. Her father was apparently called Francis Fielding and according to the subsequent engagement announcement now lived at Lake Tahoe, Nevada. I don't know if Anita saw her father at all. Her mother, who came from Fleetwood and from whom she was partly estranged, was a Roman Catholic and had fairly recently married a professional soldier, Colonel M. G. Hughes, known as Spike, who by 1969 was stationed in Hong Kong. Anita had spent some of her earlier life in Kenya where she had distinguished herself as an equestrian. She still had several friends in the sporting world, including Peter Robeson, sometime captain of England's show jumping team, and Muriel Gross, who wrote to her from the Westwood Country Club in Nairobi. In London, she had a large circle of friends and acquaintances, including our older brother Julian, and had recently taken a flat at 21 Cale Street, off Chelsea Green. She was now twenty-two years old, traffic-stoppingly beautiful and worked in public relations. A few weeks before meeting Jonathan, she had set up a firm called The Publicity Machine with a man called Tom Cave. Their office was a house called The Cottage which was located at the point where Gilston Road meets the Boltons. Anita wrote poetry in her spare time and, one gathered, had had several boyfriends.

I don't know the exact date of Julian's party when Jonathan and Anita first met – I must assume I was away at the time – but I do have an account of this meeting written by Anita on smart Cale Street writing paper shortly after-wards. She states, 'His eyes did not leave mine as he left the person he was talking to and walked slowly towards me.' She continues, 'I wanted him to take my hand and leave the room completely without saying more.' Instead she gave him her card and left the room completely confident that he would ring her up. It seems he did not do so immediately: her notes conclude with the information that five days after the party Jonathan stopped his car – the red Mini had been discovered in a Battersea backstreet – to let her cross a road, did not recognise her but smiled fleetingly, which reassured her 'that it would all happen anyway'.

According to Jonathan's diary their first date was at 6 o'clock on Thursday, 18 September. How things proceeded from there isn't clear and the word 'Librium' noted on the following Sunday may have no significance. On Thursday, 25 September, Anita's name appears again and that weekend they went together to Scotland to stay with friends of Anita called Alan and Patrea More Nisbett who lived in or outside Edinburgh at a house called Buckstane. Jonathan claimed later that the house party had sat up late at night talking about fatal car accidents. One of those present had described being 'first on the scene' at a triple fatal, opening the door to find blood gushing out of the driver's head and his eyes – Jonathan seemed delighted at this detail – 'revolving'. What psychologists would make of this I cannot guess but I can only remind the reader that from all outward appearances Jonathan remained healthy and happy.

The startling contrast between my brother's inner and outer selves had also hit Michael Thomas, a partner in the literary agency A. M. Heath to whom Jonathan had shown some of his recent writings, including presumably the *London Magazine* stories which had at last been published. Writing on 25 September, Thomas began, 'This is a hard letter to write because I enjoyed talking to you the other day, and I believe we could work together happily, but I have to be frank and say that I really don't like what you showed me at all. It seems to me to be extremely self-indulgent, full of writing which achieves its immediate purpose of shocking, but only briefly and thereafter, to my mind at any rate, merely becomes repulsive and boring.'

Though similar views could be expressed about *The Queue* itself, as yet unwritten, Jonathan treated such rejections as a joke, pressed on in the same style and, in due course, got warmer receptions from the agent Diana Crawfurd, who represented Jonny Gathorne-Hardy and a host of stars like Freddie Forsyth, and from the small but up-and-coming publishers Allison and Busby. He had also, at around this time, negotiated his move from Ogilvy & Mather to an even bigger and more prestigious firm. On Friday, 3 October, he had his last day at the place he and others sometimes nicknamed Ogilvy & Graveyard and the following Monday started work on a salary of £2,000 a year at J. Walter Thompson in Berkeley Square, then the largest advertising agency in London, surely not deserving its nickname, J. Walter Tombstone.

Here, of course, he would say little about his work – aside from claiming that one of his accounts was Carter's Little Liver Pills – but quickly set about glorifying his colleagues whose names meant very little to me. 'Jane Folkard's on every corner. Anne Isaacs is next door,' he soon told me – and he had much to say about a fellow copywriter called Hugh Bredin who became agitated when Jonathan smoked a cigarette in his office and told him, 'You're about to have an ash crisis!' He also kept in touch with his Ogilvy & Mather colleagues, especially Gathorne-Hardy, with whom he lunched regularly at Le Petit Café in Stafford Street where items on the menu included best end of lamb and raspberry water ice, and at the French Club in St James's where the fare included braised sweetbreads in sherry sauce and *Poulet au Riz avec Sauce Supreme*. I drag in these details to remind readers of Jonathan's previous life. Should I also have mentioned that his new office was only a street away from Claridge's, his one-time power base?

But of course Jonathan was by now swept off his feet by Anita Fielding and her world. He was hardly ever at 52 Tite Street, though I see from his bank statements that he continued to pay rent to Felix Hope-Nicholson until mid-November. Anita's flat in Cale Street was now his home and his love nest. Love letters, notes and telegrams flew between them which I feel slightly uncomfortable reading and quoting from. A telegram dated 23 October reads GUESS WHO LOVES YOU MORE THAN ANYONE IN THE WORLD: JONATHAN sets the tone and there were also memos from Anita suggesting that they should get engaged, over one of which Jonathan has scribbled, 'I don't know what we should do. But I love you terribly badly and that is what matters.'

From my perspective Anita's world seemed even more exotic than Jonathan's. I was stunned by her cat-like beauty, her mane of hair, her jet-set self-assurance. She knew aristocrats and politicians. She had friends in places like Devonshire Mews West, which reminded me of the world of Dr Stephen Ward and Profumo. She was a friend of a senior police officer based in Chelsea called Dave Woodland, and had recently hired an air-taxi to get to a meeting in Belfast. And among her possessions, I would later find invoices from Dr Tony Greenburgh, a society doctor practising at 73 Eaton Place. I would also find disconcerting items like a pawnbroker's ticket recording that she had pawned a ring for £3 under an assumed name. One cannot help concluding that, like Mary the dachshund or Mr Grant himself, Anita often led a precarious hand-to-mouth existence.

There is also her poetry to consider. Among their shared papers I would find several poems with a distinctly morbid if not sensationalist tone; much more solemn than Jonathan's offerings in this area, but alarming in what it reveals about their shared morbidity, of which there was so little outside evidence. A poem by Anita, entitled 'Death', begins, 'Why do you run so fast/when I long for you/with open arms?' and concludes, 'Oh death take me to/your breast/caress me/make me yours'. Another poem, with the same title, begins, 'I long for the penultimate breath/when I can reconsider/judge myself/and better/know what substance it was of/my life/my little futile life.'

Perhaps self-knowledge was displayed here and real humility. Anita was certainly a wild cat who needed restraining, a far cry from Jonathan's well-connected deb friends of the past, a new departure. Yet their worlds fused comfortably: I see from Jonathan's diary that Slatter joined them for dinner at the Casse-croute on 9 October. Anita's love for Jonathan also extended to seeing the point of Mr Grant. During the autumn of 1969, Jonathan was in permanent touch with Grant, sometimes paid for his overnight accommodation at the Church Army Hostel in Great Peter Street and in December – times were more difficult for guides in cold weather – invited the old schoolmaster to stay with Anita and himself in Cale Street. Here, Jonathan remained open-eyed about Grant's faults, indeed appeared to celebrate them. 'Anita found Grant in the kitchen at three in the morning, mixing red wine with cider,' he soon told me with glee. And on another occasion, 'Grant was sent to the launderette to dry some clothes. He came back with them *sopping wet*.' Grant, meanwhile, supported and buttressed the Anita/Jonathan relationship. 'You are a young man going places who can go a long way,' Grant wrote to Jonathan on 4 December. 'You have an excellent aide in Anita.'

I suppose I got a little closer to them, though I never visited the flat in Cale Street. On my twenty-fourth birthday, 5 November 1969, Jonathan and I had breakfast together at one of our old haunts, Lyons in Piccadilly, famous for its 'bottomless' cup of tea, a feature memorably written up in Jonathan Routh's *Good Cuppa Guide* – 'The record is held by a certain Barnsley woman, rumoured to have drunk 86 cups.' Soon afterwards, Jonathan gave me two amphetamine tablets, telling me that they would enable me to walk past cinema queues without feeling awkward, but also warning – an odd admission – that they could make me impotent.

He also claimed that Anita's policeman friend had told him that the Kray Twins were nothing compared with a South London couple called the Nash Brothers and then gossiped about a peer he was about to nick. Lord Fuck?

I knew much less about Jonathan's working life, and only learnt after his death that he had undertaken various freelance advertising jobs at this time. He had been recommended for one of these by the whizzkid Peter Mayle, later famous for his books about living in the South of France but then running a fashionable agency called Papert, Konig and Lois in Hans Crescent. Alas, this particular assignment hadn't worked out – a rare hiccup for Jonathan – and Peter Mayle had written to him on 2 December, 'I'm desolated to hear your news. I feel I owe you a soothing drink and I'd like to hear all about it. Perhaps you could give me a call and we can fix a time.'

During this period Jonathan also edged closer to our brother Julian, who had written to him from New York on 19 November, urging him to send photographs of his latest artworks to David Mann at the Bodley Gallery, with a view to a New York exhibition the following year. The differences between my world and Jonathan's had meanwhile been emphasised by further publicity about him, organised by Anita, who had also arranged for the pair of them to be photographed strolling in the snow by a man called Richard Clive. On 6 December, a particularly absurd piece about Jonathan Head-Barrow, as he now called himself, appeared in the *Evening Standard*'s 'Londoner's Diary'. There was no 'peg' for this story and it was full of falsities. He claimed to have left Harrow 'under a very dark cloud' at the age of fifteen, trained privately as an artist in Rome and that he and our brother Julian did not see eye-to-eye. 'I hate his work and he hates mine,' Jonathan is quoted as saying. He had gone along with all this nonsense, treating it as a big joke.

Considering their grand and busy life together it was perhaps slightly surprising that, on 17 December, Jonathan and Anita appeared at a large drinks party given in the studio at 33 Tite Street by James Graham and two friends. I recall that they had arrived late – Jonathan had had his 'soothing drink' with Peter Mayle earlier that evening – and made a triumphant entrance. This had enraged Jonathan's old friend Margaret Peile, who had flung her glass of champagne at his feet and stormed out of the room. In the resulting kerfuffle I had told my brother, '*Go after her!*' but found I no longer had any power over him and he made no attempt to do so. Anita had subsequently circled the room like a film star.

Late on 24 December, Jonathan drove me to Wiltshire for Christmas, leaving Grant and Anita together in the flat on Cale Street. During the journey he regaled me with remarks uttered by his J. Walter Thompson colleague Hugh Bredin, references to 'waistcoated tally-ho's', and Bredin's reasons for not driving home till early on Christmas morning: 'By that time all the drunks are either asleep, in jug or in

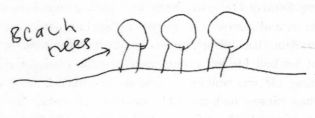

the morgue.' At Turig, Jonathan did more stone carvings and made further morbid jokes. Serving the surviving dogs their supper, he said, 'Shall we have a plateful sent down to Gilda's grave?' and later he asked me: 'Who do you like best? Tiger, Tom, Amber or Gilda's corpse?' When our grandmother, now ninety-one, and soon to move to a care home in Cumberland, shuffled into the room, he remarked more brightly, 'Frank Sinatra's entrance.' On our return journey he pronounced judgement on aspects of the world we had known and shared and declared that Mike d'Abo now had 'little to offer us'.

Back in London, Jonathan soon filled me in on how Grant's festive season had gone. On Christmas Day itself, the old man had apparently wandered down to the King's Road. 'All the down-and-outs were there,' he had reported. 'All the thieves, no-hopers, misfits. And, of course, I'm one of them.' Soon afterwards, Jonathan had more serious news to impart about his house guest. 'Grant has blotted his copy book at Cale Street,' he began. He then launched into an intriguingly long, open and honest account of recent events. 'Grant had become very difficult,' he told me. 'He's back to square one on Sunday. He hasn't been able to save any money. He comes in and annoys me when I'm working. Yes, very like Father. Anita had bronchitis recently and Grant came in and lay on her bed. He left a smell and a mess in the lavatory this morning. He was walking around in a blanket. If he doesn't earn any money he'll die. Of course he still comes up with superb material.' The reference to Sunday and being 'back to square one' was a reminder – or Jonathan's way of telling me – that they were all about to leave Cale Street anyway. Since before Christmas, Jonathan had started renting the basement of a house in Cheniston Gardens Studios near High Street Kensington. His landlord here was the up-and-coming young

Old Harrovian painter Richard Foster, already a family friend. Here, Jonathan and Anita moved early in January 1970.

Their exit from Cale Street seems complicated – Jonathan was soon boasting about a £300 solicitor's bill in connection with the move – and seems to illustrate the wild way in which Anita sometimes behaved. Among the sad muddle of their papers, I would later find a letter dated 22 January from a man called George, upbraiding Anita about some curtains she hadn't made: 'I do not intend to lose £290 plus the material I delivered to you and go to all the trouble of starting again from scratch without someone's head rolling.' A much more serious matter was suggested by a letter to Anita from Sidney Balcombe & Co, insurance loss assessors, about an apparent burglary at Cale Street. The subsequent arrival, on 23 February, of a cheque for £722.3s.08d. in settlement of what one fears was a bogus claim coincided with my discovery around the same time of a drawer full of jewellery and other knick-knacks in a back bedroom at Turig. The fact that Jonathan knew about this business suggests that he too, hitherto so businesslike and responsible, enjoyed living dangerously, and throws further light on the state of his mind during the last few months of his life.

And, of course, further evidence of his inner demons is offered by *The Queue*, which he had now started writing as if his life depended upon it – the whole manuscript has all the appearance of being a rushed job. When occasionally that spring I called at J. Walter Thompson's, I saw the densely typed pages on his desk, if not actually in his typewriter, and for the first time in our semi-collaborative relationship he refused to show them to me. The contents, style and plot of *The Queue* will now be familiar to readers but its actual writing owed a great deal to Jonathan's circumstances at that time. Grant and Anita were now to a large extent dependent on him – Grant had also been given a lot of Jonathan's old clothes – and the various qualities of these two very different individuals are neatly encapsulated in the dog Mary, ultimately a lovable and forgivable character in spite of her misdeeds. Did Jonathan know what he was doing when he invented this creature and set about describing her adventures – or did the whole book pour unedited and undiluted from his subconscious?

Whatever the answer, this was a dramatic and erratic phase of Jonathan's life. Like the young narrator in *The Queue*, he was now moving from place to place – and his wanderings were reflected on a more hazardous scale by those of Mr Grant. Following the loss of Cale Street, the old man was homeless again and, apart from exercising some dogs belonging to a businessman called Sir Patrick Hamilton, who lived in Cheyne Walk, very much at Jonathan's mercy. As before in these circumstances, Grant now turned against his benefactor, again blaming him for the pickle he was in. On 16 January 1970, Grant had written Jonathan another angry letter, severing the friendship for the second time. 'I appreciate your many kindnesses but I do not wish to have my present misery exploited,' he wrote. 'Please do not try to find or contact me.' For a day or two, Jonathan wondered if Grant had thrown himself into the Thames but this particular crisis was quickly resolved. First, Jonathan heard Grant's voice on the J. Walter Thompson switchboard trying to get through. Then he appeared at the office in person. 'I gave him a quid and a cup of tea,' he said smugly. And, from this point on, the old man was even more in his care. During the next few days, Grant would leave begging letters at the office, often pleading that my brother should meet him after work at Farm Street Church – 'For heaven's sake be there as I am in a crisis' – and spend several nights in Jonathan's car parked outside his flat in Cheniston Gardens. One evening, Jonathan had cheekily shown me Grant's hunched and totally covered figure in the back of the vehicle. After one such ordeal, Grant had written to Jonathan along the following whimsical lines: 'I had a child last night in the red mini,' he began. 'I shall christen it reddi-mini, it may mean ready money, which is what we all need . . .' Grant's idea was that Jonathan and Anita should import cigarette lighters from the Continent and get firms like Guinness to advertise on them. I imagine Jonathan did nothing about this idea but he sent me a copy of Grant's letter, with the covering note: 'Received yesterday: surely it is genius.'

Around this time he had also sent me a J. Walter Thompson house magazine showing pictures of couples swirling together at a staff party, over which he had scrawled: 'Final proof that JWT is of no consequence.' Such frank and irreverent communications narrowed the gap between us. As did a rather dramatic little dinner at Cheniston Gardens, also attended by David Gillies. That night the dish, containing a homemade beef and oyster pie, had exploded in the oven and Jonathan had calmly retrieved the situation, laying out more strips of instant puff pastry to accompany or adorn the rescued meat. Another evening we had dined together in a restaurant in Elystan Place, Chelsea, and Anita had thrown back her head, looking drugged or drunk. I also got a little closer to Grant, arranging for him to be photographed by a new acquaintance of mine named Graham Lemane, whom I had met when looking for a job.

I did not know at the time what a rollercoaster life Jonathan and Anita were leading. On 4 February, they attended the Winter Ball at the Hilton Hotel, presided over by the Conservative leader Edward Heath. They had both served on the young committee for this event and Jonathan supplied the wildly unsuitable, harshly abstract pen-and-ink drawing used on the programme cover. Later that night, if a graphic drawing is to be trusted, they made love in Hyde Park, copulating in slanting rain. Whenever apart, or even sometimes when in the same room together, they raised the tempo by writing rude, crude notes to each other and I noticed a new coarseness penetrating Jonathan's language. On finding a note from his new landlord politely pointing out some loose wiring in his flat, Jonathan retorted by muttering joke obscenities out of earshot.

Perhaps unsurprisingly, Jonathan's tenancy of the basement flat at 3 Cheniston Gardens Studios had not worked out. After his exceptionally courteous notes had been ignored, Richard Foster wrote formally on 29 January, giving his fellow Harrovian seven days' notice to quit. In early February, Jonathan and Anita moved to a tiny single room at 99 Oakley Street, Chelsea, part of a flat belonging to a vivacious Irish girl with ducal acquaintances, called Mary-Geraldine O'Donnell.

Going through their papers later, I found a revealing letter that Anita's mother had written to her at this time, announcing that she was coming over from Hong Kong on an indulgence flight to see Anita's 'Grandpa' up in Fleetwood. 'If I don't hear from you soon,' she concluded, 'I take it you don't want me to contact you on arrival or you're maybe busy or away or something.' The defeatist tone of these sad, final words suggests that the estrangement between mother and daughter was partly based on Anita's social insecurities. A few weeks later, Jonathan would bolster these pretensions by telling me – I had no reason to disbelieve him – that Anita's mother was staying at Claridge's.

★

With or without these pressures, Jonathan continued his busy life from the new base in Chelsea. That spring, he began to contribute drawings and prose to a magazine called *Synthesis*, edited by the young Peter Fuller, and developed other contacts elsewhere. On 3 February he had lunch with Diana Crawfurd, who had now agreed to become his literary agent. And the following day had a date with an arty type called Adam Pollock, who invited him to participate in a theatrical project similar to the Edinburgh Festival one and appealed to the mischievous side of his nature by telling him that their mutual friend, Jimmy McMullan, had been in prison. 'Most people have,' Jonathan added when he told me this news soon afterwards. 'Grant's been in three times . . .'⋆

His chief preoccupation during these exhilarating final months was *The Queue*, which mirrored the life around him as well as containing so many curious flashbacks to his early life and times. Grant's potentially suicidal behaviour and escapist nature is often echoed by Mary's behaviour, not least when she hires a paddleboat and throws herself off into the deepest part of a pond. 'For a moment she splashes desperately and I think she is going to keep herself up,' the narrator tells us, but soon he has dived in after her. Luckily the friendly pike mentioned earlier comes to the rescue and 'this strong, experienced fish' soon surfaces with Mary clasped firmly in its *arms*. Jonathan then adds a bit about the pike expecting a tip, taking offence and threatening to upset the boat.

There are several ingredients here which echo the pressure Grant put on Jonathan, but *The Queue* also quotes the old man verbatim. The way the narrative lapses into intimacy, confidentiality and joke self-pity is reminiscent of the

⋆ Pressed on these matters, Grant had apparently replied, 'Yes, I've had three convictions. I'd rather not talk about it if you don't mind.'

endless letters Grant now wrote to Jonathan, awash with statements like, 'I am very tired of all this, day in day out, and wonder how much longer I'll hold out,' 'I have not had a soul to talk to (properly) since I saw you on Friday,' and 'I have suffered enough and can take no more.' Chapter Twelve of *The Queue* actually begins with several sentences lifted from one of Grant's letters: 'I am in Cattel Street NW1 with no money, no hope and only the clothes I stand up in,' the narrator tells us. 'I cannot go on very much longer like this. There is no way out. The daily strain is too much. Am sorry to be so dreary.'

And of course Jonathan put a great deal more into *The Queue* than just Grant. While he was writing it, painful matters resurfaced, like the oppression suffered at the hands of various schoolmasters – to whom I have suggested Grant had acted as a kind of antidote. As I stated earlier, he was still raging against the Head Master of Harrow during the final weeks of his life. God knows what other painful matters he addressed and then submerged in humour. I only know that writing *The Queue* was not sheer pleasure for him. 'I have not felt too well for the past few days,' he wrote to Anita around this time. 'I think it is the book. It takes a lot out of me. I love you. I love being with you. So please don't go away.'

CHAPTER TWENTY-ONE

Engagement

I expect you are knee-deep in 'wedding-itis' . . .
I'd love to be there but I don't suppose you want
murderers and shabby genteels bobbing in their
ugly little heads. I can imagine you introducing
me to your father and a quick stock-taking of my
get up and recognition of the Head–Barrow
wardrobe . . .

Letter from Mr Grant, 13 March 1970

IN THE MIDDLE of February 1970, Jonathan surprised me by
insisting that I should not go down to Wiltshire the following
weekend. It soon emerged that he was planning to take Anita to
Turig for the first time. The seriousness with which Anita
took this first encounter with my parents emerges from a
letter she had already received from her mother, to whom
she seems to have been reconciled. Back in Hong Kong, Mrs
Hughes had written on a forces airmail form, saying, 'Good
luck this weekend and I know you will be happy.'

All seems to have gone well and the following Monday
or Tuesday Jonathan telephoned Tite Street to say that he
and Anita were getting married. 'We're putting it in *The
Times* next week,' he told me. At first, a Register Office ceremony was mentioned, but soon they were consulting Father
Wilfred Tighe about getting married at the Brompton

Oratory. When I asked where they would live, Jonathan replied, 'We'll probably get a little house.'

I had played no part in the run-up to this decision, but got the impression that Jonathan had been hand-in-glove with our oldest brother over the matter. 'Simon openly passed water when we announced our engagement,' Jonathan joked, but had in fact consulted him closely about the arrangements. He would soon also inform me, 'Father has written two letters to Anita, both incredibly funny.' Anyway, this was a crucial turning point. I was no longer in a position to direct or organise my brother's path. For years, Jonathan had been a useful ally in my battles against so much. Now it had been finally rammed home to me that I stood alone.

At the same time, there was something faintly disquieting about the arrangement. Jonathan did not seem quite as happy as he should have been, but since he had never discussed Anita with me, or hinted at any problems or doubts they might have had, I did not know what to think. James Graham shared my concerns, remarking, 'It's a very rum do,' and adding, 'With any luck your turn will come.' In those days marriage seemed a much bigger thing, a much bigger commitment than it does today. Julian had now returned from a long absence abroad and was also faintly critical of the match, remarking, 'Jonathan doesn't need security. Anita does.'

The engagement was officially announced in *The Times* on Tuesday, 24 February. I still have some of the letters that poured in for Jonathan. Uncle Gurney, who had tutored Jonathan for Common Entrance ten years earlier, wrote offering 'very many congratulations', and adding, 'You do seem to have taken everyone by surprise.' Kenneth Slatter wrote from Brussels where he now worked for Holiday Inns International, 'Congratulations – well, well, well, you made it . . . I hope all goes well for you both.' And from Northumberland, there came an immensely generous letter from Margaret Peile. 'I send you all the wish in my power that you will be happy,' she wrote and added her deep apologies for the incident at the party before Christmas. 'It is quite a long time ago now, meant very little and really didn't and certainly doesn't matter. But if it upset you at all, I am sorry.'

It was soon decided that the wedding would take place at the Brompton Oratory at 5 p.m. on 23 April, followed by a reception at the Belgravia home of Anita's friends, Peter and Renee Robeson. In due course, an engraved copperplate invitation was printed by Smythson, giving Anita's mother, Mrs M. G. Hughes, as the hostess but making no reference to her father, Francis Fielding. Jonathan invited Jonathan Gathorne-Hardy to be his best man, a fact that particularly pleased my father when he learnt that Gathorne-Hardy's mother-in-law was now married to the Marquis of Bath. In the weeks that followed Jonathan blew hot and cold with me. I attended parties in the first-floor flat at 99 Oakley Street, hosted by Mary-Geraldine O'Donnell. On 4 March, I had dinner with Jonathan and Anita and learnt about some of the people being invited to the wedding. The Michael d'Abos had accepted immediately, he told me chirpily, and he was also inviting Frere, sending the ex-Chester Herald's invitation to the address he gave in *Who's Who*, i.e. care of the Society of Antiquaries. He then added spikily, 'And a lot of people you don't know.'★

And where was Grant during all this excitement? My brother's friend's life had taken a bizarre turn around the

★ I had already seen the invitation on Quentin Crisp's mantelpiece. Quentin claimed that Jonathan had only sent it to 'tease' him. Other prospective guests included the future TV chef Clarissa Dickson Wright and her parents.

time of the engagement announcement – a turn that may have greatly appealed to Jonathan on some levels. Certainly he told me about it with relish. After living in any number of different places, Grant had returned at the end of February to the Church Army Hostel in the East End where he had been staying the previous year. Here he had immediately plunged into an extremely dramatic situation. A murder had taken place on the premises and Grant had been arrested and held on suspicion. The police had even interviewed Jonathan for an hour in his office at J. Walter Thompson about it. On 11 March, Grant had appeared in court and been given an absolute discharge, muttering in the dock, 'I must get away to the country.'

This event is so fanciful – Grant had apparently said later, 'The room service in prison is always a bit slapdash' – that I thought Jonathan could easily have invented it all, had I not later found essential details confirmed in an eight-page letter from Grant to Jonathan. After his court appearance, Grant took the train from Paddington to Oxford, seen off by Jonathan who gave him a first-class ticket and was as delighted as ever by Grant's conduct as the train departed. He now pronounced him 'an adult deb's delight', and praised the 'brilliant pompous expression' on the old schoolmaster's face, especially considering that he had absolutely no money at all in his pocket.

This railway station parting would also provide Jonathan with the closing scene of *The Queue*. The character of Grant fuses easily into that of Mary, though Jonathan is extremely playful with the details, and presents Mary as more troublesome than Grant ever was. But the bare bones of this description of a court appearance, a kindly magistrate and departure from a railway station, are broadly true of Grant's experience:

The gaoler knocks on the door at ten. Mary is badly hung over. I have to steady her and, at the suggestion of the gaoler, take a sick bowl into court. The magistrate is kind and thoughtful. He deals with our case quickly, giving Mary an absolute discharge providing she agrees to attend Colter Hill Maternity Home. Mary bursts into tears. She breaks away from the gaoler and runs to the magistrate's dais. Court officials wave their hands at her. Stop it. Get back to the dock. You've no business to behave like this. But the magistrate raises his hand, ordering the officials to be silent. The court is hushed. Mary is on the magistrate's lap and all that can be heard is her sobs. He is stroking her: everything will be alright my dear. This is the best thing for you. Magistrate has a dachshund of his own at home. He is almost in tears and so upset that he is unable to take the rest of the cases. He goes home in a taxi and the relief magistrate is summoned by telegram. However, he refuses to make the journey and the court is closed for the day. Major offenders are returned to their cells. Minor offenders (drunks, exposures, petty thefts) are set free.

A telephone call is put through to the super-intendent at Colter Hill. Mary will be arriving on the one-thirty train. A car will meet her. The gaoler and a police officer accompany us to the station. We must meet Mary's fare ourselves, so I ask Sparrow to distract the newsagent's attention and lift some money from the till with his beak. The police officer notices, but, realizing the circumstances, ignores the offence. Unfortunately, just as Sparrow has gripped onto a five-pound note, the drawer is shut and Sparrow is trapped inside. Anxiously, we wait for another sale and the till to open. He loses several feathers but otherwise is unhurt. The train is delayed and the gaoler buys cups of tea at the canteen. Mary will not sip and clutches me. It is pathetic. She urges me not to leave her like this. The train pulls in and she begins to weep again. The gaoler, normally brutal, is visibly upset and takes a napkin to wipe his eyes. Mary, thinking this a good moment to escape, slips her collar and runs. Soon she is lost in the crowds. The angry gaoler organizes a search and all station personnel are summoned. Meanwhile the train is not allowed to leave. After half an hour I hear the gaoler cry out. He has found Mary hiding in a wastepaper basket (her tail stuck out). The gaoler has now no patience and marches her onto the platform, kicking her whenever she lingers . . . All down the train, passengers lean from their windows and boo: they are furious at the delay. A compart-ment door is opened, but, as Mary steps in, she trips and falls between platform and coach. The gaoler goes down on his knees and curses. She has fallen nine feet and is straddled across a line. I think she is unconscious. The stationmaster brings a rope-ladder and I volunteer to descend. I place wet flannels on her head and, in a few moments, she comes round. She has lost her memory. She wants to know where she is.

Now the impatient engine-driver is beside us: I must take my train away now. I cannot delay further. Put her on, or travel later. There is no alternative. I wrap Mary in my pullover and place her in a compartment. But the occupants do not want her and ask for her to be removed. I try next door. Three businessmen tell me to clear out. Finally I am forced to leave her on the corridor floor. As the train begins to move, she staggers to her feet and I see the old grey face pressed against the glass. She tries to say something, but her voice cannot be heard. Sparrow's tears are running down my sleeve and we wait till the last carriage disappears.

This moving end to *The Queue* was written very soon after Grant's departure from London, but was not the last thing he wrote as he continued, perhaps until the day of his death, to produce material that could be added to his story. But this final sequence is charged with emotion and provides further evidence of Grant's hold over him.

Nor was this Jonathan's last encounter with his old friend. From Oxford, where Grant was staying, care of a certain Captain Oxley at Cambridge Terrace, he wrote the next day thanking Jonathan for all his help and apologising for dragging him into the incident. 'I do hope there is no more trouble from the evil bluebottles,' he writes with reference to the detectives who had called at J. Walter Thompson. In the same post Grant wrote about the forthcoming wedding, explained why he would not be attending and finally, true to form, declares, 'I'm sorry this is such a dreary letter.'

Whatever his anxieties, this was not a dreary time for Jonathan. He had entered into the wedding arrangements high-spiritedly, attending regular sessions and meetings with Father Tighe at the Brompton Oratory, though probably not telling this former army officer that he was trying to hew the wedding ring out of oak – 'It's almost impossible,' he told the *Daily Express* gossip columnist. 'The wood starts shrinking as soon as I start carving it' – and planning to get the surviving dachshunds, Tiger, Tommy and Amber to act as bridesmaids.

But this was a wild rather than a happy time. On Sunday 15 March, Jonathan and Anita took a suite for one night in the Carlton Tower Hotel, registering as Mr and Mrs Barrow, and paying £21.5s.3d. for the privilege. After spending that weekend at home – while there I learnt that Jonathan's old pony Flash had died of old age in a neighbour's field – I arrived in London and was summoned to the hotel and had drinks in their sitting room. Here Jonathan did a pen-and-

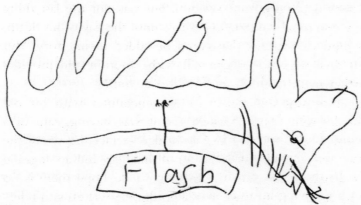

ink of Flash lying upside down in her field and, into the bargain, gave her a penis.

Jonathan and Anita paid further visits to Turig. My father loved having them to stay and was excited about the wedding. Rather amazingly, he had swallowed whole a story by Anita that she was of old landowning Lancashire stock – 'The sort of family that laid out places like Fleetwood,' he had told Aunt Jean. After spending the last weekend of March under my father's roof, they had driven back to London via Oxford where they had seen Grant at his hostel. On the mention of Father Tighe, Grant had remembered that a priest of this name had once advertised in *The Times* for a steward at the Oratory. 'The job meant looking after the wines and spirits.'

Will it surprise the reader that at this wild time a certain pace or sparkle had at last entered my own life? And that I had now slept with a titled woman twice my age? And, perhaps more oddly, that this woman was vaguely known to Anita, who soon issued instructions via Jonathan that I should on no account bring my raffish new lady friend to their wedding? And that, though I would not become a car driver until the 1980s, I had at last begun to take part in the sort of country-house weekends Jonathan had enjoyed for years?

Anyway, there were other changes afoot. James Graham had now left 33 Tite Street and taken a room at 90 Oakley Street, only a few doors away from where Jonathan and Anita were staying. And, on 30 March, my life was further lit up by the unexpected return from California, via Italy, of my old colleague David Kaye, whose first novel was due to be published that summer by Calder & Boyars. David Kaye had done well abroad and arrived in England in a saucy red sports car. In the midst of this excitement, he would tighten the net by moving into the same ground-floor room in 52 Tite Street which had once been mine. The following day we drove together to Berkeley Square and visited Jonathan in his office. On the next night, Wednesday, 1 April, David had dinner with Jonathan and Anita. 'She made me very nervous,' he said afterwards. 'I couldn't eat and things.'

I do not know where this dinner took place or how Jonathan and Anita spent the rest of the week. I do know that Jonathan continued to work on his book – perhaps it was now that he wrote that last scene at the railway station

– and that he also worked on some new pictures, again macabre, possibly commissioned by Adam Pollock or some other figure in the Redfern circle. I still have some of the very rough inky sketches that he did for this project, featuring ancient executions and decapitations, which used as a source *Foxe's Book of Martyrs*. At the weekend, they drove off – was it Friday or Saturday? – to stay with their friends the Robesons at Fences Farm, Newport Pagnell, Buckinghamshire. Jonathan took his typewriter with him and appears to have written the paragraph about a wedding turning into a funeral while under their roof. I do not know how the weekend began. I only know that before lunch on Sunday, 5 April, they went for a drink with a couple called Hartigan who owned an antique shop and lived a few miles away at a magnificent old house called Lavendon Grange with fishponds, ancient earthworks and a wood known as 'The Rookery' in its grounds.

In the euphoria of the moment, I had meanwhile invited David Kaye to come home with me to Wiltshire. My friend's possession of an Italian sports car would, I knew, reassure and amuse my father. Indeed, I soon noticed how well the two men got on together and how David had 'appreciated' the Turig drawing room. On Sunday morning we set off again and on the way back to London visited a new friend of mine called Nicholas Phipps who lived on the remains of his family estate near Westbury. Before lunch David and I walked around the empty Phipps mansion. On sighting our host at an upper kitchen window in the lodge, David observed, 'He looks like a chemist. He was mixing something.'

On our return journey to London I remember giving my friend careful advice about oncoming traffic, his car being a left-hand-drive one. I also remember that we had somewhat ghoulishly driven into the precincts of Roundway Mental Hospital, near Devizes, and seen what the narrator of *The Queue* would have called 'imbeciles' lying on the grass. We reached Chelsea at 5.40 p.m. There was a summery atmosphere. I rang 99 Oakley Street but there was no reply. I went upstairs to the studio but my brother Julian was on the telephone in his little lobby, so I went downstairs again. Presently I heard Julian coming into the flat. He said my name and entered the front room. Then he said, 'Prepare yourself for the worst possible news. Jonathan and Anita have been killed in a car crash.'

EPILOGUE

Despite sodden and almost illegible pages, the book was published on April 11. It was an immediate success and the young writer was acclaimed, posthumously, as a genius. His body was exhumed from the Salvation Army graveyard, where he had been given a pauper's funeral, and taken to London for a memorial service at Westminster Abbey. Unfortunately, the hearse collided with a No. 5 bus in Parliament Square. The coffin split in two, fell open in front of a crowd of gasping celebrities. Screens and capes were rushed to the scene. No press photographers allowed.

The Queue, Chapter Nine

I HAVE GIVEN a lot of thought to my initial half-crazy reactions to the news of my brother's death. The buzz in the air, the electric feeling that I had never experienced before – or since. And how, almost immediately, I had thought of Jonathan's impishness and impudence. Had he pulled off the ultimate trick? Was it all a brilliant hoax?

I remember how Julian quickly left the flat to go and see our oldest brother Simon in Notting Hill, and how I had limply declared, 'I'll spend the evening with David Kaye.' Summoned by telephone, my friend had arrived from across the road, dressed in a dark blue or black poloneck and with a profoundly quizzical expression on his face. 'Have you flipped your top?' were his first words.

A few minutes later I telephoned Oakley Street again, got Mary-Geraldine and broke the news to her so badly – I had hardly taken it in myself – that she went berserk. I then sent David to console her and minutes later, deciding that this might not be enough, ran through the streets after him. On arrival at the first-floor flat, I had found Mary-Geraldine sitting on the floor talking on the telephone. My appearance must have told her that this was no hoax because she said immediately to the person on the line, 'It's true.'

Today, I still feel grateful for, even amazed by the role David Kaye played in comforting and consoling me – and lifting my spirits during the next few hours and days. And my gratitude is mixed with sadness that, a few years later, our friendship would peter out. During that time together – he spent the first night in the flat at my request – he helped me come to terms with the news and helped me break the news to others, some of whom found it as difficult to believe as he had done. He also reminded me that all was not lost, that Jonathan's spirit still permeated our lives and enlivened the atmosphere by making nettle-grasping remarks such as Jonathan himself might have made. On our second evening together, he even remarked, 'The novelty's worn off.'

I also remember that I could not cry – the event was of too massive a magnitude for tears. Instead, I went mad, placed Jonathan on an even bigger pedestal than before and talked incessantly about him. For someone obsessed with death, his own demise was an utterly extraordinary event. During those early days I felt I had entered a pagan topsy-turvy world. And I was acutely aware of the excruciating, super-cruel irony that Jonathan could play no part in events that followed his death. Though he had, according to the evidence of his writing, foreseen this tragedy, his odyssey was over now and he had swiftly vanished into the past, heading away from me speedily with no farewells.

And yet, in many respects, Jonathan's death brought him closer to me than he had been for many months. In the days that followed that catastrophic weekend, Jonathan's life, writings, pictures and possessions, hidden from me for many months, were suddenly accessible and even back in my control. In a sort of trance and without speaking to each other, Julian and I had gone to 99 Oakley Street and packed up our brother's suits, ties, unframed pictures, stone carvings, books, including Muybridge's *The Human Figure in Motion* and *Foxe's Book of Martyrs*, and alarm clocks. We also bundled up the love letters and telegrams that lay strewn about that small room. And I also found, fingered and pocketed the sweet wooden wedding ring which, as readers of the *Daily Express* knew, Jonathan had been carving.

At the beginning of this book, I mentioned that I had also gone to Jonathan's office at J. Walter Thompson to pick up his things there. In a drawer of his desk I found the closely written typescript of *The Queue*. I had been aware that Jonathan was working on a book but refused even a glimpse of it. Now I had the whole thing in my possession, to which I would soon add the last scraps of writing which my older brothers would retrieve, along with his typewriter, from the Robesons' house in Buckinghamshire. I now fell upon the book, feasted privately on it and found it an immense consolation.

I was not involved in the practical, administrative side of Jonathan and Anita's deaths. Julian had taken that first terrible telephone call from the Buckinghamshire police and had driven with Simon that night to be with our parents in

Wiltshire – God only knows what Anita's mother was going through far away in Hong Kong. The following day, my brothers had gone together to Newport Pagnell to identify the bodies and pick up their personal possessions from the police, including the cylindrical silver cufflinks Jonathan had been wearing at the time of his death. They also visited the spot where the crash had occurred and found spent morphine cartridges beside the road where the emergency services had struggled to save one or both victims.

I would eventually learn that Jonathan and Anita met their deaths at 2 o'clock in the afternoon as they drove back to the Robesons from Lavendon Grange. Both had been drinking and were over the legal limit. They had stopped on the way for some sort of lunch at a roadside café, which might have come from the pages of *The Queue,* and which Julian later described as 'a miserable little place'. Minutes later, on the edge of a bridge over the Great Ouse, the red Mini had collided with another vehicle, the occupants of which were taken to hospital but eventually survived. Jonathan appears to have been killed outright. Anita died on the way to hospital. The question of who was driving the car at the time – this issue later obsessed my father – was never fully resolved. The fact that Jonathan had foreseen this violent conclusion to his life so often in his writings – and drawings – makes it all the more peculiar. More than once in *The Queue* and elsewhere, he had even imagined his death occurring in the way it did: the words spoken by onlookers and even the strap (or 'girth') placed around his waist. While lightening the load by satirising the language of medical handbooks, it is still unbelievable that Jonathan ended up under the red blankets he had so often described.

★

Jonathan's death gave me much more than his novel and his cufflinks. It also gave me immediate access to his inner circle. The day after the tragedy Grant telephoned me from Oxford but was too overcome to speak. In the next post, letters began to arrive from this champion vintage figure – I now saw him in this light – the first of which began, 'Words fail me re all this,' and went on to describe Jonathan as the son or grandson he had never had, and to stress the innocence of the relationship. 'All the fools who looked askance were looking well up the wrong tree.' I also formed immediate bonds with other key players in my brother's world. After picking up his stuff from J. Walter Thompson, I had lunch with Jonathan's colleague Hugh Bredin and in the months and years ahead would get to know him better than my brother had. Later that same afternoon, I received a buoyant call from Jonny Gathorne-Hardy, who said with dynamic zest, 'I'm coming over to you *right now!*' and indeed was soon sitting on my bed at 33 Tite Street, filling me with optimism and excitement and saying that he was planning to write a tribute to Jonathan in *The Times*. The following day I took the typescript of *The Queue* to Ogilvy & Mather, where Gathorne-Hardy still worked. Together we photocopied the script, laughed over its contents and noted that Jonathan had recorded the number of words on each page. 'I know that so well – adding up,' Gathorne-Hardy remarked, and praised Jonathan for succeeding in being funny in his first paragraph. 'Most writers, myself included, don't get their first laugh for *at least* two pages.'

My spirits rose. Many of those already in my life were hugely understanding, and gave me the strength to cope with the despondence around me. On the Wednesday of that week, a newly married friend drove me to the Redfern Gallery where I met John Synge's assistant, Maggie Wales, for the first time, kissed her immediately, retrieved four or five large framed drawings which had been on sale there and began a friendship which lasts to this day. That night I had dinner with James Graham, who had also taken the tragedy in his stride, in the sense of not being downtrodden about it. Over dinner in a slightly better Italian restaurant than we normally went to, he volunteered that there was 'a very strange smell' to the whole affair and subscribed to my tiny, lingering suspicion that it was still a hoax by declaring that there was one thing he was absolutely certain of, that was that we would eventually meet Jonathan again.

Bolstered by offbeat, upbeat comments from friends of Jonathan, I began to feel that I had at last formed a power base independent of my relations, if largely fuelled by Jonathan's aura and sense of humour. On Thursday, 9 April, I took Margaret Peile to dinner with our Old Harrovian friend Jim Vakeel at his parents' plush flat in Chelsea, and he too raised the tone, though in a different way, by talking about his bitter disappointment with the latest Barbra Streisand record, instead of the tragedy closer to home.

The following evening, I took Margaret Peile with me to Wiltshire, asking a woman carrying flowers on the train if I could have some of them to give someone who'd been bereaved. This failed gesture apart, my selfishness towards my parents may raise some eyebrows. I had not thought to telephone them to offer kindness or sympathy. To this day I do not know how they took the news and who held their hands, or even whether they held each other's hands. During that weekend, I was delighted, anyway, to find that my father's sense of humour had not deserted him – 'I may be the next to go,' he threatened. 'Just like that. Taken straight off. And not necessarily to heaven either' – but saw that he was mainly preoccupied with replying to letters of sympathy. Or noting who had so far failed to write.* And, I dare say, already focusing on the financial aspects of the tragedy. As for my mother, I learnt she had drawn comfort from an encounter with a squirrel at the time of Jonathan's death. 'I was sitting in the kitchen,' she explained, 'when it jumped up onto the window and went up and down, up and down, trying to find a way through. It scrabbled up on the glass, trying to find a way through.'

Back in London on 13 April, I was excited by the publication of Gathorne-Hardy's tribute to Jonathan in *The Times*, which ended with the inspiring phrases quoted in the Prologue. His words must have rung in my mind as I made my way later that day to witness the Induction of the two coffins at the Brompton Oratory. Do I need to describe this event or the crowded funeral the following day in the very place where the wedding was due to have taken place? Or explain that my brother Martin, now living in Bangkok, was not present at the Brompton Oratory on account of the baby his wife was expecting later that month? I chiefly recall being sustained by a comment on my clunking footwear by Guy Hungerford – '*Mourner's shoes!*' – and the way that Jonny Gathorne-Hardy had waved wildly at me from the pavement as I was driven off to the burial in Putney Vale. Here, at the graveside, I was further moved by the way my mother, normally shy and inhibited, had suddenly put her arm around the woman I now knew to be Anita's mother.

Do I need to describe the party afterwards in Julian's studio? Or the heightened tensions between me and the rest of the family? I can only say that it was *The Queue* and the idea

---

* He had already receive an inspiring letter from Rosemary Leventon's father: 'Hold your head high. Jonathan would not want you to mourn for too long.'

of Jonathan, as it were, having the last laugh, that kept me afloat for the next few months. And my madness. Perhaps I was too batty to respond properly to the loss? Instead of being downcast, I often felt on top of the world. Jonathan's death had made me feel important. For the first time in my life there was a sense of doors opening and possibilities presenting themselves. I found I was liberated by his death. I no longer felt upstaged by him. His death removed some of the shackles of adolescence and family life and cleared the decks for the relationships and projects that came later. I saw

at last that Jonathan was no longer my boss or my protégé, but was also intensely proud and flattered when Aunt Jean, whom I visited in Cumberland later in April, declared, 'He was *your* creation. *You* brought him out. He was *your* discovery.'

And of course I remained obsessed by him. I started to wear his clothes, shirts and ties, even the cylindrical cufflinks he had worn at the moment of his death and, on one drunken occasion, even pretended to be him. Hardly surprisingly and perhaps to my benefit, I also dreamt constantly about him, perpetuating in my sleep the conspiracy between us and the rest of the world. In those early months, I often dreamt that Jonathan was still alive, shaken by the accident, in a wheelchair perhaps and, once, in a hospital-cum-prison-cum-hotel – but still planning his wedding to Anita. In these dreams I told Jonathan what had been happening since his death, and woke from these reveries amazed that *he* was dead and *I* was alive, rather than the other way round. I also, just occasionally, wondered how Jonathan would have reacted if this *had* been the case. And from time to time I still brooded on the remote possibility that the whole accident had been an elaborate hoax, a piece of subterfuge, an attempt by Jonathan to change his identity.

The posthumous extension of Jonathan's world was partly perpetuated by the letters that now arrived in almost every post from Grant, addressing me on the envelope Andrew Head-Barrow Esquire – and I was touched by his joy when I announced I would visit him at the hospital near Oxford where he was now receiving treatment. Here I found this surviving member of my brother's entourage in sparkling form, a sprig of heather in his lapel, trotting around the hospital canteen like a child and enjoying a chirpy dialogue – 'Cup of tea, James?' 'I'd love some if you're doing some, Jackie' – with another inmate. Perhaps predictably, Grant had already refocused on the adventure of his own life, and Jonathan was no longer for him of primary interest.

By now I had also linked up with others in Jonathan's circle. I had telephoned Jimmy McMullan at his gallery off Baker Street. 'My dear,' he began in his rather over-the-top style, 'you nearly lost me too, I was on the bottle for three weeks. Let's just pretend he's still alive. It's the only way.' Faintly hollow and theatrical though this sounded, McMullan would ask me round to his flat in Porter Street more than once in the following months, where he would drawl on about Jonathan in a drunken but unrevealing way. From his office in Brussels, Kenneth Slatter had sent me a rather colder typewritten letter beginning, 'Words fail, but I can only tell you how sad I was when I heard the news about Jonathan,' and ending 'I will call you when I am next in London and we will meet.'

More immediately welcoming was Patrick Procktor, whom I had never met. On 28 May I had tea with this immensely tall, melancholy-looking artist in his drawing room in Manchester Street where Jonathan had met the likes of Cecil Beaton the previous summer. Procktor took ages to prepare tea but then spoke revealingly about my brother. 'He came to me as a complete loner, he just came knocking on my door one day. I never knew he had a girlfriend.' Later Procktor would visit me at 33 Tite Street, walking all the way from his own house and accepting, on second thoughts, my offer of wine and telling me to forget the tea I had started making.

Meanwhile, I had run into our comedian friend Tommy Deane at a street corner. On hearing the news, the small Australian had punched the air and stated, 'It's all a great mistake!' and then launched into a defence of Jonathan's driving skills. 'He was the only person I felt really safe taking a lift off,' which surprised me as I was unaware Jonathan had ever given him a lift anywhere. Tommy's parting words concerned the As You Like It's proprietor, 'Barrie doesn't know, does he?'

What did I learn or hope to gain from these encounters? Some people may have said what I wanted to hear, acquiesced with my own views of my brother's talents. Others were more guarded in their responses. From Quentin Crisp, to whom I had now shown a copy of *The Queue*, I got the view of Jonathan I quoted at the beginning of this book, namely the differences between his outer and inner selves. When the author of *The Naked Civil Servant* later lunched with me at Tite Street, he mocked me for saying that I planned to live off Jonathan's talents for ever.

Others had agendas of their own. One evening in Rossetti Gardens Studios, the grief-stricken portrait painter Brenda Bury, a close friend of Anita, whom I had not met until the funeral, held forth about my brother's fiancée in a highly revealing way. 'Anita had to lie, had to move, had to cheat,' she told me. 'She was lying all the time. Robert Spencer-Barnard thought Jonathan was Anita's *half-brother*. She told a lie right up to the end. She was a liar. That was half the attraction. Nine-tenths of the time, she was motivated by fear. She had a foul reputation. She looked used, slept with. I know she got money out of men – Mark, Robert, Neil, Dicky . . .' Of Anita and Jonathan, she said, 'They were hopelessly together. I could do nothing. I tried to stop it. She was making Jonathan into something he didn't want to be. It was too fraught, too worrying for both of them.' But she also acknowledged Anita's magic: 'She was brave and strong. You had to admire that woman for what she did for herself. You had to admire her courage and panache. She had a great many people who *returned* to her and loved her . . .' Riveting though these comments were, I was more intrigued by the emerging similarities between Anita and the fictional Mary. I now knew the dominant character in *The Queue* well but was full of wonder as to whether Jonathan knew when he wrote about his heroine's delinquent, promiscuous, difficult, impossible, adorable character that he was also writing about Anita?

★

I had also run into the first of various problems with the hitherto staunchly and poetically supportive David Kaye, still my neighbour in Tite Street. In the immediate aftermath of Jonathan's death, David had struck all the right notes, even to the extent of smiling and murmuring, 'Jonathan's alive,' when we met in the street. He had praised and attributed to Jonathan a *Citizen Kane*-like persona and not shirked the gruesome details of the crash itself. 'In high-speed collisions,' he told me, 'the shoes always come off.' Now, with a new girlfriend at his side, he had less time for me. When I pleaded with him to come over the road, he replied, 'Can't you bear the loneliness?' And when I accosted him once too often, he snapped at me, 'Call me when you turn twenty-one.'

In other respects that summer became busier and richer. The weather was nice. My engagement diary shows that I was out almost every night. I saw a certain amount of the titled lady and a lot of Margaret Peile, who radiated goodness and understanding and promised, when asked if I would run into Jonathan and Anita again, 'It's only a question of time.' I also saw a lot of James Graham who, to make matters more complicated, had briefly moved into the very room Jonathan and Anita had occupied at 99 Oakley Street. He claimed to have had a very bad first two nights there, heard all sorts of creaking, seen a figure and poured with sweat . . .

Over the summer, I also saw the surviving members of my family regularly. Simon and Julian had not shared my views of Jonathan. Nor had I inflicted these on them. Though closer to me in age and experience, Martin had to some extent been insulated from the tragedy by living on the other side of the world. At sentimental moments, I felt like Abbott without Costello, or Bootsie without Snudge, but Jonathan's death had left no obvious gap in my other brothers' lives. They remained more interested in his advertising work than his novel – and Simon had even had one of Jonathan's advertisements framed. Though patient, good-natured and initially prepared to tolerate Jonathan's pictures which I had hung up around the flat, which we now to some extent shared, Julian showed a detachment, which was reassuring rather than offensive. I remember how, during dinner in a Chinese restaurant, he sketched on a napkin the image our late brother had presented on the mortuary slab. By returning so soon after the funeral to Italy, where he had friends and work waiting, he showed he had another life to lead. Back in England later in the summer, he said of Jonathan and Anita's wedding, 'It would have been an absolute fiasco. The funeral only went smoothly because it was brilliantly organised by Simon.' He was also able to make jokes about the tragedy. Setting off somewhere in his car he now told me, 'Expect a call from Buckinghamshire police in two hours' time.'

Over the years, I have wondered if Julian attributed Jonathan's death to his stepping out of the ordered and basically conventional world that he himself inhabited. He certainly regretted being away at the formative time of their relationship: 'If I'd known they were having an affair, I'd have made absolutely certain they didn't get married.' He spoke of Gathorne-Hardy's piece in *The Times*. 'Thousands of people have seen it,' he said, 'but many have said they didn't know he was my brother.' And he also mentioned Anita's insurance fraud, and speculated that had she survived the accident she would have very likely gone to prison. Or a loony bin. And that Jonathan had treated the whole business as a joke.

I saw less of my brother Simon, but occasionally had rather deadbeat encounters with him which left us both deflated. Early in May, he had telephoned about the Inquest results and the ruling that Jonathan's car had been at fault and that probably Jonathan was driving. 'It all seems a long time ago now,' he said. And to Martin I learnt he had written, 'Thank God it's all over. You have no idea of the sheer administrative details of the tragedy . . .'

And, of course, I went home often to Wiltshire. At some stage, Julian had reported that our parents had 'got over it' and were now 'making jokes'. My father was also making plans to move to the Isle of Man and somehow managed to combine these chores with all the paperwork generated by the death of his youngest son.* Immune to such diversions, my mother, as always, sought and found comfort in nature. She planted her pansies and button daisies and spoke to them as she did so. And soon had another mystical experience to report. 'A little white butterfly sat on my hand in the greenhouse,' she said one weekend, 'and it remained there all the way down the path . . .' More remarkable, and more in tune with events in *The Queue*, was her dramatic revelation: '*Some animal has been at Gilda's grave.*'

In London I began to see more of Mr Grant. Or perhaps I should write, saw the last of Mr Grant. On 1 August, I had had a drink with him at the Builders' Arms in Chelsea, a session that I learnt later had ended with him being arrested for being drunk and disorderly. When I asked Hugh Bredin what form Grant's drunkenness would have taken, he replied, 'Being abusive, like Mary in the book.' On 11 September I met him in a pub called The Gaiety, in the Strand, and found him in exceptionally good form, but five days later I was called by the Samaritans and advised that Grant, apparently a client of theirs for a long time, was in very low water. An hour later, I met him in the King's Road and sat with him on a bench in Royal Avenue. 'I'm sorry I'm not very bright

---

* One of my father's ideas was to endow the Jonathan Head-Barrow Short Story Prize at Harrow, still presented more than forty years later.

this morning,' he began, but cheered up after a drink and walked with me to Rossetti Gardens Studios, where Brenda Bury was happy to welcome him – perhaps, like me, she wanted to cling on to this last surviving human part of Jonathan and Anita's world – and even offer him a bed for the night. This was all very well but before the end of the month, Brenda would telephone me and scream, 'Your friend has stolen a hundred pounds from me!' A few hours later, I was telephoned by the Chelsea police. Had I any idea where they might find Mr Grant? I did not make any suggestions and in fact doubted if I would ever see or hear from my brother's friend and mentor again.

The winter came. When snow fell in Tite Street, I thought of it also falling on Jonathan and Anita's unmarked grave in Putney Vale. Their lives would soon be commemorated by the planting of two copper beeches – the ceremony was performed by Anita's friend Peter Robeson on 29 November – and the placing of a bench at the spot where they died. But it now began to dawn on me that Jonathan's legend might not be perpetuated. None of the publishers who had seen *The Queue* had shown any interest in it. And when on 14 December, I had a visit from my old comedian friend Reg Gray, who had now made a hit record under another name, I did not tell him my brother had died. I thought of other things, like the abandonment and tearing apart of Turleigh Combe, which had been Jonathan's home since he was seven, and my parents' strange move to the Isle of Man.

What more is there to say? Do I need to describe all the other obsessions which have diverted me during the last forty years? Is it worth recording that in 1973, Jonathan's hero Silvino Trompetto opened champagne for me in his office

317

off the Savoy kitchens where he still ruled – and at least twenty years later I would attend a memorial service for him at the Savoy Chapel and find myself choking back unexpected tears which I knew had something to do with Jonathan?

Should I say how others featured in this book fared later? How Mike d'Abo kept going and continues, at the age of sixty-five, to give concerts which fill places like the London Palladium? How, in November 1974, Anita's chatterbox friend Mary-Geraldine O'Donnell had materialised in the public eye at the side of the stricken Countess of Lucan? Or how in 1978, following an item in the *Daily Express* gossip column about my first book, I was telephoned by Mr Grant, but after deep thought and consultation told him I wished him well but could not see him? Do I need to say that Kenneth Slatter later opened a restaurant called Slatter's off the Haymarket and died after a long illness in the early 1990s – and that a psychoanalytic appointment prevented me attending the funeral? Or that Jonathan's own therapist, Dr Edward Griffith, author of *Modern Marriage*, died in the summer of 1987 at an advanced age, and that Jimmy McMullan had died ten years earlier after discharging himself from hospital where he'd been recovering after being beaten up in the street?

On a happier note, it's worth recording that Brenda Bury now lives in Canada and has become one of that country's best-loved portrait painters, that Rosemary Leventon is now a successful land installation artist and that John Cox, director of *Pharsalia*, went on to become boss of the Royal Opera House and still has the same telephone number he had in 1969. I've never met John Cox but I saw a lot of Patrick Procktor up to his death in 2004 and on one of our last meetings in Manchester Street drank a bottle of whisky with him.

And what about those eerie figures from our shared past? In 1994, I wrote a long obituary of James Frere in the *Daily Telegraph*. The ex-herald had ended his days living in a cottage in Wales. On the schoolmaster front, I see that Dr R. L. James stayed on as Head Master of Harrow till 1971, retired to Oxford, and died eleven years later. And that Mr Hankey, Head Master of Clifton College Preparatory School, lived latterly at a house called Linnymead somewhere in Norfolk and died on 14 February 1996. Mark Tindall died in 1994 but, as far as I know, Mr Frampton, Mr Lemmon and many of the other school-masters Jonathan knew are still alive. If they read these words, I can only apologise for dragging their good names into this murky tale.

Among Jonathan's contemporaries, I still see Margaret Peile – I have proved a pretty useless godfather to her son Noel, now a fashionable milliner – but have lost touch with most of the other girls in Jonathan's life, if I ever knew them in the first place. I still see James Graham regularly, though he now lives mainly in Cumberland where he has inherited his father's estate and title. We have lunch together at the Beefsteak Club when he is in London, after which he usually takes me to another, grander club where we drink vintage port and are sometimes joined by other surviving toffs – or Nicky Shits.

And what of the rest of the family? Two years after Jonathan's death, my grandmother died in Cumberland at the age of ninety-three – an eerie misprint in *The Times* stated that her funeral would take place at 2.30 *a.m.* – but I saw quite a lot of Aunt Jean until her death in 1981, stayed often in her extraordinary cottage and questioned her closely about the past I shared with Jonathan. 'I don't think your love of Gilda was unhealthy,' she pronounced after some serious thought. 'Sometimes rather stupid. Gilda was a tremendous character *but I think you exaggerated it slightly.*' A few months before my mother's death in 1977 she had remarked, while driving me to the Isle of Man airport, that she no

longer felt sad about Jonathan, only grateful that she had known him. My father, whose offbeat personality may have affected Jonathan more than any of us, died less than two years later without losing his sense of fun. The rest of us survive and, as I wrote at the very beginning of this book, are now dancing or hopping towards retirement.

Soon after the events described in these pages, my brother Julian got married, but has continued to paint and travel and still keeps 33 Tite Street, the scene of so many dramas, not least the first meeting between Jonathan and Anita, as his base today. Do I need to say that Simon, now seventy-two years old, today runs a small business a few yards from the old Talk of the Town, where Jonathan and I did our audition in 1964? And how Martin flourished in the East, remained happily married to Noriko, the mother of his two boys, eventually received the OBE, later upgraded to a CBE, for services to export and now lives in England again? And is it necessary to mention that, after years of clinging to straws and pursuing derelict geniuses like Philip O'Connor, I have been twice married and have four children, the youngest of whom, Blossom, is still only seven? And that I am now, heaven help me, a grandfather? And, perhaps more significantly, that neither of my wives had ever heard of Jonathan?

And what, one wonders, would Jonathan make of us all today? He would surely recognise some of the family furniture in my flat and in the West Country farmhouse I now share with Julian. He would recognise some of the pictures which once hung at Turig, even some of the spoons and forks he once ate with, but would he recognise me? And would I recognise him? And what would he make of this book? James Graham's prediction has not yet come true, and today Jonathan and I are almost entirely detached. In my flat in Eldon Road, only one of his pictures adorns the walls: a primitive oil painting of a solitary huntsman which he painted in the art school at Harrow, long before he was bitten by the creative bug I have described in these pages. On the other hand, several easy-on-the-eye canvases by my brother Julian, which I once colluded with Jonathan in describing as 'absolute stinkers', now occupy prime space, even holding their own against Picasso prints belonging to my wife.

And yet I still have many of Jonathan's possessions with me. I still have the highly distinctive butter board bought from Elizabeth David's shop in Cliveden Place on 12 April 1967. I still have many of his cookery books, including Joseph Donon's *Classic French Cuisine* and *The Pleasures of the Table* by Sir Francis Colchester-Wemyss, and still refer to them today. In a hut in the garden of my Wiltshire retreat is a large egg-shaped ashtray Jonathan carved out of stone and then spilt varnish on. And in various moves I have made since

Jonathan's death, I have carried with me three suitcases containing his letters to me, on that thick yellow Truslove & Hanson paper, his unframed drawings, the original manuscript of *The Queue* and a bundle of notes and telegrams that he and Anita exchanged in the days leading up to their double death. These suitcases, large, dented and cheap, have reminded me over the years of the unfinished business that I have at last attempted to tackle in this book.

Today, nobody talks about Jonathan. My brothers and I rarely mention his name and certainly do not reminisce about him. And I frequently meet people who know my family well but are unaware that Jonathan ever existed. And yet he still features in my mind and occasionally, especially since I started writing this book, in my dreams. And he still leaves a gap. I rarely return to Chelsea and those redbrick mansion blocks without thinking tenderly of him. And occasionally I find myself on the concourse of Euston Station where the narrator of *The Queue* first meets the extraordinary, almost magical dog Mary. And, just occasionally, things happen in real life which remind me of the wonderful events Jonathan dreamed up.

At the beginning of 2006, on the day I started writing this book, a gigantic Northern Bottlenose whale got beached in the Thames, causing consternation and wonderment to the thousands of Londoners who crowded the riverbanks near the Savoy Hotel. I have written this book to fill the gap, open a window, redress the balance and capture some of that same wonderment.

BIBLIOGRAPHY

Barrow, Jonathan *The Queue* (1970)
Barrow, Otto *The White Dachshund* (2010)
Behrens, Tim *The Monument* (1988)
Bennett, Alan *Untold Stories* (2005)
Buchan, John *The Thirty-Nine Steps* (1915)
                 Huntingtower (1922)
Channon, Henry *Chips: The Diaries of Sir Henry Channon* (1967)
Colchester-Wemyss, Sir Francis *The Pleasures of the Table* (1931)
Crisp, Quentin *The Naked Civil Servant* (1968)
Dendrickson, George *The Truth About Dartmoor* (1954)
Donon, Joseph *The Classic French Cuisine* (1961)
Fabre, J. H. *Social Life in the Insect World* (1911)
Foxe, John *Foxe's Book of Martyrs* (1563)
Frere, J. A. *The British Monarchy at Home* (1963)
Freud, Sigmund *The Interpretation of Dreams* (1900)
Graham, Stephen *London Nights* (1925)
Griffith, Edward F. *Modern Marriage* (1935)
                 Ups and Downs in Married Life (1966)
Howard Hay, William *Health via Food* (1934)
Hutchinson, William *The History of the County of Cumberland* (1794)

Johnston, Edward *Writing and Illuminating and Lettering* (1906)
Kafka, Franz *In the Penal Colony* (1914)
Kaye, David *The Australian* (1970)
    The Demise of a Poet (1973)
Kennedy, Ludovic *Ten Rillington Place* (1961)
Montsarrat, Nicholas *The Cruel Sea* (1951)
Moran, Lord *Winston Churchill: The Struggle for Survival* (1968)
Muybridge, Eadward *The Human Figure in Motion* (1901)
O'Connor, Philip *Memoirs of a Public Baby* (1958)
Ogilvy, David *Confessions of an Advertising Man* (1963)
Orwell, George *Down and Out in Paris and London* (1933)
Pevsner, Nikolaus *Pevsner Architectural Guides: Buildings of England*
Potter, Beatrix *The Tale of Peter Rabbit* (1902)
    The Tale of Jemima Puddle-Duck (1908)
    The Tale of Little Pig Robinson (1930)
Routh, Jonathan *Good Cuppa Guide* (1966)
Stacey, Barrie *Ticket to the Carnival* (1987)
Wildeblood, Peter *Against the Law* (1959)